SEXUAL HARASSMENT

OTHER BOOKS BY
AMBER COVERDALE SUMRALL AND DENA TAYLOR

Amber Coverdale Sumrall and Dena Taylor are the editors of
Women of the Fourteenth Moon: Writings on Menopause, published by The Crossing Press, 1991. Their anthology on women's
sexuality in midlife and beyond will be published by The Crossing Press, 1993. Sumrall is also co-editor of *Touching Fire:Erotic
Writings By Women* (Carroll & Graf, 1989), *Catholic Girls*
(Penguin, 1992), and editor of *Lovers* (The Crossing Press,
1992). Taylor is the author of *Red Flower:Rethinking Menstrua-
tion* (The Crossing Press, 1988).

SEXUAL HARASSMENT

WOMEN SPEAK OUT

EDITED BY
AMBER COVERDALE SUMRALL & DENA TAYLOR
WITH INTRODUCTIONS BY
ANDREA DWORKIN & MARGARET RANDALL
CARTOONS SELECTED BY ROZ WARREN

THE CROSSING PRESS, FREEDOM, CA 95019

Copyright © 1992 by Amber Coverdale Sumrall and Dena Taylor
Cover Design by AnneMarie Arnold
Interior Design by Sheryl Karas, Amy Sibiga and AnneMarie Arnold
Printed in the U.S.A.

ISBN 0-89594-544-4
ISBN 0-89594-545-2

THIS BOOK IS DEDICATED TO ANITA HILL

EDITORS' PREFACE

The treatment received by Anita Hill as a result of the Clarence Thomas Supreme Court confirmation hearings enraged women the world over, including Elaine Goldman Gill, co-owner of The Crossing Press. When she asked if we would compile an anthology of women's sexual harassment stories, we said yes and put our other projects on hold. We, too, were outraged.

Calls for submissions went to newspapers, radio stations, colleges, and individual women. Hundreds of manuscripts arrived in response: painful, angry, humiliating, humorous and empowering.

Sexual harassment is a form of sex discrimination and is unlawful under Title VII of the 1964 Civil Rights Act. The effect of this Act was minimal until 1986 when the Supreme Court established that sexual harassment, including a hostile work environment, was a violation of civil rights. And in January 1991 the Ninth Circuit court ruled that a hostile work environment must be judged from the perspective of the victim.

Sexual harassment is sexual pressure that one is not in a position to refuse, it is deliberate or repeated sexual behavior that is unwelcome. It is about male privilege and dominance, and it is not necessarily explicitly sexual: a woman carpenter on a job who is asked to clean the toilets and a wife who is hit by her husband because he doesn't like what she says are both experiencing sexual harassment. The Equal Employment Opportunity Commission defines it as unwanted sexual advances, requests for sexual favors, or other verbal or physical conduct of a sexual nature. But as a recent letter to the editor of *Z Magazine* states, "...women get to determine what is and isn't sexual harassment. Just as blacks should determine what is racist and gays what is homophobic. And if we say it happened, it happened."

Women all over the country—in their homes, at work, in the laundromat, at the hairdressers, in classrooms—watched Anita Hill's testimony, and the repeated questions, insinuations, disbelief, and laughter from the senators. For countless numbers of women, the Hill-Thomas hearings opened the gates of denial, and long-repressed memories came tumbling out.

In *Sexual Harassment: Women Speak Out*, women write not only of their experiences but also of how they responded to them. Some went into extreme depression or experienced physical symptoms; some fought back; some denied the harassment was happening, wanting to believe it was unintentional or something they themselves provoked. Some found humorous and creative ways of dealing with the harasser.

There have been and will be many responses to the testimony given by Hill; this book is one. What happened in Washington in October 1991 has forever changed the character of millions of women. They will not tolerate sexual harassment; they will speak out; they will name names; they will fight back. The "click!" of recognition was heard.

We considered grouping the stories by category: workplace, doctor's office, school, on the street. But some accounts described a lifetime of harassment, defying categorization. We decided, therefore, to present the accounts alphabetically, interspersed with quotes and cartoons by women.

A resource section is included at the end of the book. Women who have experienced or are experiencing sexual harassment can contact these organizations to find out what to do.

We want to thank all the women who sent their stories to us, stories that took courage to put down on paper. We were not able to include them all in this collection, but we hope that the very act of writing them has been empowering.

Deep appreciation goes to our families and friends who gave us the space to do this work. We lived with these women's experiences for weeks, and thus were not easy to live with ourselves.

Dena Taylor
Amber Coverdale Sumrall
Santa Cruz, CA, January 1992

CONTENTS

WOMEN IN THE PUBLIC DOMAIN: SEXUAL HARASSMENT AND DATE RAPE

Introduction by
Andrea Dworkin

The Prostitution Paradigm

In the European tradition, men have tried to keep women from working for money except as prostitutes. As with so many enduring Western ideals, the roots of this social model can be found in the Athenian city-state. The most protected woman was the married woman, a prisoner in her own home, except, of course, that it was not hers, any more than the cage belongs to the bird. She had no rights and no money. She did, however, have responsibilities. It was her duty to submit to intercourse, have sons, and run the house. Her virtue was maintained by keeping her an isolated captive. She was physically confined to the house to guarantee the husband that his legal children were his biological issue.

Any woman less isolated was more collectively owned. Foreign women taken as plunder were slaves. Adult Athenian women who were not married were, in the main, either high-class prostitutes, social and sexual companions to a male elite, or prisoners in brothels. The high-class prostitutes were the only women with any real education or any freedom of movement. The courtesan class in many societies was the social location of women of accomplishment and foreshadowed the professional woman of advanced capitalism: highly educated compared with other women, highly skilled, she worked for money and appeared to exercise choice.

The wife was the private woman in the private (domestic) sphere, protected inside, legally bound there. *Inside* meant confinement, captivity, isolation; high value; a reproductive as well as a sexual function; a privatized ownership. The prostitute was the public woman—publicly owned. She lived outside the home. *Outside* meant the breaching of one's body by more than one, how many and under which circumstances depending on one's closeness to or distance from the male elite—the small, wealthy ruling class. The low-class prostitute, kept in a brothel, was outside the bounds of human recognition: an orifice, a nonentity, used for a mass function. *Outside*, money paid for acts and access. *Outside*, women were for sale. *Inside* meant that a woman was protected from the commerce in her kind; the value of a woman was high only when she was immune from

1

the contamination of a money exchange. A woman who could be bought was cheap. This cheapness signified her low value and defined her moral capacity. A woman was her sexual function; she was what she did; she became what was done to her; she was what she was for. Any woman born outside or left outside or kicked outside deserved what she got because she was what had happened to her. For instance, the rape of a lady stole her value from her but she was not the aggrieved party. Her husband or her father had been injured, because the value of his property had been destroyed. Once used, she might become the wife of the rapist, or she was cast out, exiled to the margins, newly created common property. Rape could create a marriage but more often it created a prostitute. The deeper her exile, the more accessible to men she was—the more accessible, the cheaper. This was an economic fact and an ontological axiom, status and character determined by the degree of her sexual vulnerability. In the public domain by virtue of the male use of her, she became venal by male definition and design, according to male power and perception.

These zones—private and public, inside and outside—continue to suggest a real geography of female experience under the rule of men. The insularity of the domestic sphere for women has been treasured or honored or valued even in poor or working-class families; a man's honor is compromised or contaminated when his wife works outside the home for money. The gender-specific exclusiveness of housework creates a literal and symbolic synthesis between woman and house. She is wedded to it as much as to him. The repetitive, menial work by which she is judged—her competence, her devotion, her womanhood—establishes the house as her indigenous habitat. Her tribe, woman, carries the housekeeping gene. By nature, she rubs and she scrubs. The male lives out his wider life in the wider world, a hunter (he brings home the bacon) with a biological imperative to spread his sperm. He works for money by right, and with it goes freedom of action. After work he can range over miles, bar to bar, or library to library; he roams the big world. When finally he enters the domicile where she belongs as a natural, unpaid worker, he is both master and guest. He eats, he sleeps, he dirties the floor. Inside the domestic sphere, she lives the best life for her. Too much association with the obligations of the domestic sphere make his life too small for him. He resents the taming of his wild nature; he will not accept the limits appropriate to a female life. He will not do housework. He will not jack her loose from it. Her association with the home is nativist and in the wider world, which is his real domain, she is an unwanted alien, at best a guest worker with a short-term visa, a stigmatized immigrant.

In the workplace, her money is seen to supplement his. He is first, she is second. She is paid less than men are paid for the same work, if men do the same work; she may be segregated into female-only work, menial and low-paid. Usually, whatever her work she makes less than her husband whatever his work. Two features of female labor are so familiar that they seem to have all the permanence of gravity, or is it gravy stains?—(1) she does unpaid work in the home, a lot of it and (2) in the marketplace she lines the bottom. This makes her poor relative to him; this makes women poor relative to men. Women, then, can buy less shelter, less food, less freedom than men. Women, then, need men for money, and men require sexual access to make the exchange. Women's poverty means that women stay sexually accessible to men, a submission seen as natural instead of economically coerced.

The Athenian ethic prevails, however camouflaged. Working women are attached in marriage to the *inside*, mostly by cleaning it. The ideal is still the isolated captive but she is increasingly honored in the breach, since both the isolation and the captivity have been massively rejected by Western women. Ideologically, the right continues to promote the house as the natural, even exclusive, locus of virtue for a woman. The media, construed to be liberal in its social advocacy, continue to insist that working for money outside the home makes women depressed, infertile, stressed, more prone to heart disease and earlier death, while all extant studies continue to show the opposite (see Faludi, *Backlash*, Crown, 1991; Barnett and Rivers, "The Myth of the Miserable Working Woman," *Working Woman*, February 1992). The left—ever visionary—continues to caretake the pornography industry, making the whole wide world—street, workplace, supermarket—repellent to women. And while men use pornography to drive women out of the workplace, civil libertarians defend it as speech (it is, indeed, like "Get out, nigger"); and some ask, "Why can't a woman be more like a man?" i.e., why can't a woman flourish in a workplace saturated with pornography? Thus, each tried-and-true political tendency combines the best of its theory with the best of its practice to force women out of the workplace, back into the house, door locked from the outside. Pretending to argue, they collude. And if one don't get you, the other will.

And we, the women, of course, remain touchingly naive and ahistorical. We believe that women are in the workplace to stay, even though men have engineered massive and brutal social dislocations to keep women poor and powerless or to return us there. In Europe, the mass slaughter of the witches over a three-hundred-year period was partly motivated by a desire to confiscate their property, their money—to take what wealth women had. During the Crusades, women took over land, money, aspects of male political sovereignty—and were pushed out and down when the men returned. In the United States, of course, Rosie the Riveter was pushed out of the factory and into the suburbs, unemployed. We have been playing Giant Steps throughout history, trying to advance on the man while his back

3

was turned. Each time we get an economic leg up, the man finds a way to break our knees. Of course it will be different this time; of course. We want equal pay for equal work and we wait, patiently, quietly; let them have one more war. Especially, we believe that the workplace is a gender-neutral zone, a fair place; we believe that we leave gender behind, at home, with the polish on the linoleum; we believe that a woman is a person, at work to work, for money. We may wear our little skirts but we do not expect them to mean anything, certainly not that the men will try to look up them. Even though we know that we have had to fight bias to get the job and to get the money, we present ourselves at work as workers, a final prayer for fairness. We have given up on the streets; we have given up at home. But, this time, we entered the workplace *after* some legislative promises of fairness and we believe in law, we believe the promise. Our immutable assumption, synonymous with our deepest hope, is that we do not go into the workplace sexed: which means, always in our experience, as a target.

But the men, classics scholars each and every one, honor the old road map: a woman outside, a woman in public, is more collectively owned than a woman inside. Each woman may be bound to her husband by the rites and rituals of domesticity, but when she crosses the periphery, exits the door, she belongs to them that see her: a little or a lot, depending on how the men are inclined. The eyes own her first; the gaze that looks her up and down is the first incursion, the first public claim. The single woman inhabits this old territory even more fully. She is presumed to be out there looking for him, whomever—his money, his power, his sex, his protection (from men just like him). There is virtually no respect for a woman without a man and there is virtually no recognition that a woman's life is fully human on its own. Human freedom has him as its subject, not her. Always, she is an adjunct. Her integrity is not central to the imperative for human rights or political rights or economic rights. And, indeed, this is what matters. It may be all that matters. The solitary woman must incarnate for us what it means to be human; *she* must signify all the dimensions of human value; she must set the standard. The inability to conceptualize her individuality amounts to a morbid paralysis of conscience. Without her as a whole human being in her own right, a sovereign human being, the predations of men against women will appear natural or justified. The tolerance of these predations depends on the woman's life being, in its essence, smaller, less significant, predetermined by the necessities of a sexual function, that function itself formed by the requirements of male sexual tyranny, a reductive and totalitarian set of sexual demands.

So, outside, the woman is public in male territory, a hands-on zone; her presence there is taken to be a declaration of availability—for sex and sexual insult. On the street, she may be verbally assaulted or physically assaulted. The verbal assaults and some physical assault are endemic in the environment, a given, an apparently inevitable emanation of the male spirit—from the breast-oriented "Hey, momma" to, as I saw once, a man in a suit walking rapidly down the street punching in the stomach each young, well-dressed woman he passed—wham, bam, punch, hard, they keeled over one after another as he barreled by them—each was incredulous even as she folded over, and he was gone before I could take in what I had clearly seen on rush-hour crowded streets. It is a fiction that male assaults against women are punished by law. In any woman's life, most are not. The casual, random violence of the stranger has nearly as much protection as the systematic, intimate violence of the lover, husband, or father. None of us can stand up to all of it; we are incredulous as each new aggression occurs. We hurry to forget. It can't have happened, we say; or it happens all the time, we say—it is too rare to be credible or too common to matter. We won't be believed or no one will care; or both.

In the workplace, the woman hears the beat of her unsexed heart: I am *good* at this, she says. She is working for money, maybe for dignity, maybe in pursuit of independence, maybe out of a sense of vocation or ambition. The man perceives that she is close to him, a physical and mental proximity; under him, a political and economic arrangement that is incontrovertible; poorer than he is, a fact with consequences for her—he perceives that she is in the marketplace to barter, skills for money, sexuality for advancement or advantages. Her genitals are near him, just under that dress, in the public domain, his domain. Her lesser paycheck gives him a concrete measure of how much more she needs, how much more he has. In the academy, a grade is wealth. In each arena, she is a strange woman, not his wife or daughter; and her presence is a provocation. His presumption is a premise of patriarchy: she can be bought; her real skills are sexual skills; the sexuality that inheres in her is for sale or for barter and he has a right to it anyway, a right to a rub or a lick or a fuck. Once outside, she is in the realm of the prostituted woman. It is an economically real realm. The poor trade sex for money, food, shelter, work, a chance. It is a realm created by the power of men over women, a zone of women compromised by the need for money. If she is there, he has a right to a piece of her. It is a longstanding right. Using his power to force her seems virile, masculine, to him, an act of civilized conquest, a natural expression of a natural potency. His feelings are natural, indeed, inevitable. His acts are natural, too. The laws of man and woman supercede, surely, the regulations or conventions of the workplace.

Every regular guy, it turns out, is a sociobiologist who can explain the need to spread the sperm—for the sake of the species. He is a philosopher of civilization, a deep thinker on the question of what women really want— and he thinks old thoughts, rapist thoughts, slave-owning thoughts. He thinks them deeply, without self-consciousness. He is a keeper of tradition, a guardian of values: he punishes transgression, and the woman outside has transgressed the one boundary established to keep her safe from men in general, to keep her private from him. If she was at home, as she should be, she would not be near him. If she is near him, his question is why; and his answer is that she is making herself available—for a price. She is there for money. The workplace is where a woman goes to sell what she has for money. Her wages suggest that her job skills do not amount to much. Indisputably, she is cheap.

It stuns us, this underlying assumption that we are whoring. Here we are, on our own, at last, so proud, so stupidly proud. Here he is, a conqueror he thinks, a coward and a bully we think, using power to coerce sex. We feel humiliated, embarrassed, ashamed. He feels fine. He feels right. Manly: he feels manly. And, of course, he is.

Male Sexuality

Now, I have had this experience. In my work I have described the sexual philosophies of Kinsey, Havelock Ellis, De Sade, Tolstoy, Isaac Bashevis Singer, Freud, Robert Stoller, Norman Mailer, Henry Miller. Each has an ethic of male entitlement to women's bodies. Each celebrates male sexual aggression against women as an intrinsic component of a natural, valuable, venerable masculinity. Each suggests that women must be conquered, taken by force; that women say "no" but mean "yes"; that forced sex is ecstatic sex and that women crave pain.

I have written about the gynocide of the witches, one thousand years of Chinese footbinding, serial rape and serial killing.

I have written about the misogyny in the Bible and in pornography, about the advocacy of rape in male-supremacist psychology, theology, philosophy, about the cruelty of dominance and submission, including in intercourse.

In every case, I have used the discourse of men as a source, without distorting it. I have said what men say about women, about the nature of sex, about the nature of nature. The men remain cultural heroes, Promethean truth-tellers; surely they mean no harm. I am excoriated (surely I mean some harm) for saying what they say but framing it in a new frame, one that shows the consequences to women. The ones they do it to have been left out. I put the ones they do it to back in. In exposing the hate men have for women, it is as if it becomes mine. To say what they do is to be what they are, except that they are entitled, they are right, in what they do and what they say and how they feel. Maybe they are tragic but they are never responsible: for being mean or cruel or stupid. When they advocate rape, that is normal and neutral. When I say they advocate rape, I am engaging in the equivalent of a blood-libel (this is the meaning of the "man-hating" charge); I slander them as if I invented the sadism, the brutality, the exploitation, that they engage in and defend.

Now: men describe their masculinity as aggressive, essentially rapist. Feminists have challenged the rape itself. We have agitated for changes in law so that we can prosecute all acts of forced sex. Men continue to speak as if we are ultimately irrelevant; they say that force is a natural part of sex and a normal expression of masculinity. We say that force is rape. Men continue to rationalize the use of force in intercourse as if force indicates the degree of desire, the intensity of the urge. Feminists are charged with hating sex (rape) because we hate forced sex. We are charged with confusing the horrible crime of rape (rape with the most brutality imaginable) with intercourse (which involves less force, though how much less the men will not say), thereby making it impossible to prosecute real rape, horrible rape (rape done by someone else) because the force a good guy (me) might use can be confused by some nasty or dumb woman with the worse force used by a real rapist (not me).

Until about twenty years ago, men did what they wanted and called it what they liked. They decided all meaning and value. (Not all men decided all meaning and value; but men, not women, decided.) They could describe sex as conquest, violence, violation, and themselves as rapists (without using the word), because they were never accountable to us for what they said or did. Men were the law; men were morality; men decided; men judged. Now we have pushed our way out from under them, at least a little. We see them owning and naming. We have a critical new distance. Still screwed in place as it were, we have swiveled loose a little, and we see the face where before we only felt the heavy breathing. We see the brow knotted in exertion, the muscles of the brain flexing in what passes for thought: discounting us, ignoring us, ignorant of us, celebrating rape and leaving out the cost to us. In the last two decades, feminists have built a real political resistance to male sexual dominance, i.e., to male ownership of the whole wide world; and it is clear that we are not saying no because we mean yes. We mean no and we prosecute the pigs to prove it. More and more of us do, more and more. We prosecute and sue our fathers, lovers, bosses, doctors, friends, as well as the ubiquitous stranger. For all our cultural brazenness, men have learned that no might mean no because we take them to court. It started as a rumor. The rumor spread. The bitches are really pissed.

Uses of force that men consider natural, necessary, and fair are being confronted by women who take those same uses of force to be intolerable violations without any possible extenuation. In 1991, two events clarified the state of conflict between male sexual hegemony and female political resistance: Anita Hill charged Clarence Thomas with sexual harassment;

and William Kennedy Smith was prosecuted for rape.

Clarence Thomas was George Bush's nominee for the Supreme Court, an African-American conservative whose origins were rural and poor, in the segregated South. Anita Hill was a law professor who came from the same background. She had been Thomas's subordinate at the EEOC, the administrative agency responsible for pursuing complaints of sexual harassment and other civil rights violations. In other words, Clarence Thomas was in charge of vindicating the rights of victims. His record at the EEOC was one of extreme lethargy. Feminists saw a relationship between his record, a poor one, and his own behavior as alleged by Hill—he was a perpetrator. Hill described a continuing pattern of verbal assault, especially the recounting of pornographic movies that featured rape, women being penetrated by animals, and large-breasted women. In one incidence of harassment, Thomas asked who had left a pubic hair on a Coke can. Ms. Hill could not make sense of the remark but those of us who study pornography identified it immediately: there are films in which women are penetrated by beverage cans. Mr. Thomas talked about the size of his penis and his ability to give women pleasure through oral sex. These confidences were forced on Ms. Hill in the workplace, in private, without witnesses. Ms. Hill was Mr. Thomas's chosen target, a smart, ambitious African-American woman whose future was linked with his. In the narrow sense, their political destinies were linked. He was a favorite of the Republicans and she could travel with him: up. In the wider sense, as an African-American conservative, he was pioneering the way for other black conservatives, especially women who would follow because they could not lead—Mr. Bush has shown no interest in even the token empowerment of African-American women. The verbal assaults humiliated Ms. Hill and pushed her face in her sexual status. They emphasized the servility that went with being female. They put her in her place, which was under him; in the office; in the movie; in life—her life.

Anita Hill testified before the Senate Judiciary Committee and fourteen white men evaded the issues her testimony raised. Rightwing senators, with deft diagnostic skills, said she was psychotic. He was a lunatic if he did it but he could not be a lunatic and therefore he could not have done it. He would have to be morally degenerate to watch such films and he could not be morally degenerate. They sputtered trying to say what she must be—to bring the charges. *Psychotic* was their kindest conclusion. Leftwing senators, presumably out to destroy Clarence Thomas the black conservative by any means necessary, did not ask him questions on his use of pornography, though the answers might have vindicated Anita Hill. The topic was barely mentioned and not pursued. The claims of sexual harassment were essentially ignored; they were buried, not exposed. Panels of women were brought forward to say that Clarence Thomas did not sexually harass them. When I rob my neighbor, I want all the neighbors I did not rob to be asked to testify; I am very kind to my neighbors, except for the one I robbed. The chairman of the committee, Democrat Joseph R. Biden Jr. from Delaware, who is sponsoring the first federal bill to treat rape and battery as the sex-based crimes they are (the Violence Against Women Act), said that terrible things always come to his attention during confirmation hearings. He specifically mentioned charges of wife-beating (the aforementioned "battery" of the Violence Against Women Act). The press ignored this information; no one demanded to know which men confirmed by the Senate Judiciary Committee and then the whole Senate beat their wives. Clarence Thomas himself was reported to have beaten his first wife, an African-American woman, though she did not come forward to make the charge in public.

Clarence Thomas was confirmed and is now a sitting Supreme Court Justice.

Mr. Bush gave several interviews in which he deplored the sexually explicit testimony. His granddaughters, he said, could turn on the television and hear this dirty talk. He did not seem to mind the dirty behavior or having institutionalized it by putting an accused pornophile on the court that would make the law that would govern his granddaughters. If Clarence Thomas enjoys films in which women are fucked by animals, George Bush's granddaughters, like the rest of us, are in trouble.

Since the fourteen white men on the Senate Judiciary Committee did not ask, we do not know if Clarence Thomas still uses pornography. (This presumes that he would tell the truth, which presumes a lot. He stated under oath that he had never discussed *Roe v. Wade*, the decision legalizing abortion in the United States. My cat hasn't discussed it.) Thomas's friends from college confirm that he used pornography when he was in law school at Yale (1971-1974). Then, and even in the early 1980s when Anita Hill alleges he detailed the pornographic scenarios to her, pornography showing women being penetrated by animals was still underground. It was available in film loops in stalls in adult bookstores and live-sex theaters. A man goes to the prostitution-pornography part of town; he finds the right venue; he occupies a private stall with the film loops—women being fucked by animals or pissed on or whipped; he keeps depositing tokens or quarters to see the loop of film, which keeps repeating; when he leaves, someone mops up the stall—usually he leaves semen. Clarence Thomas asserted the absolute privacy of what he called his bedroom when one senator broached the topic of pornography. If he used the pornography when his friends say he did, his bedroom includes a lot of geography. That is one big bedroom. The patriarchal standard the Bush administration wants to defend is a familiar one: a man's privacy includes any sexual act he wants to do *to women* wherever he wants to do it; a woman's privacy does not even extend to her own internal organs. The pornography Clarence Thomas was accused of using is viciously woman-hating; it is the KKK equivalent of destroying women for the fun of it, annihilating women for sport. The President used every resource at his command to defend Thomas's nomination. So did the rightwing senators. The liberals sacrificed the women of this country to the usual imperatives of male bonding. How many—left, right, or center—harass the very low-paid, low-status women who work for them (they exempted themselves from the reach of sexual harassment laws)? How many use pornography? How many, in fact, beat their wives?

William Kennedy Smith, thirty, a rich white man, recently graduated from medical school, nephew of Senator Edward M. (Ted) Kennedy, was prosecuted for rape in December 1991. The woman who accused him was white, his approximate age and social status, an unmarried mother of one. They met in a chic bar in Palm Beach, Florida, Smith accompanied by his uncle and his cousin Patrick, a Rhode Island state legislator. The woman went with Smith to the Kennedy home in Palm Beach. (Who would not think it safe? Which citizen would not go?) According to her, Smith tackled her and forced himself on her. His defense was that she had had intercourse. The jury believed him and acquitted him with less than an hour of deliberation. He had a story that was consistent; she had memory lapses. The judge refused to allow testimony from an expert on rape trauma that would have explained how commonplace such memory losses are in victims of rape. The trial was televised. The woman's face was obscured from view. The shock to the nation, the shock to ruling-class men, the shock to male dominance, was that Mr. Smith was prosecuted at all. Feminists call the crime date rape or acquaintance rape. In the good old days, in the 1950s and 1960s as well as in the Athenian city-state, rape was a crime of theft; the woman belonged to a man, her husband or father; and raping her was like breaking her, smashing a vessel, a valuable vase; the man's property was destroyed. Until two decades ago, men raped women and men made and administered the laws against rape. Rape law protected the interests of men from the aggressions of other men; it punished men for getting out of line by taking a women who belonged to someone else. With the advent of the women's movement, rape was redefined as a crime against the woman who was raped. This seems simple but in fact it overturned over two thousand years of male-supremacist rape law.

In order for the crime to have happened to her, she had to be someone (when it happened to him, she was something). In order for her to be someone, the law had to revise its estimation of her place: from chattel to person in her own right. As a person, then, she began to say what had happened to her, in the courtroom but also in books, in public meetings, among women, in the presence of men. She began to say what had happened, where, how, who had done it, when, even why. The old law of rape, it seemed, barely touched on the reality of rape. The crime had been defined by male self-interest. Men had demanded as a legal standard that women be prepared to die rather than to submit; this degree of resistance was required to show, to prove, that she did not consent; her visible injuries had to prove that she might have died, because he would have killed her. Resisting less, she would be held responsible for whatever he had done to her. Her testimony had to be corroborated—by witnesses or by physical evidence so overwhelming as to be incontrovertible. The legal presumption was that women lied, used false rape charges to punish men. One of the law's purposes was to protect men from vindictive women, which all women who charged rape were presumed to be. In practice, every effort was made to destroy any woman who prosecuted a rapist. A woman's sexual history was used to indict her. The premise always has been that loose women—prostitutes, sluts, sexually active women—could not be raped; that the public woman was for sexual consumption however achieved, by money or by force; that any woman who "did it" was dirt, took on the status of the act itself (dirty)—that she had no value the law was required to honor or protect. If a woman could not prove her virtue, she could be found culpable for the lack of it, which meant acquittal for the rapist. Empirically speaking, it did not matter if she had been forced to do what it was presumed she would be happy to do anyway—even if under different circumstances or with someone else. If the rapist's lawyer could show that the woman had had sex—was not a virgin or a faithful wife—she was proved worthless. No one would punish the accused, hurt his life, for what he had done to a piece of trash—unless he needed to be punished for some other reason, for instance, his race, or social hubris, or some other scapegoating reason, in which case she would be used to put him away.

The reforms seemed so minor; frankly, so inadequate. We need more and better but the changes have had an impact. Trial rules were changed so that the woman's past sexual history was generally inadmissible. Corroboration was no longer required—the woman's testimony could stand on its own. The procedures involved in collecting and keeping physical evidence were scrutinized and standardized so that such evidence could not be lost, contaminated, or tampered with. Before, evidence had been collected in a haphazard way, giving the rapist a big headstart on an acquittal. Doctors in emergency rooms and police were trained in how to treat rape victims, how to investigate for sexual abuse. Rape crisis centers were created, some in hospital emergency rooms; these gave victims expert counseling and a sympathetic peer on the victims' side in dealing with the police, doctors, prosecutors, in going through the ordeal of a trial, in surviving the trauma of the event itself. In some states, the definition of consent was changed so that, for instance, if a woman was drunk she could *not* give legal consent (rather than the old way: if she was drunk, she had consented—to whatever would be done to her; she deserved whatever she got). Laws that protected rape in marriage—the right of a husband to penetrate his wife against her will, by force—were changed so that forced intercourse in marriage could be prosecuted as what it was: the act of rape. "But if you can't rape your wife," protested California state senator Bob Wilson in 1979, "who can you rape?" The answer is: no one. And women began to sue rapists, including husbands, under civil law: to expose the crime; to get money damages. The law remains tilted in favor of the rapist. For instance, prior convictions for rape are not admissible as evidence. The woman still almost always looks wrong, stupid, venal, and the prejudices against women—how women should dress, act, talk, think—are virulent, nearly deranged by any fair standard. Most rapists are acquitted. Usually this means that the woman is told by a jury, as Smith's accuser was, that she had intercourse. (In some cases, the jury acquits because it believes that the wrong man has been apprehended; it accepts that the woman has been raped.) The acquittal that declares she was not raped, she had intercourse, upholds and reifies the patriarchal view of rape: a monstrous act committed by a monster (invariably a stranger), it is an excess of violence outside the force sanctioned in intercourse; the woman is, in fact, subjected to so much violence that no one could interpret her submission as voluntary or think it was at her invitation, for her pleasure. Just some violence does not take the act out of the realm of normal intercourse for male supremacists because, for them, sex is a sometimes mean dance, and aggression against the woman is just a fast and manly way of dancing.

The progress is in this: that, increasingly, incursions against women are prosecuted as rape; that rape is now a crime against the woman herself; that the use of force is enough to warrant a prosecution (if not yet a conviction); that a date, a friend, an acquaintance, will be prosecuted for the use of force—even if he is rich, even if he is white, even if he is a doctor, even if his family is powerful and lionized. And the progress is also in this: that a woman could go out, outside, past the periphery, at night, to a bar, chat with men, drink—a woman who had been sexually abused as a child, who had worked for an escort service, who had had three abortions—and still, force used against her was taken to be rape—by prosecutors, hardasses who do not like to lose.

Feminists have achieved what amounts to a vast redefinition of rape based on women's experience of how, when, and where we are raped—also, by whom; and we have achieved a revised valuation of the rape

victim—someone, not something. Male society, once imperial in its authority over women and rape, having operated on the absolutist principle of the
divine right of kings, has not taken the change with good grace.

"Feminists," says the rightwing *National Review* (January 20, 1992),
"have attempted to strengthen the likelihood of conviction by inventing the
concept of 'date rape,' which means not simply rape committed by an
escort, but any sexual contact that a woman subsequently regrets." Regret,
then, not force, is the substance of this charge we thought up; Pied Piper-
like, we lead and the little children—the police, district attorneys—
charmed by our music, follow.

Neo-con writer Norman Podhoretz claims that date rape does not
exist; that feminists, in order to make men sexually dysfunctional, are
putting unfair, unnatural, unreasonable constraints on masculinity. There is
"a masculine need to conquer," an "ever restless masculine sex drive," in
conflict with the "much more quiescent erotic impulses" of women (*Commentary*, October 1991)—we don't push and shove? In other words, so-
called date rape is, in fact, normal intercourse using normal force, misunderstood by women who are misled by feminists into thinking they have
been forced (raped) when they have just been fucked (forced). Mr. Podhoretz
singles me out as a particularly noxious example of a feminist who repudi-
ates women being force-fucked, call it what you will; I am indecent,
castrating, and man-hating in my refusal to accept male force and male
conquest as a good time. The liberal *Tikkun* praises Mr. Podhoretz for trying
to off me; then, with dim logic but shining arrogance, claims that "the
psychic undergirding of so much neo-conservatism" has been "the fear of
women's power, the fear that women's wishes and desires may have to be
given equal weight with those of men" (November/December 1991). Ain't
I a woman? What undergirds *Tikkun*?

In *The Wall Street Journal* (June 27, 1991), Berkeley professor Neil
Gilbert, a very angry man, seriously undergirded, claims that we lie about
rape as a way of lying about men. In particular, we lie about the frequency
of rape. We make up statistics in order to "broadcast a picture of college life
that resembles the world of 'Thelma and Louise,' in which four out of six
men are foul brutes and the other two are slightly simpleminded." We do
this because we have a secret agenda: "to change social perceptions of what
constitutes acceptable intimate relations between men and women... It is an
effort to reduce the awesome complexity of intimate discourse between the
sexes to the banality of 'no' means 'no.' " Actually, being force-fucked is
pretty banal. Didn't Hannah Arendt write a book about that?

"The awesome complexity" of getting a woman drunk to fuck her has
lost some ground, since if a woman is drugged she is held incapable of
consent in some states.

"The awesome complexity" of owning her body outright in marriage has lost ground because marital rape is now criminalized in some states.

"The awesome complexity" of driving a woman into prostitution through forced sex, however, holds its ground, it seems, since incest or other child sexual abuse appears to be a precondition for prostitution and prostitution thrives. Claiming that date rape—rape defined from women's experience of sexual coercion at the hands of an acquaintance—has created a "phantom epidemic of sexual assault" (*The Public Interest*, spring 1991), Mr. Gilbert opposes funding rape crisis centers on college campuses. A press release for Mr. Gilbert proudly states: "In a similar vein four years ago, Gilbert criticized sexual abuse prevention training for small children. Partly as a result of Gilbert's research, Governor Deukmejian last year canceled all state funding for the school-based prevention programs." The awesome simplicity of Mr. Gilbert's public discourse is more venal than banal: neither women nor children should have any recourse; keep the rapist's discourse awesome by keeping the victim helpless and silent.

Male hysteria over date rape (its recognition, stigmatization, punishment) was especially provoked in the media by date-rape charges on college campuses: where boys become men. Outstanding numbers of young women said that boys could not become men on them; by coercing them. Take Back the Night marches and speak-outs proliferated. Women named rapists and reported rapes, though college administrators mostly backed up male privilege. Even gang rapes rarely got a penalty more punishing than the penalty for plagiarism. At Brown University, women wrote the names of male students who had coerced them on the walls of women's bathrooms. To men, first-amendment absolutists in defense of pornography, this suggested a logical limit on free speech. It seemed clear to them. In a slyly misogynist profile of an actual date rape at Dartmouth College, *Harper's* (April 1991) characterized student activism against rape this way: "Sexual-abuse activists are holding workshops to help students recast the male psyche."

Indeed, male rage against date-rape charges originated in the conviction that men had a right to the behaviors constituting the assaults; but also, that manly behavior, manhood itself, required the use of force, with aggression as the activating dynamic. The redefinition of rape based on women's experience of being forced is taken by men to be a subversion of their right to live peaceably and well-fucked, on their own terms. "The trend in this complicated arena of sexual politics is definitely against us, gentlemen," warns *Playboy*'s Asa Baber (September 1991). "A lynch mob could be just outside your door. In William Kennedy Smith's case, a lynch mob has already placed the rope around his neck." Well, hardly. The boy had the best due process money could buy.

Men cannot live without rape, say these organs, so to speak, of male power. Men cannot be men without using some force, some aggression, or without having the right to use some force, some aggression. Men need rape, or the right to rape, to be men. Taking away the right to rape emasculates men. The charge of date rape is an effort to unsex men.

This male rage also derives from the perception that college-age women experience what used to be normal, sanctioned coercion as rape—real rape. These charges are not ideological. They do not come from the first generation of this wave's feminists, the sadder-but-wiser flower children who wondered why all the peace-now men pushed and shoved and what it meant. Male aggression is being experienced by young women now as violation. The pushing and shoving is taken to be hostile and unfair, wrong and rotten. This is proof of feminism's success in articulating the real experiences of women, so long buried in an imposed silence. We older ones looked at our lives—the forced sex that was simply part of what it meant to be a woman, the circumstances under which the force occurred, who he was (rarely the famous stranger). Male lies all around us celebrated force as romantic rape; male laws protected force used against women in rape and battery; in this very unfriendly world we enunciated, at risk and in pain, the meaning of our own experience. We called it rape. The younger women vindicate us. They are not bewildered as we were—stunned by how ordinary and commonplace it is. They are not intimidated by the rapist, who can be any man, any time, any place. They are traumatized by the force, as we were. The unwanted invasion repels them, as it did us. But we were quiet, during and after. The rapes were covered over by so much time, so many desperate smiles. The younger women know what date rape is. They publicly charge it, publish it, prosecute it, because it is the truth. And, as the angry men know, these young women are the future.

The male strategy in undermining the claim is simple, rapelike verbal attacks on women as such: on the inherent capacity of women to say what we mean, to know what has happened, to say anything true. The old rape jurisprudence protected men from rape charges by so-called vindictive women (any woman they might know). To undermine the validity of date rape, male supremacists claim that all women are vindictive women; that date rape is a vindictive social fantasy, a collective hysteria, invented by that mass of vindictive women, feminists. The whole political spectrum, gendered male, claims that women are emotional illiterates (heretofore the province of men; see, they can learn to give up territory). *National Review* defined date rape as any sex that a woman later regretted. Over a year earlier, *Playboy* (October 1990) made the same charge (in an article penned by a woman, *Playboy*-style, to break our hearts): "...the new definition of rape gives women a simple way of thinking about sex that externalizes guilt, remorse or conflict. Bad feelings after sex become someone else's fault. A sexual encounter is transformed into a one-way event in which the woman has no stake, no interest, and no active role." Actually, the rapist defines the woman's role (the very essence of rape) and it is about time that the guilt was externalized. He can have the remorse, too. We can share the conflict. *Playboy*'s prolonged propaganda campaign against date rape predates the mainstream backlash—usually the verbiage is in unsigned editorial copy, not written by the token girl. *Playboy* has the political role of developing the misogynist program that is then assimilated, one hand typing, into news journals left and right. The point of view is the same, *National Review* or *Playboy*, with the left political magazines paying better lip-service (for women who like that sort of thing) to feminist sensibilities while ripping us apart by critiquing our so-called excesses. Underlying virtually all of the date-rape critiques is the conviction that women simply cannot face having had consensual sex. A genetic puritanism (it travels with the housekeeping gene) makes us sorry all the time; and when we are sorry we retaliate—we call it date rape, sexual harassment, we tear the pornography off the walls. Any way one looks at it, these boys ain't great lovers. Women are not left quivering, begging for more (waiting by the phone for his call). The old-type vindictive woman used to want the man to stay but he left; she retaliated for being betrayed or abandoned. The new vindictive woman— on college campuses, for instance—can't get far enough away from him; she appears to retaliate because he has shown up. Surely, this is different. Male privilege seems to be at stake here, not any woman's sense of regret. (That is a different girls' club. Men one wants to sleep with can be bastards, too.) Regret tends to be an identifiable emotion, one even dumb women (a redundancy in the male-supremacist lexicon) can recognize. It has taken us longer to identify garden-variety rape because use of us against our will was so protected for so long. Now we know what it is; and so will he. Count on it.

Date rape and sexual harassment have emerged together—in 1991 because of the coincidence of Anita Hill's charges against Clarence Thomas and the prosecution for rape of William Kennedy Smith; politically because each challenges men's right to have sexual access to women who are not hidden away, to women who are out and about. Both date rape and sexual harassment were, as Gloria Steinem says, just life—until women turned them into crimes. Each is defended as essential masculine practice, necessary to the expression of male sexuality—he chases, he conquers. The proscribing of each is repudiated by those who defend rapist sexuality as synonymous with male sexuality. "Enough is enough," writes *Playboy*'s hired girl, this time on sexual harassment (February 1991). "An aggressively vehement sexual-harassment policy, whether in the workplace, on campus or in high school, spreads a message that there is something intrinsically evil about male sexuality. It preaches that men must keep their reactions (and their erections) bottled up tightly, that any remnant of that sexuality (in the form of a look, a comment, a gesture, even a declaration of interest) is potentially dangerous, hurtful, and, now, criminal." (A bottle is fine; in high schools they can be found in the chemistry lab.) Sexual harassment laws and policies are gender-neutral, in keeping with a basic ethic of contemporary United States law. The existence of the laws and policies does not indict men; but the frenzied repudiation does indict men—it is a male-supremacist repudiation of conscience, fairness, and, of course, equality. Some feminists say "please." Some feminists say "put up or shut up." But it is the defenders of male privilege who say that it is the nature of men to aggress against women; that male sexuality requires such aggression. It is the defenders of male privilege who say that male sexuality is essentially rapist. Feminists say that laws against date rape and sexual harassment are fair laws. No man of conscience will use force against a woman nor will he use his power to harass, pursue, humiliate, or "have" her. Men raised in a rapist culture, in conflict with it but also having internal conflict, wanting to be fair, wanting to honor equality, will not want to rape or to sexually harass; these laws will set standards and show the way. It was good of us, and generous, to pursue remedies in a principled way, without shedding blood. These things have been done to us. They will stop.

But Thomas was confirmed and Smith was acquitted. Now the question is: how do we nail them? Think.

Brooklyn, New York
January 1992

Andrea Dworkin is the author of Intercourse, Pornography: Men Possessing Women, *and the novel* Mercy. *She is co-author of legislation recognizing pornography as a violation of women's civil rights.*

Doublespeak and Doublehear, Anita Hill in Our Lives

Introduction by
Margaret Randall

From October 12 through 15, 1991, millions of women in the United States were riveted to our television sets or radios. Many men watched too, and some women and men who follow political events more closely were engaged by what was happening even earlier. But from the 12th through the 15th a process unfolded in U.S. mass media that held particular impact for women. An African American woman law professor named Anita Hill sat before a panel of fourteen white male senators and made public her accusations of sexual misconduct against a poorly qualified conservative Black male who President Bush had nominated to become an associate justice of the U.S. Supreme Court.

There was much that was noteworthy in both the events themselves and in the process behind them. Presidents Reagan and Bush have consistently nominated conservatives to the high court, as part of their overall program of pushing back class, race, and gender gains fought for and won since the sixties. As the last of the truly constitutional justices grow old and retire, these presidents have been successful at gradually stacking the court in favor of a neo-conservative agenda. Sometimes they have miscalculated, as in the case of Robert Bork. That people's victory showed the need for minor concessions in order to present an impeccable mask behind which fundamentalist ideas could hide.

Clarence Thomas—a Black man who was born and raised in Pinpoint, Georgia, and had worked his way up the American ladder to be graduated from Yale Law School—was ideal. Only 43, his tenure on the court would assure decades of anti-working class, anti-minority, and anti-woman decisions.

Sometime during Thomas's senate confirmation hearings his opponents got word of rumors that he sexually harassed one or more women who had worked for him at the Department of Education or the Equal Employment Opportunities Commission. The name Anita Hill was mentioned, and senate staffers tracked her down at the University of Oklahoma where she now teaches law. It took a number of phone conversations to convince Professor Hill to come forward with her story. An FBI investigation was concluded during the all-senate hearings, but the senators obviously didn't pay much attention to the charges. After all, they were made by a Black woman. One wonders how this part of the history might have differed, had it been a white woman charging a Black man with sexual misconduct of the type described in detail by Hill.

But some unknown someone—a member of the senate judiciary committee or his staff—leaked the report of Hill's charges to the press. Leaks are common on Capitol Hill. It is interesting how much has been made of this one. The scandal put pressure on Congress to at least hear the accusations. In the midst of the usual ruckus about who leaked the information (government is often more concerned about *how* things happen than about what the fact of their existence says about what passes for justice in this country), the judiciary committee decided to hold special and public hearings so they could air Anita Hill's story.

During the public hearings, and especially when Thomas himself was given the opportunity of answering Hill's charges, the administration used race as a clever political ploy to try to mask or divert the gender issue. The very nomination of a man with such a poor legal background but who was Black, had been a political rather than a legal choice. But then Thomas, in about as unjudgelike a posture as it was possible to assume, refused to address the charges against him. He wouldn't even hear them. Instead he relied on the effect of loaded images like "high-tech lynching" and the traditionally discriminatory over-emphasis on the sexual characteristics of Black males in a move designed to shame and subdue those white men who questioned him. As a result, for the purpose of the hearings and in spite of the moving testimony of extraordinarily credible character witnesses, Anita Hill's allegations were defeated where they stood.

Thomas got away with verbal grandstanding in lieu of any real response. Had Hill given in to emotion, had she raised her voice or responded to any number of the committee members' patronizing taunts, or had she in any other way moved from her dignified, concise, and underplayed testimony, she would certainly have been labeled strident, hysterical, even crazy. She handled herself admirably. Yet she was destined to lose before she began to speak. That is, if one sees winning or losing as exclusively circumscribed to the Thomas nomination.

Important as that nomination was, Hill's testimony goes far beyond it. The reason so many millions of women sat mesmerized before our television sets that weekend in October, the reason many of us tuned in our radios as we drove back and forth from work and even sat in parking lots, unable to tear ourselves from this woman's story, was that she was speaking for us. Her voice was our voice. Her story is one that belongs to the vast majority of working women in this and most other countries of the world.

19

And if we look at the larger picture—not only sexual harassment on the job, but sexual abuse in all its forms, wrought (most often) by men against women—we know that Anita Hill's experience and her telling of that experience belongs to women everywhere. It belongs to some men as well. It belongs to all those who in one or more ways are rendered vulnerable by virtue of our dependent positions within the patriarchy, a system supported and strengthened by a capitalist economy, imperialist expansion, and colonialism outside or within our borders.

An African American woman, a devout Christian and politically conservative woman, well educated, unmarried, with her parents standing at her side, a woman who had also been born into poverty, one of thirteen sisters and brothers, Anita Hill graduated from the same Yale Law School attended by Thomas. She worked for him at two different government agencies, and then went on to a tenured professorship at a major university.

Hill had nothing personal to gain and everything to lose by breaking ten years of silence about what she had suffered in Thomas's employ. But she finally decided to tell the story so many of us have been forced to swallow in silence. We who have lived through our own versions of her experience heard her loud and clear. We who have been sexually harassed, used and abused, and—like Hill—in order to keep our jobs or our incomes or our children or our status or our dignity itself have felt it necessary not to speak, had no trouble relating to what she said.

Anita Hill spoke for us: We who have spoken and were not believed. We who have not spoken, often because we *knew* we would not be believed. We who knew that if we told the terrible secret we would gain nothing, and lose what little we had. Ultimately Anita Hill also was not believed, at least by the mostly white male forces with the power to confirm Clarence Thomas. But her words were not spoken uselessly, or without gain. Unacceptable as is the prospect of Clarence Thomas on the bench, there is a larger picture that has to do with the fact of sexual harassment and abuse at every level of our national life. Anita Hill's testimony brought this untalked-about but ever-present reality into public view.

This is why we were mesmerized by Anita Hill's testimony. Through the doublespeak of congressional jargon, through the "rules" and all their officious interpretations, through the indignities suffered by Hill as opposed to the treatment afforded the man she accused, the sound of her single voice remains.

Doublespeak is an interesting phenomenon. The English novelist and essayist George Orwell (1903-1950) coined the word to refer to a language which appears to be the opposite of what it really is. The political agenda of public rhetoric and mass media rely heavily on this device. Additionally, the technological age provides new ways to ensure that language serves the interests of those in power. For example, it was no accident that Anita Hill's testimony was scheduled during daytime television, when some five million Americans customarily tune in, and Clarence Thomas's was at night when he would be heard by 30 million.

But when an experience is shared by a large enough number of people, *and when some of those people have been courageous enough to break the silence*, doublespeak itself may confront a kind of *doublehear*. For it is absolutely clear that those looking and listening during that weekend in October *heard* two different stories. We women and some men who experience and therefore understand the reality of sexual oppression, heard one story. Most men and those women who have sufficiently internalized the patriarchal value system, heard another. This is the gender gap of power.

Those who lack the experience and thus the knowledge, those who protect themselves when they claim that sexual harassment is infrequent or that it must be *proved*, were suspicious of Hill's words: *Could they be true? No, of course not. Why, a man who would do such things would surely be in a mental institution wouldn't he? She must be doing this for personal reasons. Probably put up to it by one of those feminist special interest groups. Or maybe she wants to write a book. Is she a woman who loved and was spurned? The experts say...fantasy...memory...why, a judge wouldn't lie, now would he?*

But to women who have shared this experience many times over, to women who have endured it in silence, sure that we would never be taken seriously if we spoke, Anita Hill's words were heard quite differently. We were listening to something we know to be true. As one of Hill's witnesses, Ellen Wells, so eloquently responded when questioned by the senators as to why she thought Hill had not written down what Thomas had said to her: You don't have to write it down, Senator. It's etched in your body forever. You only wish you could forget (a paraphrase).

Sexual harassment, sexual abuse of different kinds, incest, rape, battery, trivialization, and other discriminatory practices against women, which are facts of everyday life for most of us, evoke a picture we know too well. Those who have experienced this reality, or are close to someone who has, have no trouble believing Anita Hill. Those in whose interest it remains to protect themselves from this knowledge, particularly the perpetrators, will of course claim that she is lying.

We have all been wronged in the person of Anita Hill. Black women, faced in this case with a false choice between race and gender, suffered the most profound abuse. All women who carry in our bodies a memory of sexual harassment and how it is protected under patriarchy, know that our reality has been publicly denigrated and that once more the power of the male hierarchy has won out. And the American public has what we have allowed the administration to foist upon us: a Supreme Court weighted against our best interests as a people.

Nevertheless, Anita Hill's voice is a part of our process now. It thunders in the chorus of voices—voices that have been raised at great personal risk, with courage, in ever-widening circles of reclaimed power— by women and men who are no longer willing to allow the perpetrators to go unchallenged. We tell our single stories and we tell a collective one—of minds and bodies damaged by abuse, of unredressed grievances, or a travesty that will no longer give in to silence. Increasingly, our stories are also about the healing and the rechanneled energies unleashed by our ability to speak the pain.

This collection of personal testimonies is one of many responses to Anita Hill's conviction and courage. Those who have spoken out before her contributed in tangible ways to Hill's ability to go public with her story. She in turn strengthens the resolve of many who will speak out now. We give and take from one another. In our individual and collective refusal to suffer in silence, we make it easier for others who might have been afraid to speak to do so.

Together we are creating a safe space where we may call abuse by its name, identifying our abusers and making them responsible for their acts. When our rage speaks louder than a status quo that would protect the abuser, our lives and the lives of our children will be different. Less damaged. More whole. Freer and more creative. Blessed with the dignity of all our memories retrieved.

Margaret Randall is a poet, photographer, teacher, and activist.

DOUBLECROSSED

Mary Allison

By the time I was about ten, most old men gave me the creeps. I hated how they'd paw at me. "Give me some sugar," they would say. Then they'd reach out and grab me like they were the grandfathers of the world. They thought I would just love to be petted or patted, to catch their eye or their praise. Deep down I hated them and I knew why. Because I couldn't trust them.

They hardly ever spoke when they'd do certain things. Things like sneak their hand up my leg and inside my panties. It wasn't just one of them who was the problem, it was not knowing who'd turn out to be that way. For instance, Uncle Bill wasn't that way. Mr. Thompson was. So was Father Reynolds.

The worst was the electrician, the one who cornered me and fondled me in the school hallway, then threatened to kill me if I ever told anyone. He meant it; I believed him. I spent half that night in terror before it came tumbling, crying out of me.

I was almost twelve when it happened. The Sheriff's deputy came to the house, talked to my parents and then to me. He had a clip board and a ball point pen that he kept clicking. He was filling out forms and shaking his head. "Well, I can take all this down but I'll be honest with you folks, most of these cases never make it to court," he said.

The next day I had to go back to the school with the police to point the man out. I was afraid to go without my mother. They told me this man would never get near me, that he couldn't hurt me anymore. I knew they were wrong. I was afraid I wouldn't be able to forget.

Just imagine it, first you're molested, then you're threatened, then you have to identify this man who you never wanted to see again. On top of that, your mother hasn't stopped crying since you told her what happened, and that drives you crazy because she hardly ever cries and you know you're the one who caused it. It was definitely not my week.

It was summer. School was not in session, I was glad of that. I didn't know what I could tell anyone who asked why I was riding in a police car. There was another unmarked squad car in the parking lot when we arrived. From where we stopped, I could see the man's panel truck, dingy grey with maroon lettering. I recognized it because it was the only vehicle parked outside the school on the day before. He was inside the school building. My stomach sank, feeling like it was full of river rocks. I swallowed. I wanted to run. I wanted this morning to be over. I wanted this thing to have never happened. "All you have to do is let us know which man it was," they said. Easy as pie, right? No, not right. Not easy. "O.K.," I said.

The first man they escorted out of the school was not the right one. "That's not him," I announced. They knew that. They were just clearing the hallway "in case there was any trouble." There had already been too much trouble, as far as I was concerned.

A few minutes went by and the police emerged, surrounding the man who had messed with me. I was glad they didn't bring him over to the car I was now standing behind. I knew if he broke free, he would run straight to me and make good on his promise to kill me, especially now, so I was poised, ready to escape. I knew there were paths in the scrub palms that surrounded the school, and I knew this time I could outrun him. He would not get within a hundred feet of me again, not if I saw him coming.

They loaded him into the back of a squad car and off they drove. It was over, I thought.

It wasn't over.

"He won't bother you or anyone else for a very long time," they told me on the drive back to my house.

We went to a small office downtown for the preliminary hearing. Two men in business suits were asking all the questions. "Had you ever seen this man before?" No. "Were you friendly to him?" "What did you say?" "What did he say?" My mother began crying softly; the men went on with their questions. "What did he do then?" Her tears began to streak down both her cheeks as my father consoled her.

So much about that day I did not understand, sitting in that room, trying to be braver than my mother, wishing she would not cry here in this place. "Then what did you do?" I hate to cry, and I hated even more to admit it but that's what happened after that man in the hallway at school had slid his hand inside my blouse and felt my breast.

My mother folded into a mass of sobs. "That will be all," the man behind the desk ended. Someone put a dime into the Coke machine, brought me a drink.

A few weeks later the trial began. I did not want to see that man, the molester. If he was in the courtroom, I did not look at him. Everyone stood when the judge entered the courtroom. "The State of Florida vs. Jacob C."

I was scared to death. I was the only kid in a room with dozens of adults. I had to go on the witness stand and I had to do this alone. I was to answer questions about the time I was trying my hardest to forget. And what if they asked me who else had done such things to me? I would be under oath. God himself would get me if I lied. My mother would kill me if she knew that Mr. C. was not the only man who took his turn with me.

They called my name and I had to place my hand on the Bible and swear to tell the truth. They asked how old I was, where I went to school, what grade I was in, how I was doing with my studies. All the easy questions were first. Then they asked about Mr. C. and what happened. "Had you ever seen him before?" No. "What were you doing in the school hallway after hours?" I was on my way home and that was my usual shortcut. "What did he say to you?" He asked where I lived. I showed him; we could see my house from the end of the hallway. That's when he cornered me and slipped his hand inside my shirt. "I like them small," he had told me.

"Did you offer any resistance?" I was asked. Chills ran through me when I heard that question. Had I done something wrong? Would I be found guilty?

"Did you offer any resistance?" he repeated.

"Have you ever wrestled with a man twice your size?" I asked. The courtroom filled with laughter.

The judge smacked his gavel on the desk. "Court will reconvene in the morning," he said.

That night two strangers came to the house, an older woman and a young man. I was sent to my room. I snuck up the hall to try to hear what was being said in the living room, but all I could hear were muffled tones. Then the strangers left.

My parents stayed up late that night talking in their bedroom. My head was full of questions that had no answers, feelings that had no names. In a way this whole thing was like a bad dream I couldn't wake up from.

The next morning my mother told me we were not going back to court any more. The people who were at the house last night were Mrs. C. and the son who was just finishing seminary. "I think Mr. C. has learned his lesson," my mother said.

"What?" I asked, shocked.

"If we continue with this and Mr. C. is sent to jail, it could ruin his son's career as a minister," she explained. "Besides, I really feel sorry for Mrs. C. She's been through so much already. Now, what I want you to do is go get dressed for school, and just forget about all this."

I did forget about it for twenty years or so. That is to say my memory misplaced it, because there's a part in you that never truly forgets, it simply guards you, helps you stay two steps ahead of strangers, and maybe friends as well.

I never married. In fact, by my mid-twenties I began to realize I was gay. I don't mean to say Jacob C. caused it, but I do feel he played a part. When you learn that nothing is safe, for sure and certain, and that men will mess with you if they get the chance, there is an automatic wall you put up to protect yourself.

Sometime after I understood this connection, I was riding in my mother's car; we were alone. "You know, I've begun to wonder if that incident with Jacob C. hasn't in some way affected my ability to get close to men," I said.

She was silent for a moment, then said, "The person I always felt sorry for was his poor wife."

"Yes, I remember," I answered.

She reached over and snapped on the air conditioner.

Mary Allison is a nurse, caterer, carpenter, award winning photographer, and unsubmitted, hence previously unpublished, author.

Halcyon Days

AnneMarie Arnold

Richard and I are having our afternoon caffeine fix: coffee and chicory brewed to a thick syrup served with hot milk and sugar, listening to jazz while discussing our latest art project. I love my life, New Orleans, and my good friends like Richard. I'm young and free and happy in my new house, a little 1920s Victorian shotgun in the Irish Channel. Like the house next door it has recently been renovated—complete with a dishwasher and an alarm system. This is considered a fairly good neighborhood, but because the house has a lot of windows, I sleep more easily at night having this security. I could be even safer if I installed burglar bars on all of my windows, but I like my view unobstructed.

I can see Dr. Steve Kook as he pulls up in his new red hot Alfa Romeo convertible. Steve is nervous, jerking his head from side to side as if worried about being seen by someone—his wife, maybe? Steve is my former boss. He probably wants to know if I need a ride somewhere since I don't own a car. I don't need a car, I like to walk. Or he might try to coax me into going shopping for something; I like to make my own clothes. Steve is a consumer. He wants to consume me. He wanted to consume me from the first moment he met me.

"Let's do lunch," Steve would say, or rather drool down my neck. He embarrassed me. I knew he had an erection under his white lab coat and he should be the one embarrassed, not me. I did not want to be his lunch.

Steve does not know that I have company. He rings the doorbell. I yell from inside that I am busy and to go away, I have work to do. Steve wants my attention. I find him incredibly boring and, no, I'd rather walk to the store. I remember when he used to tell me to leave work early and to buy his daughter a little present. "Part of the job," he would laugh nervously. And while I was shopping I could "buy something, too; aren't credit cards great, just sign 'Mrs. Kook'!"

"Yeah, sure, that's normal," his secretary would say, "since Dr. Kook has nothing else for you to do. After all he's the boss." Steve would then follow me downtown in his Alfa and suddenly appear with his arm around me offering food, wine, and romance. I just wanted to go home—without him. I called my girlfriend

27

and asked her to meet me downtown for dinner.

Richard has never seen me so rude. I apologize to him and attend to our project. Steve walks around the house and jumps up and down calling to me from outside the window. I again tell him to leave. I lock the doors, slam the windows shut, and turn on the alarm. I assure Richard that Steve is harmless and that we should continue with our task.

Yes, everything seemed so "harmless" to everyone but me up to the moment Steve fired me. I can remember the first day at work when I didn't even have an office space in which to work. I was supposed to sit outside his office and be "on call" for him. My office and drafting table were just ordered, he said, and it might take a while. Then, when Steve noticed how highly visible I was to the other doctors and how they were starting to flirt with me, he quickly removed me to an obscure corner of a back office and I sat in a chair waiting for work to arrive. I don't know what I would have done if any work did arrive since I had no supplies.

Steve's yelling is too distracting and I turn up the music. Now Richard and I cannot even hear ourselves think. Shit! I can't stand it! I tell Steve that if he doesn't leave I will call the police. I call the police and tell them that a crazy man is jumping up and down at my windows and that I can't even leave my own house without this person harassing me and would they please tell him to leave.

"Nice car this guy's got, would you please talk to him, ma'am?" This is unbelievable, I'm a prisoner in my own home. "No, I don't want to talk to him, I have freelance work to do and he is disrupting my business." They look at me and roll their eyes. "Oh, come on, he seems like he's a nice guy and he is really upset."

I can't believe it. I'm upset. Steve is ruining my nice afternoon. "Yeah, I'll talk to him but don't leave till he's gone." The police go back to their car across the street. Steve whines for a few minutes about how his wife denies him carnal pleasures. "So, you want me to hire you a prostitute?" I don't want to talk to Steve. Steve says, "How can I get you to talk to me?"

"Okay, Steve, write a check for a thousand dollars and we'll talk." I grab the check, wave at the police to let them know that all is well and tell Steve that he can't come in because I've got to leave for an appointment, and no I don't need a ride. Richard and I decide to work again tomorrow. I go to the bank immediately to cash the check. Soon after, I sell my house, buy a car and leave town.

AnneMarie Arnold is an artist and mother.

PLEADING IGNORANCE

Carol Atkins

I am a 68-year-old woman who has experienced sexual harassment in the workplace, in social situations, in school, from the medical profession, and from religious groups. Rather than focus on one or two incidents, I want to speak out on how I responded to the harassment and how it affected the way I regarded myself.

My response to harassment in the workplace: I got out of there. Always. I just left. Even though it cost me jobs I liked, I left. I did not know that sexual harassment was endemic; I thought some other place would be free of it. I also thought that something in my behavior had triggered the harassment (though I did not call it that). So I did not say anything to anyone about it, and used other reasons for leaving.

Once I applied for a job on a weekly newspaper and was told that they put the paper to bed on Saturday night, when I would be working with an all-male staff, and I would not be "comfortable" there. I knew what that meant and did not pursue the job further.

My response to sexual harassment socially, in school, with the medical and religious communities was the same. I removed myself as soon as possible. Socially I tried to make a joke of it first, but always, always I wanted out of there. You have to remember that there were only two kinds of women then—the madonna/whore syndrome held full sway—so I spent many hours blaming myself for what happened, trying to find acceptable solutions, and regarding myself as inept, incapable of coping, socially clumsy, stupid and somehow "bad."

Now I know better and see what happened to me over the years as classic, predictable and even trite. But I write this because I want all women to know better than I did.

Another thing. Recently men have been pleading ignorance about sexual harassment. They say they did not know their behavior caused distress, discomfort. I don't buy this. They knew. Men know what a bully is and bullies know they make people miserable. They do "get it." It is time we faced this fact.

Carol Atkins is a 68-year-old Anglo-Saxon free-lance writer who is looking for another planet to live on.

Cath Jackson

PRESENTATION

Sheila Benson

I was working as the secretary to the director of the research department at a network owned and operated television station in Los Angeles. Annually the station participated in a presentation to affiliated stations throughout the country in order to demonstrate positive ratings and shares of audience figures. I was asked to type the presentation and I was flattered to do so. After finalizing the presentation, the station manager held a meeting in his office to present the project to the sales department. I was asked to join the meeting, which was held after the business day. I was the only female present. The presentation was read aloud simultaneously as a slide show was displayed on a screen.

When it came time for bragging about the local station's recent ratings accomplishments, the slide which appeared was of a naked woman with the numerals painted on her buttocks. At that point, the several males present looked at me and laughed. I felt humiliated. I was speechless, in shock, and my face was crimson. I felt betrayed by this group of males, now known as the "good old boy network." I was powerless to do or say anything to anyone. There was no one to whom I could report this incident, even if I had the confidence to do so, because the general manager of the station and my boss were participants.

It did not occur to me until I watched Anita Hill during the Thomas hearings that I had been a victim of sexual harassment in the workplace. Even though this incident occurred twenty-five years ago, when I was twenty years old, I can still recall the incredible humiliation that I felt on that day.

Sheila Benson is 45 years old, Caucasian, and self-employed in medical insurance services.

LIFE IN AMERICA: SEXISM AND SEXUAL HARASSMENT

HENRIE BENSUSSEN

This is a scene that pops into my mind at all hours of the day or night: some man assaults me; I respond with a hurricane of anger, scratching out his eyes, stabbing him with my handy Swiss army knife, strangling him with his necktie, stomping his balls, bashing his head on the sidewalk. I have observed the way men behave toward women in this society over the past fifty years and it has brutalized my soul.

Was it sexual harassment when I presented myself to a dermatologist at my health clinic with a contact rash that turned my breasts red and itchy, and he had me wait half-naked while he rounded up all his doctor buddies to come and stare, as if I were a circus sideshow?

Was it sexism or sexual harassment when a neurologist, testing my neck and arm reflexes with an open safety pin, began to nonchalantly and, seemingly in all innocence, pull the hospital gown off my shoulders?

Talking of innocence, was it sexual harassment or just frisky love when my young husband wrestled me to the floor in front of my parents as we were saying goodbye after a visit?

Was it child pornography or sexual harassment when an esteemed psychology professor gave a public lecture to a mostly female audience about sexuality and development and during his slide show presented a photo of his naked granddaughter, age 13? She looked straight into the camera, without expression. I know that look—of taking oneself out of the moment, of being psychically absent. She has given him her consent, he tells us, to take this picture. Has she given her informed consent, I wonder, for him to continue to use the slide in his college classes, as he says he does, five years later? What would she feel like if, as a young adult, she happened to be attending one of those classes?

You find this going on every day, every place. The train conductors stand in the stairwell opposite the boarding door, their eyes at a level to get the best view of women in tight skirts climbing up the steps. There are all those movies with the obligatory scene of the naked female star, a scene totally irrelevant and unnecessary to the movie's plot, unless the plot is really sexual harassment. The actress doesn't have to sleep with the director any more, but she does have to undress for the camera and the audience. Many times I find these scenes uncomfortable; it's not as if I knew before I bought my ticket that this is part of the price of admission.

I've worked in places where the office was full of women and the warehouse full of guys. When I went to the women's room, at the rear of the warehouse, I held my head high and just shut out the remarks, the gestures, as if they weren't there. Those guys. In another job, on my first day, the office Romeo finished smooching one clerk and moved in my direction. When he tried to put his arm around me I shrugged him off and stepped away. He got the hint. And that is how I've managed in a lot of situations. When a man looked at me as though he was shopping for a sex toy, I would put both physical and psychic space between us. I didn't join in. I acted naive, unknowing, unapproachable.

That's the way I've been forced to be in this culture. My grandmother used to make me read rape stories reported in the newspaper so I would always be aware of lurking danger. You build a wall, a glass shell, to protect yourself. Then it becomes part of you so you can't get rid of it, even with a lover, even when you want to. In the work world, women are bent to the role of the respectful daughter serving the male patriarch, who could banish her if she's not obsequious in the correct way. She takes on the role easily; she's been trained to think this way in her family and by her school.

This is my experience. I've been so busy defending my space and tending my glass shell that I've never made it out of the pink-collar ghetto. Maybe it's that repressed anger shining in my eyes that has put off job offers. Now I just look forward to early retirement and having a little business of my own—secretarial in nature, no doubt. But at least I won't be under some man's thumb. My answer is to opt out of the male-controlled establishment. A better answer would be for women to organize together and support a new party, as N.O.W. has suggested, since we can trust neither the Democrats nor the Republicans to pass or enforce legislation to protect women.

Henrie Bensussen is a 54-year-old Jewish lesbian secretary and grandmother.

MERCY

Abby Lynn Bogomolny

Rita Mae Brown in *Rubyfruit Jungle* calls Gainesville, Florida, "the bedpan of the South." Gainesville is also the home of the nation's largest facility for the study of cockroaches. Before the University of Florida was placed in "hogtown," as it was known, its main industry was agriculture. But the University of Florida put Gainesville on the map for solar energy development, journalism and communications and gave the town a new reason for tourism: Florida Gator football. The university also houses the original writings of Zora Neale Hurston and attracts liberal thinkers and students, one of whom invented Gatorade. The balmy weather also attracts transients who, when mixed with the town's good ol' boy establishment, give Gainesville the honor of being the rape capital of the United States.

I was a second-year graduate student working on a degree in communications. My assistantship had run out. I needed to work and was looking forward to having a job which left me some energy to think about my research project. When I answered the secretarial ad for National Surveyor's Seminar, it seemed like the perfect office job.

T.G. Minson II was an attorney who had built himself a small publishing and mail order business. He also toured the United States lecturing on land surveying. Minson's son, Bill, also worked for him as "the shipping department." My job was to type up the book orders, lecture registrations and answer the phone. I would be a one-person office. Simple and boring. I took it.

Minson was pale with red hair and stood six feet four. He came from old Southern money, namely his father's estate in Largo, Florida. At 45, Minson was finally doing well. The guy was making money. He had been a drinker and rebel in his twenties and thirties, but had straightened up in a period of five short years. After working there for six months, he confided that he had converted to the Mormon church, saying that it helped him in his efforts to rid himself of caffeine and alcohol. He was also intent on getting richer.

The assault on my self-worth began slowly. It began with nonchalant references to my appearance. After two months, Minson preferred that I call him "Ted." The job wasn't the type of position where I had to meet the public or other professionals, so I never wore dresses. Somehow it didn't make sense to dress up in order to work in an office in a trailer park; plus, the only people there were Ted and Bill. Often Ted Minson was out of town and he rarely wore a suit himself. Bill never came to work in anything more formal than jeans. So I was surprised when Ted one day asked me, "Why don't you wear dresses?" I said that I was more comfortable in nice blouses and jeans. That day's conversation ended there. However, the subject of my appearance became a theme over the next few months. He would comment on my lack of makeup and would continue to ask me why I never wore a dress and almost always wore long sleeve shirts. "Do you have scars on your legs or something?" he asked me one Friday. He then told me that men liked "to see a little skin now and then in the office."

My response to these comments was silence. I was too insulted to reply. My work for Ted's business had been excellent. He had entrusted me with the editing of his monthly newsletter. He consulted with me on advertising issues, fully taking advantage of my graduate school experience in communications. We discussed business issues that he would never talk about with his son. We had a professional relationship. And I respected Ted's intellect in business matters and his accomplishments. Even though our worldviews were entirely different (he was blatantly sexist and very racist), I was learning a great deal about how men like him did business. Somehow, these remarks seemed so out of context that I refused to believe I was hearing them. They increased in frequency.

He began to call me "hotlips." "Hotlips, bring your buns in here. I have a job for you." I began to picture him as a type of simple dog who snarls at intruders, then turns and bites one of his own family. Looking back now, I should have walked out that day or told him that the nickname was unacceptable. But in the social fabric of that office, telling him anything was unacceptable. It was so difficult. I would have had to confront him immediately. The obvious result would be that I lose my paycheck. And that appeared to be more difficult than putting up with a few silly comments. There was only one role I could play to continue working for Ted at that time.

He then started to ask me why my boyfriend never came to pick me up. "The reason he never comes to pick you up is that he's probably black, right?"

Ted never said much to me about his wife, Doris. One day she came to the office and strongly hinted to me that the restroom was dirty. Suddenly my position as secretary was enlarged to that of cleaning woman, too.

I complained to Ted. He said to Doris, in front of me, "You've got to stop this, dear. You're upsetting the help." But that comment didn't stop Doris from leaving a toilet bowl brush on my seat, which I found when I came back from lunch that day.

"You left your toothbrush on my chair," I told Ted. He just laughed.

After that day, Ted took the opportunity to lapse into complaints about his wife, which continued over the next few weeks. He would usually talk about her in the middle of another project we were discussing. I would try to bring the conversation back to our work, but Ted was intent on letting me know that he and Doris were not "doing it" any more. I would leave his office and go back to my desk to resume working. He seemed to accept this nonverbal message that I didn't want to hear his personal problems. Then one day he asked me if I would take "mercy" on him.

"What?" I replied.

"When I was in high school," Ted began, "there was a guy who was a loser. He could never get a date, and if he had a date he never could 'get any.' Sex I mean. Well, a few of us felt sorry for him and finally arranged for a willing girl to have 'mercy' on him. We called it a mercy screw." I picked up my papers and started to walk away. Ted followed me to the door of his office. "I really feel like that guy. How about it?"

After that day my silence grew larger. It enveloped my every movement. I no longer made conversation with Ted that was unrelated to business. I told no one of the incident. I looked for a new job. Then I asked for a raise. He denied it, citing his inability to pay more. I gave notice. He asked me to stay another month because his stepdaughter was having surgery soon and it would be too much stress to train someone new during that time. I stayed another month. The two women I trained to take my job didn't come back to work after the third day. By my last day, the business had not yet found someone to take my place.

Today, I would never tolerate such abusive working conditions.

Abby Lynn Bogomolny is a writer and certified hypnotherapist living in Santa Cruz, California.

An Open Letter To All Of My Harassers—
They Know Who They Are

Claire Braz-Valentine

I just wanted to say that I have followed you throughout your life
and I am happy to report
that you, my college journalism T.A.
who tried to rape me,
have never been published anywhere,
probably because you were more interested
in chasing women than deadlines.
And you, the minister who kept visiting me in the name of God,
who took the laying on of hands seriously,
were defrocked,
and not in a woman's bedroom the way you always wanted.
And the owner of the restaurant where I got fired,
because I wouldn't put out,
you got put out permanently by fire one night.
You always wanted things to heat up.
And to the supervisor who pinned up
the playboy centerfold
that looked like me,
you lost your job,
the way I lost my dignity.
And let's not forget the manager who whispered foul
messages in my ears.
You lost your whole company.
What a shame.
And my boss, the sales consultant,
who wanted me to travel with him
and share his bed,
took to drinking and died one day,
while giving a lecture on how to sell yourself.

I know the lecture, he tried it on me.

Isn't it strange that all of you ended up so miserably
and I did not.
While you were planning little rendezvous,
I was planning little promotions.
While you were focusing on what was between your legs,
I was focusing on what was between my ears.
While you were thinking about having sex with me,
I was thinking about having your job.
And guess what I got it.

Condolences,
Your victim.

Claire Braz-Valentine teaches writing at Soledad State Prison, and worked for many years at UCSC as a Sexual Harassment Advisor.

SO MANY CHOICES, SO LITTLE TIME

Jan Buckwald

Women and harassment. It's a question of choice, isn't it? With so many examples, it's hard to choose just one. Well, here's mine. Not the most insidious, or complex, or even the most disgusting. But it did make me Superwoman for a day. And it is for that reason that I share the story.

It was a normal, sunny day in the city. People going to work (well, it was more normal back then, in 1983) or going for coffee or going out to jog. Some other people—carpenter people—were wandering around on the roof of my apartment building, getting ready to carpent. Me, I was just going out for a run.

Do the carpenters have anything to do with this story, you ask? You needn't ask. You already know the answer. Because you, yourself, have crossed the street probably a jillion times to avoid that scene. You've felt your face burn red in that confounding mix of anger and embarrassment and helplessness. While trying to look as if you didn't even notice them, you, too, have wished for some recourse, some response to their whistles and grunts and gestures and stares. I have, too, only I didn't actually come up with a super good one until that day I went out for a run.

I had tried a few different things before. Staring back doesn't work. Looking critically at the beams and joists only works once in a while; it works while you're facing the crew. (Once you've passed, it's hunting season for them again, and there may be an added backlash against your questioning their ability). Spitting, I find, works more effectively with this type of jerk and the ones who drive by hanging out of their car windows. Something about superimposing the image of a woman spitting onto that of a Playboy bunny just doesn't work for them.

Anyway, the city. I'm just walking down the steps from my apartment when I hear the whistling of carpenters on the roof, whistling and yelling at another jogger (female, of course) running by. She does the usual, used to this treatment from the time she was a teenager. She pretends not to hear, looks straight ahead, and keeps on running. I head the other way, my best plan at the moment being to avoid them altogether. (This does work, but sets something brewing inside.) And something was a-brew as I continued running. When I got back to the building, in my shorts and T-shirt, they saw me. They whistled. They couldn't know what was coming. To them I looked like just another defenseless female. My cape was tucked in and hidden beneath my T-shirt.

My heart had started pounding several moments before, when it started seeping into my consciousness that this time I would have to do my part to save the city for myself and other women who ran. Blood raced through my body. My mouth was dry. But I knew what I had to do. I stopped. I took a deep breath. I looked straight up at one of them and said I wanted to speak to the person in charge.

"He's not here."

"Where is he and when will he be back?" (Can he see me shaking?)

"He's at lunch."

"What's his name?" I pushed.

A shaky voice mumbled his name. (Funny how fragile they become.)

"You give him a message," I said. "You tell him that if there is one more instance of harassment from anyone here, you all are off this job."

Silence.

"You understand what I mean by harassment?" I pursued.

"Yes." Gulp. More silence.

"What? Tell me what I mean!" (Not the loving teacher approach.)

Pause. "You mean that if we harass anyone." (Hidden genius.)

"That means whistling, ogling, yelling, or anything that makes anyone feel uncomfortable."

He nods to signal that he has comprehended.

"What's your name?" (Well, why not, now that I see he's scared? I want him to take this seriously and personally.)

He mumbles a name.

I repeat his name out loud and tell him to make sure everyone gets that message. Things have become unusually quiet. He returns to working on a piece of wood, slowly, quietly, slowly and quietly like everyone else up there on the roof. After getting the company name and number, I leave the quiet carpenters working humbly on the serious roof of my building.

I'll tell you the truth. I didn't know what I could realistically threaten. It wasn't even my building. I hadn't hired them. It was 1983, before harassment had been discovered by the boys on Capitol Hill. But something told me that I would call the mayor if I had to, and she would handle it.

The rest of the truth is that my legs were jelly, but I got them to carry me around the corner, to the stairs, where I grabbed the railing just as my knees buckled beneath me.

For the rest of the week, the carpenters continued to putter around up there. I heard not a peep from any of them. The way I see it, if they can learn to be jerks, then they can learn not to be. Sort of like how I learned a long time ago that I had to put up with it. And then, that day, I learned that, as Superwoman, I didn't. My choice.

Jan Buckwald is a writer and restaurant person, 39 years old, white, with flecks of gray in her hair.

Marian Henley

A WOMAN'S CHOICE

Eleanor Capelle

In late 1941 when World War II began for Americans, I was twenty-one. Two years later I joined the Women's Army Corps. I dated a sailor from a naval base in Maryland. One night when he had a car for a change, after we had some drinks, we went for a drive outside the city. He stopped in the gravel at the side of the road and we had sex. Although I had been fitted for a diaphragm at Planned Parenthood in New York, I evidently wasn't wearing it that night. To my dismay, I missed my period. When I was sure I wasn't just late, I saw a doctor off the base for a pregnancy test which turned out to be positive. I was scared. I just couldn't be discharged from the service for pregnancy. And my conservative mother and relatives, as well as myself, would be shamed if I had a baby out of wedlock.

"You can get some pills from a pharmacist," said my friend Shirley. "They're supposed to bring you 'round. I'll find out what they are."

The next Saturday night, after getting the pills, Shirley went with me to a room I rented. I lay down on the bed and inserted the pills in my vagina. But nothing happened that night or during the week. There was no welcome sight of blood.

My best friend in New York told me about a doctor there who would do an abortion for three hundred dollars. I had saved a little over that amount for a trip to Europe after the war ended. But I took out the money. I managed to get a weekend pass to New York. In a Queens apartment house, I waited nervously for two other patients to see the doctor, a sixtyish man with a pot belly. When he called me into his office, I told him I was pregnant and needed an abortion.

"Do you have three hundred dollars?" I assured him I did.

"How far along are you?" he asked.

"Two months."

He felt my stomach and breasts.

"Come up next weekend and I'll take you to a doctor who can help you."

I had expected to get the abortion while I was on this pass and was worried that I wouldn't be able to get another pass the next weekend. During the week, I was transferred to Ft. Myers from Arlington Hall. To my relief, I was granted a pass for the second weekend.

I had phoned the sailor and told him I was pregnant. "Are you sure?"

"Yes, I'm sure."

He wanted to get together on the weekend and talk. "I can't," I said. "I'm going to New York."

"Well," he said, "if you'd rather go to New York and have fun!"

And he hung up.

Although I wrote to tell him how much the abortion cost, I heard nothing more from him.

On my second pass, the doctor I had seen the previous weekend drove me to the apartment house where the abortionist lived and had his office. He told me to wait in the car and he went in alone.

"He's nervous," he said when he came back. "Just relax. We'll have to sit here a while." He put an arm around my shoulders.

"You girls are really horny, aren't you?"

I pulled away. "No harm being a little friendly," he said, squeezing my thigh.

I pushed his hand off my leg.

"Please...don't!" I moved as far from him as I could.

I was feeling nauseated as I tried to discourage his passes. Did the delay mean this man was just going to mess around with me and I wouldn't get the abortion I needed so desperately?

Finally, after struggling for what seemed ages to escape his persistent hands, the man gave up and took me into the apartment house.

A baldheaded old man with a huge nose said, "I can't use ether, you know. Neighbors would be suspicious if they smelled it on a Sunday."

I was ready to stand pain, anything. During the surgery as I lay on the table, the two men fondled my breasts. I was repulsed but didn't try to resist. What could I do? Just let it be over, I thought—these old men touching me, the pain.... When the fetus was removed, I never asked whether it would have been a boy or a girl.

As soon as I could, I phoned my girlfriend and she came to pick me up in a cab. That evening, I took a train back to Washington.

The next day, I could hardly get out of bed at reveille. I didn't know how I could possibly go to work on my new Ft. Myers assignment in Recruiting. I signed up for sick call where I complained of severe menstrual bleeding and cramps. But I was given a pill and sent to work. Getting through that day was a nightmare.

I didn't have sex again for three months.

After the war ended, when Shirley became pregnant and was discharged from the Army, she went to the same abortionist. He took advantage of her too and, what was worse, somehow neglected to remove the fetus. She ended up at Harlem Hospital with high fever from an infection.

At seventy, I took part in my only protest march when there was the threat of abortion becoming illegal again. I remembered with anger those two doctors in the bad old days and marched for a woman's right to choice and power over her own body.

Eleanor Capelle is a 71-year-old retired librarian.

Angela Martin

Misogyny has done and is still doing the greatest harm to humankind.

—Victoria Branch

It starts early, the buildup of tolerance for sexual innuendo. It comes along with being female, is established before there are words to understand that one is constantly being weighed, measured, and judged by the males who run the world.

—Catherin Malcolm

Have I ever been sexually harassed? Ain't I a woman?

—Kate Huard

We are only beginning to break through denial into truth. Both incest and sexual harassment occur with tragic frequency. I feel strongly that women must honor one another's credibility, and as we stand together, we will gather the strength to face these issues head on with greater clarity.

—Marcia Noren

I believe that if even one victim goes to the grave without blowing the whistle on her perpetrator, it is one victim too many.

—Terry Kennedy

The line differentiating the acceptable from the unacceptable is so gradually drawn that it is nearly invisible.

—Jane L. Mickelson

THE PARK DISTRICT

Jamee R. Carlin

I am a professional woman, thirty-nine years old. I am currently a consultant with the Chicago Park District. During my approximately thirteen-month relationship with the Chicago Park District I have been subjected to both overt and covert forms of discrimination and harassment. Some of the incidents were subtle, some brutally aggressive. All involved forms of psychological rape and intrusions upon my privacy and integrity as a woman and a human being. Some were calculated to hinder my performance as a professional. All were structured to debase and humiliate me as a professional woman. All were inexcusable.

I attempted to resolve issues on a one-to-one basis as they occurred. When I confronted the perpetrators of these episodes I was told that I should have a better sense of humor. I should, in other words, write off behavior designed to degrade me, as a joke. What intelligent adult could be expected to turn her back on such behavior? Obviously, women aren't considered intelligent adults at the Chicago Park District; therefore it is apparently justifiable to attribute their complaints to a lack of humor. If I got angry, I was told I was unreasonable or too sensitive. In fact, whenever I was angry, I said so and articulated as logically and as simply as possible, the reason for my anger. I feel that I am very reasonable and if I am sensitive, it is because I am sensible and unwilling to let anyone humiliate, harm, or insult me. When I spoke to a manager about what was going on, his reaction was that they were just teasing me. He trivialized my experience by reducing it to the word "tease."

I would like to share a few of my experiences. In attempting to deal with these and other incidents it became increasingly clear that these men had certain expectations about the way they could treat women. They also had double standards about how women should behave in the workplace. This meant that women should be subservient, not swear, act "ladylike" and not express anger. This made it very difficult for me to respond to harassment without incurring further harassment.

A number of times a man claiming to be a decent and moral Christian, Mr.

46

A, said to me, "Jamee, I like to imagine you in leather." This occurred after a conversation between Mr. A and Mr. B regarding sado-masochistic women who dressed in skimpy leather outfits and carried whips. There could be no mistaking Mr. A's meaning. This kind of behavior is a form of psychological violation, a verbal rape.

Another day I sat down at Mr. C's desk to discuss a Park District project that we were working on. Mr. C proceeded to acquire an erection. I had done nothing to provoke this. I would have been willing to overlook the incident if he had at least made an attempt to be modest by pulling his chair up to his desk or picking up papers on his desk and putting them over himself, both options available to him. Instead, he leaned back in his chair, put his hands behind his head, and spread his legs so that "his problem" was even more visible. I chose to ignore him, not look at him, and referred to the notes I was holding in my hand. The problem went away but I was enraged.

It was another example of the lack of respect in general that some men feel towards women and especially towards those women determined to assume their rightful place in the work force and in society. Again, it was an action conceived to debase, humiliate, and demean. Again, it was uncalled for and unprofessional.

A Mr. D let me know that I should not say "damn" because, according to him, "Ladies should not swear." I told him that if the word lady defined a certain way that I was supposed to be and act than I preferred not to be called a lady because it limited my potential as a human being. To this he replied, "You mean you want to be a man then." I tried to explain to him that I had absolutely no wish to be a man, only to be left to live and define my life as I saw fit, that no one had the right to dictate to me how I should act or not act.

I had similar conversations with Mr. A, the decent and moral Christian who imagined me in leather. He persisted in telling me that I should be a lady and act in a certain manner and not "use cuss words" because it offended him as a "Catholic and a Christian." I had to ask him not to call me honey, dear, a lady, or a girl. He responded that his wife didn't mind being called these terms and that I should be flattered. I pointed out that I did not call him any of these terms, including boy. I tried to explain to him that it was not his prerogative to call me by anything but my rightful name, and that if he for any reason could not call me by my first name then he could feel free to call me Ms. Carlin instead. I pointed out to him that I was a woman, not a girl. He actually sat in his chair looking at the floor and while vigorously shaking his head, repeated, "No, no, then you're a man."

The incidents related here are only a part of what I have had to endure at the Chicago Park District. There are more, many more. I was finally forced to file a complaint with their Affirmative Action Department. I submitted twelve pages of documentation detailing these and other incidents. It also included incidents of racial discrimination I had witnessed. I felt that one page alone was a page too many. My complaint initiated a two-month investigation, the results of which are still pending. In the meantime I have been providing services to a different department. The manager of this particular department has been very supportive. As a result he is beginning to experience severe backlash from the same management that supported what happened to me.

Jamee R. Carlin is a 39-year-old Irish Jewish Lesbian currently providing professional consulting services to the Chicago Park District.

Viv Quillin

THE DOVER PRICK

Karen Carlisle

Have you ever been sexually harassed? Get real! Many times. Eventually I thought it was a standard result of being female in a male-controlled world. Most of my sexual harassment stories occurred in my twenties, when the second wave of feminism was in its infancy and I had not heard of it or of sexual harassment. I thought I was the only one and I believed it was my fault.

<u>1963</u>: As a second-year college student, I thrice weekly sat through a Western Civ class taught by an ultra-misogynist professor who spoke only of three women in the entire school year: Elizabeth, Eleanor of Aquitane and Catherine the Great. He didn't tell us that Elizabeth kept peace longer than any other monarch in history; that Eleanor and Catherine instituted democratic reforms that bettered the lives of peasants and raised the status of women. No, he told us in great detail about their sexual behavior. When he told us that Catherine died as a result of fucking a bull, he entertained the boys in the class, and humiliated me. When I was with him asking for help in the course, he always stared at my crotch and said as many shaming, woman-hating things as possible. I felt disempowered and avoided him at all costs. Told by my T.A. that no woman ever received an "A" from him, I turned in all work labeled with only my initials so I could receive a fair grade.

<u>1964</u>: As a senior, I worked as a research assistant to a professor of Russian history on a book he was writing about Soviet/Latin American relations. Mostly, I translated articles from Latin American newspapers on the subject. Continuously, he made sexual innuendeos, brushed my breasts, my vulva, my buttocks with his hands and his body, and stared intimately into my face. I felt endangered academically and sexually and played the game by allowing him to do those things, but usually withdrew at the threat of further advances by making an excuse to leave. He liked the chase, probably more than the sexual act. He made veiled threats about interrupting my academic program and preventing me from graduating. I thought my choices were to submit or drop out of school. No one

had prepared me for this. My mother counseled me to give in rather than risk my degree. It never came to that. I don't know why. He had all the power, but he chose not to exercise it.

1968: I was a bartender in a very popular sports-oriented bar. My boss was a small, ex-golden gloves champion with an aggressive, macho attitude about women. Whenever he was behind the bar with me, he was forever touching my body, backing me into corners, making his eyes soft and saying subtle, suggestive things. When his wife was there, he ignored me. I hated working when Vi was absent. When I got to work each day, I'd ask if she was there.

One night, Al and I closed the bar together; Vi had gone home. It had been a Broncos football night which means lots of drinking. Al, who seldom drank, was drunk and more aggressive than usual. The bar was in a basement and he had locked us in to count the money. This time, when he backed me into a corner, and I heard his heavy breathing, I knew I was in real trouble. I said no. I gave plenty of non-verbal resistance, and finally tried reasoning with him. Try reasoning with a drunk with a hard-on. He was not deterred by my attempts to extricate myself so I began bargaining. I told him my baby sitter would call the police if I was late, that I would make a date with him for another time to have sex, but that I must leave, and I stopped struggling to allow him to maul me a little so he'd believe my offer. He let me go. The next day, he came into the bar from the office carrying the books, accused me of stealing before all the regulars, and fired me. I felt very shamed but didn't see any recourse. He wasn't pressing charges. Theoretically, I had closed the bar, but on Saturday nights, there were as many as six bartenders using the cash register; we were always over or under the cash register total and the books would show that. His word against mine. Who was going to believe me?

1972: The lawyer I hired to defend me against a felony rap of marijuana possession in Arizona (one joint could get you 20 years) sequestered me in his office an hour prior to my trial. He had already offered to trade sex instead of money for my defense several times. I had refused. Then he got serious. If I didn't have sex with him, he would plead me guilty, when we had good evidence that I was not. Terrified of losing custody of my child but furious, I refused. We went into the courtroom and he pleaded guilty, which reduced the charge to a misdemeanor. This cost me $300 and a criminal record. I wanted to kill him as I listened to the judge condemn and chastise me. I had paid the lawyer in advance, so I had no option but to remain silent. Tell about the extortion? Tell whom? With what evidence?

For a period of several years, I worked exclusively around women as a teacher and then as the co-owner of a feminist bookstore. I came out as a lesbian. I stayed as far away from the company of men as possible so I didn't experience much sexual harassment.

<u>1986</u>: At age 44, I entered a creative writing master's degree program. In a poetry explication class, the professor brought in photocopies of poems about women that were sexual and violent or degrading, ostensibly to study the style of that particular poet.

The women finally had enough when the professor brought in a poem called "The Dover Bitch" by Arnold Hecht—a parody of "Dover Beach" by Matthew Arnold. There was a muffled explosion of subterranean remarks that quickly surfaced when a hitherto compliant woman said, "Tom, why did he use the word bitch?" With a smirk on his face, Tom answered, "Said in just the right tone of voice, bitch is an endearment." That night, I wrote a parody of the parody and called it "The Dover Prick." At the end of the poem, I wrote, "Said in just the right tone of voice, prick is an endearment. Too bad my 19-year-old daughter isn't here. She would say 'dick brain' instead; 'The Dover Dick Brain.' It has nice alliteration, don't you think?"

The next day, I distributed a copy to every student and put one on Professor Passive Aggressive's desk, and delivered a copy to the English chair's mailbox. The other students, male and female, moved their chairs away from me as if I had typhoid. When his Royal Maleness entered, he glanced at it but did not read it. He read it later in his office. I know because I followed him there to ask what he thought. He said it was a good parody. That's all. He brought no more misogynist poems to class.

But I paid for my rebellion (though probably not as much as Anita Hill is going to pay). That professor taught most of my writing classes. He was my advisor. Half the time, I received "B" grades—a low graduate-level grade. He lost my writing files at least twice, didn't keep appointments, left his office door open when we were conferring and chatted with anyone who walked by. He did not advise me of thesis requirements and then penalized me when I didn't perform correctly. I was left with a huge amount of work to finalize and most of my poetry had not received an evaluation. Finally I was harangued abusively by the other writing teacher during my graduate committee meeting. The female professors (who always gave me As) did what they could to support me as long as it involved no risk to themselves or to the newly approved Women's Studies program.

I took the degree (although I thought about refusing it) but without joy or pride. I had to fight hard to value my writing after that treatment. It was two years before I could reclaim my writing of that period. I chose not to pursue a university teaching career because of heterosexist university politics.

Even after twenty years of working in the women's movement, I saw nothing but trouble for me in pursuing a sexual harassment grievance. The old motivator about making it better for women who come after me doesn't motivate me any more. After years of risking myself to effect change for women, I have seen those changes eroded and washed away after I left: I am a tired warrior. In the second half of my life, I am choosing my battles carefully and choosing myself first.

When I look back on my sexual harassment experiences, the commonality those men shared was the absolute sense of entitlement to dominance. They believed they had the right to threaten me, fuck me, extort me, libel me, deny me an education so they could practice power over me in order to feel superior. This sense of entitlement is deeply entrenched in men's minds. Most women know and accept it. What will change that?

If Anita Hill had filed a grievance ten years ago, she would have been laid off, demoted, transferred, covertly refused a good reference and she wouldn't have been able to prove any of it was related to the sexual harassment grievance. She would definitely not be a law professor today. You know it. I know it, and so does everyone else.

Karen Carlisle, 48, is an Irish-American teacher and writer who lives rurally in Alaska in a lesbian family.

THE POLITICS OF SILENCE

Erica Lann Clark

I. Three things are insatiable—the desert, the grave and a woman's cunt.
                                                    —Arab proverb

When I was five years old, a new refugee child living in a Brooklyn apartment building, the superintendent's brother, a retarded man, groped under my skirts to play with my pussy. He sat on the stoop of the building and caught lots of little girls by the arm to bring them into petting range.

He tried it once on my ten-year-old cousin, but she didn't let him. She rescued me, too, and told my mother. Mama warned me to stay away from him. "He's not a bad man," she said, "It's just that his hands are sick." We were refugees from Hitler. We never even considered reporting him to the police. We knew better.

For that man, I was no different from the dozen (or more) other little girls he yanked close and fondled. For me, he was my initiation into the World of Man. For years afterwards, I had a recurrent nightmare in which I would be enjoying myself with a boy I liked, a good friend, when suddenly a huge, Frankenstein-sized man would appear. My boyfriend and I always ran as fast as we could, veering like rabbits to stay out of his range. Often the man fell on the ground as he lurched after us. But still he reached for us, trying to trap us, to grab us by our ankles and bring us down.

By the time I reached puberty, I had learned on the streets of Brooklyn how many there were with the "sick hands" disease, just waiting to yank unsuspecting girls close enough to thrust their hands inside their blouses, up their skirts. I knew from experience that "free access to women is some sort of inalienable male right" (as Susan Brownmiller so aptly put it in *Against Our Will*).

Certainly the men held the power in the movies, in the fairy tales, in the magazines, in politics, and even in my own family. My father ruled the roost like a martinet and kept us all at bay with his rages. Childish sensitivity, neediness, vulnerability left him cold. I have no memory of his caresses. Nonetheless, Father was the emotional centerpiece of our tiny family; everything revolved around what he might feel or do.

"Don't tell your father, he won't understand," said Mama. "Go with your father, he will be hurt if you don't want to go," she added. And always there was the dreadful prophecy, "If your father finds out about this, he'll be very angry." And so I was sworn to secrecy and silence. Little did I know then that I was learning what, for hundreds of years (and very likely much longer than that), every woman had learned.

I was too young to question the androcentricity of my world. I just wanted to be loved. From where I sat in the darkened movie theater, I prayed to become worthy of a real man's yearning, his earning, his pedestal. It was an awesome task. I needed to become beautiful, with full and pouting lips, sensuous hips and breasts big enough to hold. Then, like Miss America, I needed to be self-assured, demure, wise, cute, quiet—able and yet helpless. Powerful, provocative, outspoken, quick-witted, smart and independent women were, like Bette Davis and Barbara Stanwyck, typecast to play the viper, the vixen, the wanton or the witch.

Elegant men like Clark Gable jes' tossed a Bette Davis up over their shoulders and carried her like a sack of straw. Cowboys like John Wayne spanked her like a child if she got out of line. Mean, cruel bastards, like the ones Robert Mitchum played, why they jes' slapped her silly right across her face. I was a smart girl. I knew which side of my bread was buttered and which was dry.

In high school, I learned from D.H. Lawrence that my vulva was a cosmic flower just waiting to open itself to the prick of His Gorgeous Stamen. Ernest Hemingway told me my blue heaven was inside His Cock and when He Came, the earth would move. Norman Mailer and Henry Miller—they wanted to stick elephants up my cunt to make me come more than ever I had before. And I believed them and thought I should. It never occurred to me that they were men and were defining my experience.

II. The body of a woman is filthy, and not a vessel for the law.
—Buddha

It was the early 50s. I was college bound. There were no women's studies courses offered at the Ivy League women's college I attended. We studied the classic texts (Greek and Latin) under the tutelage of a world famous professor, and he failed to tell us that Socrates had learned his philosophy from a woman teacher and was later forced to drink hemlock not because he was teaching homoerotic love to the boys of Athens, but because he was preaching female equality. I had to wait thirty years to discover that in Riane Eisler's *The Chalice and The Blade.*

In all our classical learning, never were we taught that, for many thousands of years, as human beings were emerging from prehistory, God was a woman and women were sacred because, like The Goddess, they could make life!

Our professors failed to mention the worldwide shift to phallic thinking, which gave rise to all the great modern religions (in other words, patriarchal monotheism). They didn't tell us how these institutions purposely erased all traces of women's previous superiority and set in motion two millennia of female debasement, downgrading and enslavement. That sexual hostility was part of this goes without saying.

We never read that "the Goddess had a lap of honey, her vulva was like a boat of heaven, and every head of lettuce was to be honored as one of the Lady's pubic hairs." By the time we met her in the "classics," woman, once sacred for her mysterious power of life, had been reduced to an obliging uterus. As Rosalind Miles observed in *The Women's History of the World*, "Once Mother of All, the Great Goddess, 'She of the Thousand Lovers,' was forced to present an obliging orifice to every conscienceless cock."

When we dared to question the authority of our professors, they told us we were "too young to think." Our job was "to learn the facts"—as given by them, of course.

Small wonder, then, that by the time I was working-age, I was thoroughly cunt-fused. I had not the foggiest notion of who I was or wanted to be. "On my own" was not in my vocabulary. It had been surgically removed, mainly by my father, each time I'd dared to give utterance to the idea of personal freedom.

I had resisted, but my resistance was sporadic and, all too often, abortive. Someday I would be owned by someone just as all luscious women are, so, if I wanted a good "someone," I had to catch him. That was my first priority. By now I knew what to do. I wore sexy shirts, tight skirts, high heels. I ate little and worked out hard to give proof of lusciousness under my clothes. Being seductive was like breathing. It was part of the environment, so invisible I never noticed. If a railroad conductor on the Hudson Line flirted with me and let me ride free, so much the better. I was a pretty piece and I deserved the perks. In this way did I fulfill my part of the covenant with a society which had long ago strip-mined my sense of worth, my sense of self. I became the pretty piece, the doll, the cunt, an object. I consented to that. I wanted to belong.

Of course, I needed some job while I hunted a man to boss me in my own home. No big deal. I went to work as a secretary for an ironmonger. A burly-tough looking, handsome man, he made wrought iron gates, tables, and other things. I was impressed. He soon made a pass at me—backed me into the steel gray file cabinets. I remember feeling stupid and dead, frozen. He was my boss! After that, he left me alone. But, in a few days, he hired a new woman. I saw them laughing and fooling around. She was able to give him the parry and thrust he wanted. A couple of days later, he fired me. It didn't occur to me, when I told my friends that I'd lost my job, to mention harassment. I'd never heard the term. The concept wasn't there. In fact, if some guy was not coming on to you, there was something wrong with you. So I kept silent, secretly ashamed that I had not been woman enough for a powerful boss like him.

My next encounter with sexual hostility took place at home. I had finally succeeded in getting out on my own. I was studying acting at Berghof Studio and living in a furnished room in Greenwich Village, and because I had ventured forth—had left my cloistered community (where my unpricked hymen might have been traded for a fair bride price)—I was at much greater risk.

I met a guy who drove a cab for money and studied acting with the famous Sandy Meisner. He regaled me with stories of the wit and wisdom of his wonderful teacher. I invited him to my place, envisioning an evening of great conversation and camaraderie. He brought a six-pack of beer, which, in those days, one opened with a can opener. An important detail.

As he opened his second beer, my new friend suddenly brandished the can opener as a weapon. "You see this?" he threatened. "I could scar up your pretty face, so you'd better do exactly what I tell you to do."

I became terrified: clammy skin, shallow breathing and childlike obedience. There was only one window in my room. He made me pull the windowshade and sit on the bed. Then he held the sharp edge of the can opener to my face and babbled on about how he could cut me up. I sat perfectly still, frozen, a trapped animal, playing dead.

Lacking the encouragement of screams or pleading or tears, his tone shifted. He began to talk about how he was always a pain in the ass. Everywhere he went, everything he did, every time he had a relationship, it always ended like this— with him being in the way, an unwanted nuisance. He stepped a little away from the bed, took center stage and, gesturing wildly with his free hand, bemoaned his unhappy life. In my tiny furnished room, his wildly swinging arm reached the bookcase and knocked down my unfinished beer.

As the beer poured over my treasured books, from somewhere very deep, I heard a shout well up. I saw myself spring off the bed. "What do you think you're doing?" he shouted.

"I'm going to wipe this mess up!" I heard my anger with amazement. As I stalked the length of the room to the so-called kitchenette where the sponges lay in the sink, I had to pass the door.

"You better not try anything!" he said. Mutely, I obeyed. Twice I walked back and forth, mopping up the mess, each time eyeing that door—if only I would dare! Could he reach me from where he stood? My stomach knotted up. I thought, "I can't," but something made my legs scuttle sideways to the door, where,

56

shaking with terror, my hands negotiated the door knob and my arms slammed that door shut as I ran into the street. Barefoot, I raced for safety, a beer-soaked dishcloth in my hand.

On the corner, there was an all-night coffee shop. It was brightly lit. I hesitated in the doorway, scanning the crowd. Two young men, clean-cut collegiate types, sat in a booth. Still panting from terror, I slid in beside one of them. I must have been shaking from head to foot as I poured out my story. It never occurred to me that they might well have taken advantage of me, too. It never occurred to me to call the police.

Their machismo was flattered—I was a damsel in distress. They walked back to the building with me and had me wait outside while they "took care of it." At first, he refused to open the door. Then, when he did, he lied, said we both lived there, argued, acted obstinate. Eventually, one of them had to hit him. He went out like a light. They dragged him out past me and dumped him on the sidewalk.

"You'd better call the police now, so he doesn't try to get back in when he wakes up." My knights-errant left me then.

By the time the police arrived, the guy who had held me hostage had long since awakened and left. It never occurred to me, or to the policemen who took my report, to find out which cab company he worked for, so that I could prosecute him for assault. He was just an asshole. But I couldn't sleep there that night. Or ever again. The sanctity of my first independent home had been broken and the terror wouldn't leave. For days, I walked around the city with my coat collar turned up and the brim of my hat pulled down so that, should he be driving his cab past me, he wouldn't recognize me.

For all I know, the guy, in the privacy of his mind, might simply have been doing what actors call "character work," learning to feel his way into the role of oppressor by practicing on some naive bitch. Afterwards I didn't live alone again. I learned to have a roommate and a dog, and I got serious about my search for a husband. When the powerful people in the world are men, and you are attractive enough to do so, you buy yourself an "in." At last, I was catching on.

III. Blessed art Thou, O Lord our God, King of the Universe, that Thou hast not made me a woman.
                              —Daily prayer of Hebrew males

A woman friend who has traveled widely in Central and South America told me how, in tiny villages way out in the country, she saw women staggering down muddy streets in three-inch spiked high heels. They wore these horrid shoes while they carried groceries, bundles and babies through the dirt streets of their village.

"But why?"

"To be sexy, of course."

"Sexy? What for?"

"To have a man. They need a man's protection and what else have they got to bargain with, besides sex appeal?"

As I progressed, I also used sex appeal to find a husband, and later, as a single parent, one job after another. So what if I was sexy with Ted and we made love on weekends? I got the job at the Mayor's office and it looked good on my resume.

All the time, I was unaware of trading sex as a commodity for protection, personal gain, power. Being a woman is not unlike living in a slave culture and learning how to be a "house nigger." House niggers are different from field hands. They wear uniforms, they take on the characteristics of the oppressor, they treat the spoiled brat children of the house as if they were their own, and even provide the Master with sexual favors. In return, they have certain privileges, like learning to read and write, or being allowed to develop their talents.

Thus, when the Medical Examiner for the Board of Education felt me up as he was giving me the health exam I needed to get my teaching license, I kept silent. I simply went dead inside. Never even thought briefly of reporting him for molestation.

When the playwright whose manuscript I was typing reached over me as I sat at work and grabbed my breast, I kept silent. I didn't report him to Office Temp as a molester. I just froze up inside.

That deadness was both the price I paid and my protection. At least I was not a "live target." I had learned from my mother how to avoid my father's rages: offer no resistance, play dead, withdraw. I had learned from my parents how to avoid persecution: disappear, evacuate, withdraw, assimilate. The cost was integrity. It isn't possible to be fully alive while part of you is playing dead. And which part is that? The erotic, the passionate, the self-determined pursuit of bliss. Maybe it's better to be a field hand and fully alive, but it's more profitable to be a silent, smiling, cordial house nigger.

For twenty years, from the mid-50s to the mid-70s, I waited for Mr. Right to come along. I waited like the traditional Jew waits for the Messiah. Over and over again, I found him, fell madly in love and even married him once. Only it was never right. So I changed partners. During those years, I learned plenty about the geography of harassment, molestation and the polite form of rape—date rape. But it failed to help me because I couldn't yet stand on my own and pursue my own direction. I had such a diminished sense of my potential, such fear of failure and besides, my passion always detoured me. I was obsessed with creating the kind of woman a man could love.

Finally, in my mid-thirties, I ended up in an abusive relationship with a man who turned out to be a child molester. When I discovered that, it was more than I could stand. I demanded a separation, and at first he agreed. Then, he began harassing me, visiting at all hours and banging on the apartment door until I answered, or climbing to the roof of the building and climbing back down to our rear window via the fire escape stairs. There he would try to pry the window open. I took to sleeping with the biggest kitchen knife under my pillow. I would cower in bed, listening to his footsteps on the roof. Our apartment was on the top floor and the crackle was clear. Many nights I took my sons with me and slept over at someone else's home. And still he would not leave me alone.

I began to crack. I was turning 36 and nothing had worked the way it was supposed to work. There was no blue heaven inside a man's cock and the earth didn't move when he came. I was an object, not a person. I was rated or counted by my sexuality, which had defined me from the time I was five years old. My life was a deadened routine. Every morning I went to work on the subway. Every night I came home to my mothering job and the night's hellish harassments.

My path from home to subway led through a warehouse district, full of truckers waiting to pick up goods from the factories and warehouses that lined the streets. Every day, as I walked by, they would whistle, catcall, comment, hiss, leer, snigger or laugh. Every day, I ignored them and watched the flight of seagulls headed for the dump. Then one day, one little guy walked up close to me to whisper something in my ear. I don't remember what he said, maybe something as innocent as "You look nice today," but it was too much for me. All the rage buried under years of going dead exploded and my self-control shattered. There happened to be an empty Coke bottle lying on the street. It was within easy reach. I stooped, picked it up and smashed it on the ground, hard as I could. It split into a thousand fragments. Shards of glass flew around us. The little guy got a scared look and began backing away. And I began to scream a series of epithets— and I knew quite a few—about the privacy of my ear and my person, about what I thought of him, of them all.

It worked. From that day on, I walked to the subway without a single catcall. No one harassed me again. But my rage was not only directed toward those truckers. They were just the tip of the iceberg. Though I couldn't articulate it then, what really enraged me was the politics of suppression, which is what sexual harassment, sexual hostility, expresses.

In that moment of rage, when I screamed out loud what I thought inside, I took the first step into independence. I stood my ground, I wasn't going to take it anymore. It was the mid-70s, women all over the country were meeting in consciousness raising groups and breaking their silence. I was one of those "hundredth monkey" phenomena. Though I backslid a thousand times, I kept on going, teaching myself how to flourish even in a society which had taught me to despise my potential and to behave, instead, like an object to be used for sexual purposes.

Writing about the hostile behavior we call sexual harassment is tough. It's ugly, nasty, political, enraging. But it's vital to break the shroud of silence by which I helped maintain the status quo. Once upon a time, I was doing a Bio-energetics Marathon weekend of therapy. Twenty of us, with three therapists, two women and one man, were crowded into a big room filled with mattresses. We were instructed to lie down and cry, scream, kick, have the tantrum we deserved. We were allowed to leave briefly to use the restroom or get a drink of water or coffee. I was on my way to the bathroom, when I noticed the man therapist.

He was a handsome young man, on the staff at Sarah Lawrence College. He had brought a pretty young student with him, a patient of his. He was on the mattress with her, caressing her, finger-fucking her for all I could see. I was stunned—aghast—I knelt by the mattress, trying to get my voice to say something. No words came out. He looked up at me, with an expression that chilled me.

"Oh, good," he said. His voice was smooth and friendly, professional. "Why don't you just sit there and call Lee by her name, you know, as if you were her mother and trying to stop her." Then he turned his attention back to the girl, Lee. I sat stunned in silence. I looked around at the room full of strangers; no one else had noticed what was happening. I got up and left. Upstairs, in the coffee room, I sat, morose and silent. One of the two women therapists approached me. "What's going on?" she asked. "Would you like to talk about what you're feeling?" I mumbled something lame. I could not tell her what I had seen! I felt such shame! No, I could not tell—not then. But now, I can.

Erica Lann Clark lives and loves in Santa Cruz, California, where she is a storyteller, writer, teacher, acupressure massage therapist, and a first generation liberated woman.

LIT 101

Jeannine Crane

It happened almost the first day of college. The campus smelled of autumn leaves and I was excited as I walked to my first literature class. I was only eighteen and I'd always lived at home with my parents and two sisters. I hoped wearing my brown tweed skirt and peach-colored angora sweater would help disguise the fact I hadn't developed yet. The campus was crowded with recently returned veterans; they were out of their uniforms and wore plaid shirts and jeans.

The instructor seemed like a nice, middle-aged man. Going over the course contents with us, he said we'd be discussing novels, short stories and various magazines, especially *Fortune* magazine. "*Fortune* is hard to describe," the professor said in answer to a question. "It has articles about money, business, etc." Then he added, "It's the kind of magazine a woman would never read." My head jerked up, I stared at the professor. I read that magazine. I looked around and realized I was the only woman in the class.

Lit 101 met three times a week and we had to read out loud from various books. The men read from Steinbeck, Hemingway, Melville, but the professor always assigned me Mickey Spillane. These were trashy, sexy, detective stories. So once a week I had to stand and read things like, "They shot her through the navel so it wouldn't mess up her body," followed by a description of her bust line. Some of the men would snicker, some would leer, but the smirks were the worst. Stony-faced, choking back rage, I stood there reading, determined not to let my humiliation show.

All I wanted was to get a decent grade and get out of that class. The course was required or I might have given up. On the days I had literature I wore a green, full-length coat and if we were going to read I left my coat on. I felt humiliated and put upon, but in those days we were not allowed to feel put upon. That was forty years ago, but I still remember the positions and faces of the men who were sitting around me and I still feel my rage.

Jeannine Crane is 62 years old with three adult children; she was raised in a Norwegian commune in the midwest.

DANCING FOR THE GURU

Geeta Dardick

India. 1972. I am living in the city of Ahmedebad with my husband Sam and three small children. I'm a thirty-year-old American housewife. And I've turned on to religion.

Before traveling to India (the five of us drove there from Europe in a VW bus), I had known nothing of Indian spiritual life (or any type of spiritual life). But you can't eat a meal in India without being overwhelmed by the presence of Gods and Gurus. Their photos, draped with garlands of flowers, adorn every restaurant wall.

So I quickly became familiar with the mythical Gods, like Ganesh the elephant, Hanuman the monkey, and Lord Krishna, the young prince who satisfied 108 women simultaneously. I became intrigued by the hordes of popular Gurus—dead ones like Yogananda and Ramana Maharishi, and live ones like Satya Sai Baba and Ma Ananda Moi.

After living in India for several months, I started hearing about the New Guru, someone different and unusual, someone so special that the well-known author Krushwant Singh wrote about him in the Indian equivalent of *Parade Magazine*. After the publication of the article, one of our friends, a weaver with an excellent reputation, became an enthusiastic devotee, proudly wearing New Guru's picture on a chain around his neck. In the following months, the weaver raved and raved about his spiritual teacher. "Oh, I've grown so much," he kept saying. "You and Sam really should check this out."

Sam wasn't interested, but my curiosity was piqued. I agreed to join the weaver and his wife for a trip into the mountains to attend a meditation camp conducted by New Guru.

Traveling to the camp came as a relief for me, as I was having severe marital trouble and needed time off from Sam and the kids. But once I arrived at the mountain retreat, I felt forlorn because I didn't enjoy the bizarre meditation methods being promulgated by New Guru, which included several hours of dancing and leaping blindfolded.

I was surprised on the third day of the camp when an Indian woman approached me and said that New Guru wanted to name me so that I could become his official devotee. She said that I should come to a private naming ceremony at a nearby hotel the following day, where I would be served breakfast.

Bacon and eggs. After two years of primitive traveling, this traditional American meal cast a spell over me. The New Guru beckoned me to his side, gave me a necklace with his picture on it, and told me that my name would now be Geeta (up to that moment it had been Carol); and next, much to my surprise, he pinched my bottom and winked.

After my breakfast-anointment, I returned to camp a changed woman. For the next few days, I wore my blindfold, and twirled and whirled freely, flailing my arms in every direction. By committing myself to participate in New Guru's movement-oriented meditations, I quickly bonded with the hundreds of other spiritual searchers in attendance (primarily Indians and a handful of westerners). I felt popular. And excited.

When meditation camp ended, I returned home to my family, with a new name and new ideas. Within five minutes, it was quite clear that my relationship with Sam was worse than ever before. All I could think about was the fun I had at the camp where I was free of domestic responsibilities and marital ties.

Unable to deal with my family crisis, I made the frantic decision to leave my husband and children and travel to Bombay where New Guru had his headquarters. I felt my only hope lay in the fact that I now had a spiritual teacher. Everyone I had met at the camp said that New Guru was a real avatar (holy man like Jesus or Buddha) who could lead me to a state of samadhi (higher consciousness). Now that he had named me, I knew I would make rapid progress by using his meditation methods.

After the first week at New Guru's headquarters, I made an appointment with his secretary to have a personal audience. I was extremely worried about leaving my husband and children to embark on the spiritual path, and craved New Guru's approval for this decision.

The secretary told me my interview would be at 5 p.m. "Take a bath first," she said. "New Guru doesn't like odors."

At that time, New Guru occupied a large, modern, five-room apartment. Devotees milled about in the living room and dining room areas, and New Guru remained in a back bedroom, where he met with his appointments, with whom, I presumed, he discussed the Indian Holy texts.

At 5 p.m., I knocked on the door of New Guru's bedroom/office. He opened the door for me, locked it after me, then crossed the room and took a seat. I remained standing, wondering why he locked the door.

"Ah, Geeta, Geeta," he said. "How are you doing?"

"Well, not too well," I replied. "I've left my husband and children."

"Don't worry, nothing to worry about. The meditations will take care of everything. But right now, I'd like you to take off all your clothes, and dance and move until you have an orgasm."

New Guru sat down in his chair, and looked up at me expectantly. Totally obedient to the spiritual leader, I unraveled my five-foot-long sari, and let it drop in a mound on the floor. Then I took off my blouse, my petticoat and my underpants, and tossed them on top of the sari. New Guru watched me, in silence.

I started to wiggle my hips, from side to side. New Guru watched me intently, but his facial expression never changed. He didn't smile, he didn't frown, he didn't wink—he simply stared. I closed my eyes, and danced as I had in the moving meditations at the camp. But how do you have an orgasm by moving? I gyrated back and forth. I whirled. I leaped. I twirled. I rubbed my clitoris with my finger, while pirouetting on the linoleum floor. But I couldn't have an orgasm for New Guru, who just stared and stared.

Frustrated, I finally gave up. "I can't do this," I said. "I just can't move to orgasm."

"Ah, then lie down on the bed," he said. "On your stomach."

I fell onto the bed and waited, my face buried in a pillow. I heard New Guru rise from his chair, and walk over to the bed.

What was he going to do? I could tell he was standing by the bed, but nothing was happening.

New Guru touched my back. He ran his finger down my spine. He waited a few moments, then caressed my spine again. Then he went back to his chair and sat down. I kept lying face down on the bed, wondering what he might demand next.

"You have a blocked second chakra," he said. "I want you to imagine a flame burning at the base of your spine, and that will unblock it."

"I could have told you that myself," I shouted, as I climbed off the bed, and sat down at his feet, stark naked. "I have a difficult time having orgasms."

"Well, just keep doing the meditations," New Guru said. "My meditation technique is very helpful. And you, Geeta, are a very fine devotee."

In the course of the last 20 years, I have told my story about Rajneesh (New Guru's real name) to only a handful of people. Some were incensed, some were nonplussed, but those who were Rajneesh devotees felt that I was lucky. After all, I had an intimate, one-on-one, relationship with their guru, something they longed for.

But those devotees didn't understand how disillusioning my experience was. I had really thought I was going into that bedroom to have an interview with God. Instead, after the click of that lock, I became the victim of a very clever and powerful and manipulative voyeur.

64

A few months after my "interview," an Indian friend to whom I told my story helped me break away from Rajneesh's cult. Later I was able to reunite with Sam and the kids, and we returned to the United States together in the spring of 1973.

But the confusing memory of my relationship with Rajneesh has never left my consciousness. And it never will.

Geeta Dardick is 49, Jewish, a writer and back-to-the-land farmer.

SYLVIA

POWER PLAY

Alice Denham

He was a powerful literary editor who admired my writing, an old friend I confided in, a man I'd trusted for years.

After my first novel was published, I tried to make a living as a journalist and work on my second novel. Since both are full-time occupations, my agent warned me. "You won't have time for fiction."

It was true, and terrifying. At any time I had ten projects or article ideas floating the magazines. If I lucked out, three of these would become assignments. I eked out a living and had no time for my novel.

The editor was a 6'5" grandiose gent who took me to fancy French restaurants for lunch, offered literary advice and friendship. Married, of course. He knew I was strapped for money. He didn't know I'd run out of money next month.

"You think you could write a mystery?" he asked.

"Don't know," I replied. "I've never read one."

"I'll send you a couple," said he. "If you can come up with a plot, you can write our next TV-tie-in." A TV-tie-in was a paperback novel published when a new network series began.

When he told me what his company paid, I knew I could live on it for six months. I was excited. It was a professional challenge. I read one mystery, got bored with the second, and churned up a mystery plot. I sent him a chapter-by-chapter summary. He phoned to say I had the assignment. Would I meet him for a drink at the Pierre to discuss it.

Of course, I replied. He explained the difference between a suspense novel and a mystery, and we added a few plot twists. He said I'd receive the contract in a week. We went to dinner and he was visibly miffed that I didn't ask him in for a drink afterward.

"Can't I come in for a nightcap?" he said.

"I'm exhausted," I pled.

Two weeks passed and no contract arrived. I phoned and asked where it was.

"Why should I be nice to you if you're not nice to me?" said he.

Hopes plunging, I said, "What do you mean?"

"You know I want to sleep with you. You've slept with..." and he named two writers we both knew.

Of course, I'd slept with them because they appealed to me; the editor didn't appeal to me. I remembered men saying to me, literally, "You're not a virgin so why won't you sleep with me?" As if every man had a right to claim me if others had.

I could not say, "You don't turn me on," because I was broke. I knew if I did, the mystery would vanish.

"But, I've always thought of you as a friend. For ten years now," I limped gamely along.

"For ten years, I've been wanting you and you've been evading me," he said. "Why me? What's wrong with me?"

"You're married."

"So is_____."

"That was just a one-night aberration," I gulped.

"Think about it," said he, "if you want the contract."

"What about my professional qualifications?" I said.

"Nobody's questioning those. Think it over." He hung up.

I was humiliated, furious, and helpless. Whom could I ask for help in 1968? I considered phoning other editors, then all male, and asking if they had any fast writing projects. But I knew I'd encounter the same problem.

He not only wanted me to do the work, to use my long-honed skill, but he wanted me to pay for the job with my body, a shameless power play. I was amazed that this once-friend would stoop so low.

He made me question my own ability, and I hated him for that. He made me wonder if the assignment came to me only because he wanted me. But I knew I could do it. I'd done a good sample first chapter. But he seriously eroded my confidence. I wept in frustration.

I longed to phone him and say, "Forget your stupid job." But then I'd remember the long adolescent years typing and filing for pennies in offices. I no longer typed well enough to get a typing job. He knew I wasn't involved with anyone because, as a friend, I'd confided in him.

Eventually I phoned. "Okay," I said, "you win."

He chortled with joy, took me to the Four Seasons. I brought him home and tried to get him drunk. But it didn't work. I gritted my teeth and had sex with him, hating him so, I imagined pummeling him with a sledgehammer.

At the network I watched the pilot of the TV series which established the main characters so that I could use them and their mannerisms authentically in the mystery novel of the same name.

The network producer gave me a script and information and we went to lunch at a nearby swankerie. As I rose to leave, he said he'd see me home.

"Don't you have to get back to the office?" I asked.

"No, no, not for a while," he grinned.

"Don't bother," I said.

"I insist," said he, guiding me out of the restaurant.

When I jumped out of the cab, he said, "Aren't you going to offer me a cup of java?"

"I have to get to work," said I, "on this."

Waving it away, he paid the cab and marched in with me and I made him coffee, thinking that my polite amiability was exhausting me. I offered him sugar and cream and fixed my own coffee. I settled on the sofa nowhere near him.

The instant I set my coffee down on the end table and turned back, he lunged for me and slung his arms around me and tried to plant a big wet kiss into my lips. I pushed my way clear with my elbows and stood up and raged. "Who do you think you are to walk in here and grab me? Take your stupid book and shove it," I screamed. "I won't be pawed." I slung open the apartment door. "Get out of here!" Looking nonplussed, crestfallen, the network producer departed. Still furious, I phoned the editor and told him what the producer had done.

"That bastard—doublecrossing me," fumed the editor. "I told him hands off, you're my girl." He said he'd phone the producer and dress him down, which he did.

The producer phoned me and apologized. I got #1 to protect me from #2. I'm not ashamed, just saddened by the way it was in 1968. I wrote about sexual harassment in my second novel and worked as an early feminist to change the legal disregard for women.

That's why I feel great pride in Anita Hill: for resisting and for the courage to speak truth under incredible duress.

Alice Denham is 50-something, a Southerner, and the author of two novels: Amo *and* My Darling From the Lions.

Protecting My Body

Muriel Eldridge

I am seventy-one years of age. For much of my life I was a left political activist, and I guess you can say I came from the poor side of the tracks. I was totally responsible for my mother from a very young age.

I traveled by bus late at night after attending meetings. Houses of prostitution were in the neighborhood where I had to transfer from one streetcar to another. In San Francisco in the early 1930s, these houses had red lights in front of buildings, and there were always a number of pimps on the corner where I transferred. You could always spot them; they were dressed to kill, and jingling loose money in their pockets.

When my family broke up, my mother went to Los Angeles to work as a domestic servant. My only way of seeing her was to hitchhike from San Francisco to Los Angeles, and by the time I was seventeen I had made seven round trips to L.A. by thumb.

I mention the above only to indicate that the protection of my body was uppermost in my mind from the time I was about thirteen. Perhaps that is why I acted so forcibly at times.

Once, when I was in my twenties, and working for the Union, I was asked by my boss to leave the office and go uptown to pick up some material from the main office. I was standing at the receptionist counter with my arms on the shelf waiting for the package, when I felt a hand on each of my breasts. I really didn't spend much time thinking about what I should do. I turned around immediately and lifted my right knee to the man's groin. He fell to the floor, in much pain. I knew the person, but only casually. I spit on him when I left—without the package.

Another incident happened while I was working for the same Union. It was during the winter and the office was quite cold. I was standing with my back to the heater when one of the members asked if I was warming up my lunch. I walked over to my desk, picked up the dictionary and threw it at him. It hit him in the chest. Shortly thereafter he left the office. He returned several hours later with a large box of candy and an apology. I accepted both.

Perhaps it was those experiences—after the word got around—that saved me from constant sexual harassment for the many years that I continued to work there.

Muriel Eldridge is 71, her ethnic background is Jewish, and she was a secretary all of her work life.

ON BECOMING A DANGEROUS WOMAN

Elena Featherston

I speak with a very specific voice, that of a dark-skinned African American (Black) woman. I speak against more than individual occurrences of sexual harassment in my life. My voice is lifted against the systematic harassment of women of color—Black women in particular and dark-skinned women—that permeates American culture. Speaking defies the conspiracy of racist and sexist pressure to keep Black women silent and under sexual siege.

The most consistent, overt sexual violation, in my life, comes from white men: on the street, in the workplace, on the telephone, applying for a job, dining out, driving my car, checking into hotels, traveling on business. Anytime, anyplace. Perhaps my experience would be different if I lived in a predominantly Black community. These white sons and fathers behave as if they have a right to act like boors, if the boorish behavior is directed at Black women. Many are genuinely surprised and offended when their sexual approaches are repelled. They assume the color of their skin guarantees our being flattered by their "attention."

Their acts of harassment, which are both racist and sexist, began quite early in my life. A white, middle-aged merchant closed his store, guided me to a secluded aisle and offered me "whatever I wanted" to let him touch me. Saying I was beautiful, he promised what he did would make me feel good. I was seven years old.

This sweet-tempered gentleman had exchanged pleasantries with my mother almost daily for as long as I could remember. We purchased our food and household necessities from him. In his store my mother had taught me the importance of honesty, forcing me to return and pay for a stolen Snickers bar. A few days after the Snickers incident, he had me cornered between the paper towels and the bathroom cleanser trying to molest me. I was convinced my stealing led him to think he could say and do nasty things to me. But, I knew what he wanted to do was wrong. There was no way I was going to let him touch me.

I didn't have sense enough to be afraid. At seven, I was a force to be reckoned with—a small, skinny-legged force, but, a force nonetheless. I declined his offer and left the store.

Being abandoned by my father had taught me a cold fierceness, disguised as self-reliance. I felt capable of taking care of myself. Mine was a fortuitous admixture of mother's love, father's absence and innate stubbornness, an alchemy which gave the inner strength necessary to enforce my will with a potentially abusive adult.

In the weeks and months that followed, I rebuffed all his friendly gestures and efforts to re-establish his usual patterns of behavior. Secretly, I savored what I supposed to be his fear of my family's anger. But I never told anyone and for very good reason. I felt guilty.

Only seven years old, yet insidious social messages were already clear: the burden of proper sexual conduct rested with the female, even a female child. How this knowledge was transmitted, or when, I don't know. With hindsight I could point to fairy tales, movies, jokes, or constant reminders to be "ladylike." Any one, or a combination of a thousand things, might have been the reason, but my responsibility for this man's behavior seemed clear. From this first instance of harassment, I learned to take care of myself and to keep my mouth shut, and it was only the beginning.

Four years later, as I walked home from school with several friends one sunny, Spring afternoon, another white man invaded my life. Suddenly, everyone was shrieking, laughing, or muttering nervously, "Look at that." Nearsighted, unable to see what had them so agitated, I stepped closer to the green Buick with silver ports glistening in the sun and the big, well-dressed, blond stranger leaning on it. The giggling and shouting grew louder as a result of my approach. The man smiled an invitation, and vigorously jiggled what appeared to be a set of car keys. My friends' carrying on seemed unwarranted, but they wouldn't stop snickering, pointing and backing away. Stepping a bit closer, I realized what he shook were not keys, but his penis. I was stunned. His eyes, concealed by sunglasses, were not visible, but his smile was unforgettable.

For him this behavior had some bizarre justification. Parked five minutes from our homes, he basked in the sunlight and his power to make us scream, his power to intimidate. I was furious. Not about his pathetic penis, but his supercilious smile. It suggested we deserved his filthy, degrading attention. I wanted to claw that smirk off his face, but I was unsure how. Force was not the best option, the guy was six feet tall. Then it came to me. Being a "tomboy" had its advantages. I knew boys were as insecure about their penises as girls about their breasts.

Peering analytically at his crotch, I advised him to put the "itty-bitty thing" in his pocket because it looked like a key chain. Part bravado, part truth. Staring at him, real hard, I asked my now-tittering friends if they were amused because his "weenie" was so small, or because it was so white. Our insolent flasher wilted and blushed deep maroon. As he climbed into his fancy car, he hollered, "Niggers." Once. Viciously. Face contorted. The air was charged with his impotent rage, our laughter and my churning desire to do murder. Stony-eyed I watched his car until it was out of sight. If he looked in his rear-view mirror, it was important that he see my fearless, smiling face. It was imperative he never know how vulnerable he had made me feel.

My mother called the police. Though two white officers came to our home, they didn't take the complaint seriously. Quite the contrary, they questioned *my* ability to remember so much so clearly. One asked if my mother had coached me. He then told her, sounding a bit skeptical, that I was very smart. The way it was said, instead of lending credibility to my allegations, implied that intelligence made me less believable. Nothing was done.

I didn't realize that hundreds of such men stalked the Black community, safe from prosecution and conviction. But, only eleven, I was getting the message that if you were Black no one really cared what happened to you. The flasher's disrespect, coupled with the cops' indifference, made me want to go to war. For weeks I had fantasies about kicking him in the balls, spitting in his face, watching police cars careen into trees, beating them with a bat—assorted childish revenges.

It was clear to me that white men—walking-down-the-street-store-owning-police-officer-car-driving-everyday white men—were dangerous to me. Sick sexual aberration, the need to thrust themselves at young girls, was obviously a white man's disease. This behavior, like their racism, like their belief that Blacks should be unintelligent, and their unwillingness (or inability) to be fair in their dealings with people, especially people of color, seemed genetic. My experiences and conversations with other Black girls demonstrated the truth of that analysis. (The treatment to which their own white daughters, mothers or sisters might be subjected was never considered.) But, white men were not the only culprits, as I discovered all too soon.

It was not an unduly obscene experience, and the male involved was only 18. It did not break my spirit, but it did hurt my heart. It still does.

Six of us were watching American Bandstand—three girlfriends, my "play sister," her older brother and me. He suggested that we "dance." It was a game we had played before. One at a time we sat on his lap, and were bounced up and down while he undulated playfully to the music. We "danced," we laughed, ate popcorn and were having an all-American afternoon. But this time something felt strange. His face was "funny," it looked odd. On my third turn, I noticed he had an extra "knee." The truth is, I didn't want to understand what was happening. He was Black. I thought: There is a mistake, I must be confused.

He was my friend, a protector. He had carried me on his shoulders when I was younger, bought ice cream, told stories, helped fix my bike, taught me to box. He never once made fun of me for being a tomboy. He was my surrogate big brother, my comrade. He was a good person, I loved him. Most important, he was BLACK! Black men definitely did not act like crazy, white men. I had to be wrong.

As the other girls continued to take turns "dancing," I watched his face, his body. When we finally made direct eye contact, what passed between us was ghastly. I wasn't wrong. He knew what he was doing and now he knew I knew. He was apprehensive, but composed. He pretended nothing was amiss. I can still see him seated, reaching out his hand, beckoning me to take my turn. The spasm of distrust and resentment which rippled briefly across his face when I said I didn't want a turn, reverberated deep inside me.

Heavy-hearted, wounded by an undefined sense of loss, I went home. Black men were my men—my brothers, my cousins, my godfather, my minister, my friends, even my father. I had always felt safe with them. Until that moment my battle had been with the occasional demented white man who invaded community and serenity without warning or reason. It had not been necessary to be on guard with Black men. This was a betrayal. My safety zone was gone. In truth it never existed. I began to realize that being Black and female meant there were no safe places, unless we created them ourselves.

This time I would not be silent. I sat in the window waiting for his father to come home, plotting my revenge. This time I was talking and someone was going to listen. Unlike white men who ravished minds and bodies with anonymity and impunity, this young man was going to learn he had to respect me. His father, after hearing my story, did a brutal thing. He invited his son outside and whipped him publicly with a garden hose. Curious neighbors looked on. It is only brutal in retrospect; at the time it seemed quite fair. No one ever mentioned the incident to me again. I never forgot it. It changed my life.

That evening, lying in bed, I made a decision. As a Black woman, considered fair game by everyone, having respect meant demanding it. Hell, fighting for it, when necessary. It meant refusing to spend time with men who did not respect me. I consciously crossed a line—the one defining male and female sexual behavior—into a grey zone. I would not be exploited. I would not be silent. I would not be afraid. I would choose if, when and with whom I had sex. I would discover what it meant to be me and how to express what I found. This betrayal gave me access to a part of myself unnamed until then. Rebel, fighter, outspoken, "womanish" child. I was a 13-year-old virgin.

The most recent—and hopefully last—instance of harassment occurred at an Alameda computer company in 1988. For three months, I was systematically badgered, racially and sexually, by a white manager. Let's call him Mike.

Mike and my boss, "Steve," were friendly rivals. Both had their eyes on the same Vice Presidency. Both had many women working in their departments. Mike demanded fawning loyalty from the women in his group and underpaid them. Steve, though paternalistic, treated us with respect and paid us well. Perhaps this was his downfall; he was eventually ousted. Mike gained control of both departments.

In Steve's office, on the day he told me the bad news, Mike, flushed with victory, casually placed his arm around my shoulders, hand lightly (and deliberately) brushing my left breast. Smiling into my eyes, he told me Steve's dismissal meant I would become his sex slave. Maybe it was his smile that pushed me over the top. It didn't matter, he had "torn his drawers." No corporate code of conduct was keeping me under control, or forcing me to submit to his crap. I reached down, hefted his balls speculatively, and smiling back into his face, disdainfully answered, "No, I really don't think so." The inference was that he was not well-endowed enough to carry out his "sex master" mission. Men are still very sensitive about their weenies. Turning a deeply gratifying crimson, he rushed from the office and never said anything suggestive to me again. Instead, he became the enemy and launched a campaign to have me dismissed.

For more than a year, a powerless woman held corporate honchos at bay. I would not bend. I would not betray other Black women as they wanted and I knew how to use the law to my advantage—a powerful combination. The corporate power brokers were at a loss. I finally left the company, when I wanted to. If Black women refuse to play the game, have integrity and bond with other Black women, we have more power than the system likes to acknowledge.

Sexual harassment is so subtle, so pervasive. Women are asked to betray themselves and their children, especially their daughters, to the power of male domination. This means placing power in the hands of men and allowing them to decide whether or not to abuse it. Oh, please!! I don't think so, boyz.

When my daughter was young, I made it clear to every man I knew that touching her inappropriately would result in serious bodily injury. Graphic details were supplied concerning my women friends who would help me castrate them if the need arose. Some men left and never came back, good riddance. Those who stayed treated me and my children with respect. My experiences taught me to champion my children until they could champion themselves. My responsibility was to them, not the male ego.

Recently a friend, a sensitive soul and lover of children, tried guilt-tripping my two-year-old granddaughter into letting him pick her up. She didn't want to be held. His autocratic behavior suggested she had no right to choose. He wanted contact, so she must comply. She was told to be "a good girl." Instead, she held her ground, firing back a perky little "no." He changed tactics. Pulling himself to his full height—six feet two inches—he talked down to her in a "playful" gruff voice, saying, "I said come here." She became apprehensive. Her voice faded to a whisper. This was to be her first lesson in male domination. One she would never "consciously" recall, but might react to for the rest of her life. It was imperative she feel empowered.

Suddenly, I was prepared to kill or die in that hallway, if necessary, so she could choose. I told her so. Louder and firmer, she said: no. Astounded by my "saying such a violent thing to a child," he backed off. He never admitted that his behavior was unacceptable. Instead he decided I was becoming a rabid feminist. Rabid because he recognized a "violent thing" said to him in response. My granddaughter sensed my intensity and knew she had an ally. Allies are important to a Black woman, at any age, in a racist, sexist culture. The sooner we have them the stronger we become.

These are overt examples of sexual harassment; they, like overt examples of racism, make it possible for the subtler indignities to be ignored. Men are not the only offenders; women are often covert harassers.

My humanity has been as much negated by other women as any man of any color. Often these women are white. Often they are not. This is a reality with which we must grapple if significant changes are to be made in the unjust behavior which victimizes all women.

In the circle of misconception which surrounds and protects the rights of others to invade women's lives, only Black women are systematically subjected to this invasion by other women: The women who assume Black women are as exotic and "sexual" as do their men. The women who stare when we enter a restaurant with a man not of our own race, their assumption of prostitution vibrating in the air between us.

Perhaps sexual harassment begins immediately after birth as one is wrapped in blankets of pink or blue. From that moment on we are shaped by oppressive expectations, manipulations, "shoulds," "ought tos" and "musts" which can cripple for a lifetime. In every culture there are stereotypes of what male and female behavior should be and the differences between genders are artificially exaggerated. Our culture is empowered to twist our spirits and create a mental environment which allows sexual harassment, misuses and abuse to flourish.

As Black women we must love, respect and defend ourselves. We have to combat, nay negate, the hatred and contempt that bombards us daily. Forget the night, my sisters, take back your minds.

I feel like a dangerous woman much of the time; dangerous to those who would curtail or overthrow my freedoms. I question their assumptions about themselves, and certainly those they have about me. Sexual harassment is too often seen as an issue of men and their attitudes about women. Of more importance are women and our attitudes and assumptions about ourselves. Always be vigilant. Given choices among resistance, compromise and compliance—when possible choose resistance.

Elena Featherston is a 44-year-old lecturer, filmmaker and writer who produced and directed Alice Walker's "Visions of the Spirit."

Christine Roche

ON THE DISINCLINATION TO SCREAM

Molly Fisk

If I had been a ten year old stranger
and you had tripped me in a dark
alley, say, downtown, instead of our
mutual living room
I'm sure I would have screamed.

If, in the alley, you had
straddled me as fast—
your knees clamping my
elbows into asphalt,
not the blue Chinese dragons
of our living room rug, I
might have been quiet there too.

When you opened my mouth
with your heavy flat thumbs
filled it with pain and
flesh and that awful hot liquid
I would have choked in the alley,
as anyone would choke.

But if you had groaned then,
and stood up, walked away
from the dark street leaving
me to vomit and shake alone
I might have been saved.

I could describe you to policemen.
Perhaps their composite would match
your photo in the Harvard Reunion Guide,
Class of 1950. Your finger prints,
lifted from the collar of my dress, might
be found in Coast Guard files.

If they didn't find you and there was
no trial, still I could have gone home
to people who loved me. Horrified, enraged,
they would plot revenge and rock me
to sleep in soft arms.

I would have been frightened, maybe forever,
of asphalt, small streets and the
dark—but encouraged by the world, who
would hate you on my behalf. I would
have been as safe as a ten year old can be.

Instead, I rose quietly from the Chinese rug
and went upstairs to wash. I couldn't afford
to throw up, and it wasn't
the first time.

Molly Fisk is a contract investigator for the EEOC currently on leave of absence due to the emergence of repressed memories of childhood sexual abuse.

TALES OUT OF MEDICAL SCHOOL

Adriane Fugh-Berman, M.D.

With the growth of the women's health movement and the influx of women into medical schools, there has been abundant talk of a new enlightenment among physicians. Last summer, many Americans were shocked when Frances Conley, a neurosurgeon on the faculty of Stanford University's medical school, resigned her position, citing "pervasive sexism." Conley's is a particularly elite and male-dominated subspecialty, but her story is not an isolated one. I graduated from the Georgetown University School of Medicine in 1988, and while medical training is a sexist process anywhere, Georgetown built disrespect for women into its curriculum.

A Jesuit School, most recently in the news as the alma mater of William Kennedy Smith, Georgetown has an overwhelmingly white, male and conservative faculty. At a time when women made up one-third of all medical students in the United States, and as many as one-half at some schools, my class was 73 percent male and more than 90 percent white.

The prevailing attitude toward women was demonstrated on the first day of classes by my anatomy instructor, who remarked that our elderly cadaver "must have been a Playboy bunny" before instructing us to cut off her large breasts and toss them into the thirty-gallon trash can marked "cadaver waste." Barely hours into our training, we were already being taught that there was nothing to be learned from examining breasts. Given the fact that one out of nine American women will develop breast cancer in her lifetime, to treat breasts as extraneous tissue seemed an appalling waste of an educational opportunity, as well as a not-so-subtle message about the relative importance of body parts. How many of my classmates now in practice, I wonder, regularly examine the breasts of their female patients?

My classmates learned their lesson of disrespect well. Later in the year one carved a tick-tack-toe on a female cadaver and challenged others to play. Another gave a languorous sigh after dissecting female genitalia, as if he had just had sex.

"Guess I should have a cigarette now," he said.

Ghoulish humor is often regarded as a means by which med students overcome fear and anxiety. But it serves a darker purpose as well: depersonalizing our cadaver was good preparation for depersonalizing our patients later. Further on in my training an ophthalmologist would yell at me when I hesitated to place a small instrument meant to measure eye pressure on a fellow student's cornea because I was afraid it would hurt. "You have to learn to treat patients as lab animals," he snarled at me.

On the first day of an emergency medicine rotation in our senior year, students were asked who had had experience placing a central line (an intravenous line placed into a major vein under the clavicle or in the neck). Most of the male students raised their hands. None of the women did. For me, it was graphic proof of inequity in teaching; the men had had the procedure taught to them, but the women had not. Teaching rounds were often, for women, a spectator sport. One friend told me how she craned her neck to watch a physician teach a minor surgical procedure to a male student; when they were done the physician handed her his dirty gloves to discard. I have seen a male attending physician demonstrate an exam on a patient and then wade through several female medical students to drag forth a male in order to teach it to him. This sort of discrimination was common and quite unconscious: The women just didn't register as medical students to some of the doctors. Female students, for their part, tended (like male ones) to gloss over issues that might divert attention, energy or focus from the all-important goal of getting through their training. "Oh, they're just of the old school," a female classmate remarked to me, as if being ignored by our teachers was really rather charming, like having one's hand kissed.

A woman resident was giving a radiology presentation and I felt mesmerized. Why did I feel so connected and involved? It suddenly occurred to me that the female physician was regularly meeting my eyes; most of the male residents and attending physicians made eye contact only with the men.

"Why are women's brains smaller than men's?" asked a surgeon of a group of male medical students in the doctors' lounge. (I was in the room as well, but was apparently invisible.) "Because they're missing logic!" Guffaws all around.

Such instances of casual sexism are hardly unique to Georgetown, or indeed to medical schools. But at Georgetown female students also had to contend with outright discrimination of a sort most Americans probably think no longer exists in education. There was one course women were not allowed to take. The elective in sexually transmitted diseases required an interview with the head of the urology department, who was teaching the course. Those applicants with the appropriate genitalia competed for invitations to join the course. (A computer was supposed to assign us electives, which we had ranked in order of preference, but that process had been circumvented for this course.) Three women who requested an interview were told that the predominantly gay male clinic where the elective was held did not allow women to work there. This was news to the clinic's executive director, who stated that women were employed in all capacities.

The women who wanted to take the course repeatedly tried to meet with the urologist, but he did not return our phone calls. (I had not applied for the course, but became involved as an advocate for the women who wanted to take it.) We figured out his schedule, waylaid him in the hall and insisted that a meeting be set up.

At this meeting, clinic representatives disclosed that a survey had been circulated years before to the clientele in order to ascertain whether women workers would be accepted; 95 percent of the clients voted to welcome women. They were also asked whether it was acceptable to have medical students working at the clinic; more than 90 percent approved. We were then told that these results could not be construed to indicate that clients did not mind women medical students; the clients would naturally have assumed that "medical student" meant "male medical student." Even if that were true, we asked, if 90 percent of clients did not mind medical students and 95 percent did not mind women, couldn't a reasonable person assume that female medical students would be acceptable? No, we were informed. Another study would have to be done.

We raised formal objections to the school. Meanwhile, however, the entire elective process had been postponed by the dispute, and the blame for the delay and confusion was placed on us. The hardest part of the struggle, indeed, was dealing with the indifference of most of our classmates—out of 206, maybe a dozen actively supported us—and with the intense anger of the ten men who had been promised places in the course.

"Just because you can't take this course," one of the men said to me, "why do you want to ruin it for the rest of us?" It seemed incredible to me that I had to argue that women should be allowed to take the same courses as men. The second or third time someone asked me the same question, I suggested that if women were not allowed to participate in the same curriculum as the men, then in the interest of fairness we should get a 50 percent break on our $22,500 annual tuition. My colleague thought that highly unreasonable.

Eventually someone in administration realized that not only were we going to sue the school for discrimination but that we had an open-and-shut case. The elective in sexually transmitted diseases was canceled, and from its ashes arose a new course, taught by the same man, titled "Introduction to Urology." Two women were admitted. When the urologist invited students to take turns working with him in his office, he scheduled the two female students for the same day— one on which only women patients were to be seen (a nifty feat in a urology practice).

The same professor who so valiantly tried to prevent women from learning anything unseemly about sexually transmitted diseases was also in charge of the required course in human sexuality (or, as I liked to call it, he-man sexuality). Only two of the eleven lectures focused on women; of the two lectures on homosexuality, neither mentioned lesbians. The psychiatrist who co-taught the class treated us to one lecture that amounted to an apology for rape: aggression, even hostility, is normal in sexual relations between a man and a woman, he said, and inhibition of aggression in men can lead to impotence.

We are taught that women do not need orgasms for a satisfactory sex life, although men, of course, do; and that inability to reach orgasm is only a problem for women with "unrealistic expectations." I had heard that particular lecture before in the backseat of a car during high school. The urologist told us of couples who came to him for sex counseling because the woman was not having orgasms; he would reassure them that this is normal and the couple would be relieved. (I would gamble that the female half of the couple was anything but relieved.) We learned that oral sex is primarily a homosexual practice, and that sexual dysfunction in women is often caused by "working." In the women-as-idiots department, we learned that when impotent men are implanted with permanently rigid penile prostheses, four out of five wives can't tell that their husbands have had the surgery.

When dealing with sexually transmitted diseases in which both partners must be treated, we were advised to vary our notification strategy according to marital status. If the patient is a single man, the doctor should write the diagnosis down on a prescription for his partner to bring to her doctor. If the patient is a married man, however, the doctor should contact the wife's gynecologist and arrange to have her treated without knowledge of what she is being treated for. How to notify the male partner of a female patient, married or single, was never revealed.

To be fair, women were not the only subjects of outmoded concepts of sexuality. We also received anachronistic information about men. Premature ejaculation, defined as fewer than ten thrusts(!), was to be treated by having the man think about something unpleasant, or by having the woman painfully squeeze, prick or pinch the penis. Aversive therapies such as these have long been discredited.

Misinformation about sexuality and women's health peppered almost every course (I can't recall any egregious wrongs in biochemistry). Although vasectomy and abortion are among the safest of all surgical procedures, in our lectures vasectomy was presented as fraught with long-term complications and abortion was never mentioned without the words "peritonitis" and "death" in the same sentence. These distortions represented Georgetown's Catholic bent at its worst.

(We were not allowed to perform, or even watch, abortion procedures in our affiliated hospitals.) On a lighter note, one obstetrician assisting us in the anatomy lab told us that women shouldn't lift heavy weights because their pelvic organs will fall out between their legs.

In our second year, several women in our class started a women's group, which held potlucks and offered presentations and performances: A former midwife talked about her profession, a student demonstrated belly dancing, another discussed dance therapy and one sang selections from "A Chorus Line." This heavy radical feminist activity created great hostility among our male classmates. Announcements of our meetings were defaced and women in the group began receiving threatening calls at home from someone who claimed to be watching them and who would then accurately describe what she was wearing. One woman received obscene notes in her school mailbox, including one that contained a rape threat. I received insulting cards in typed envelopes at my home address; my mother received similar cards at hers.

We took the matter to the dean of student affairs, who told us it was "probably a dental student" and suggested we buy loud whistles to blow into the phone when we received unwanted calls. We demanded that the school attempt to find the perpetrator and expel him. We were told that the school would not expel the student but that counseling would be advised.

The women's group spread the word that we were collecting our own information on possible suspects and that any information on bizarre, aggressive, antisocial or misogynous behavior among the male medical students should be reported to our designated representative. She was inundated with a list of classmates who fit the bill. Finally, angered at the school's indifference, we solicited the help of a prominent woman faculty member. Although she shamed the dean into installing a hidden camera across from the school mailboxes to monitor unusual behavior, no one was ever apprehended.

Georgetown University School of Medicine churns out about 200 physicians a year. Some become good doctors despite their training, but many will pass on the misinformation and demeaning attitudes handed down to them. It is a shame that Georgetown chooses to perpetuate stereotypes and reinforce prejudices rather than help students acquire the up-to-date information and sensitivity that are vital in dealing with AIDS, breast cancer, teen pregnancy and other contemporary epidemics. Female medical students go through an ordeal, but at least it ends with graduation. It is the patients who ultimately suffer the effects of sexist medical education.

Adriane Fugh-Berman, M.D., is on the board of the National Women's Health Network, and is a former collective member of off our backs.

I had accepted the attitudes of a society in which somehow a woman is responsible for any unwanted sexual attention that is bestowed upon her.

—Angela Marie Ferguson

Trust men on a scale of 1-10 with only dead men being a 10.

—Karen Feich

I think that for most women, it is damned hard out there, to earn a living or to do much else, without some man thinking he has the right to objectify her.

—Donna Roazen

Most men are not my allies. Male sexuality can be hazardous to your health and well being.

—Catherin Malcolm

If someone says stop it, it's harassment.

—Barbara Otto

Research has what I see as one shortcoming: it focuses on our reaction to harassment, not on the harasser. How we enlighten men who are currently in the workplace about behavior that is beneath our (and their) dignity is the challenge of the future.

—Anita Hill

Persephone's Lament

Jana Gary

When I search back for an incident of sexual harassment in my life, I immediately think of a college professor who tried to put the moves on me when I was in graduate school. I must have been incredibly naive, because I didn't even realize what he was up to until he started complimenting me during a dinner date that I thought was strictly platonic.

It wasn't even what he said as much as the shock of it coming from a man who was my teacher. He leaned across the table and spoke in hushed tones. "I love women with short hair," he said. "It really turns me on." Of course, he was looking straight at my breasts instead of my hair.

I started to panic. I felt my face blushing and I couldn't stop. Somehow, I made it through the rest of dinner, even though I stammered most of the way through. I couldn't understand why I felt so upset. It probably had to do with the fact that this man was responsible for the grade I would get on the toughest course in my entire program. From that point on, except for class, I did my best to avoid him. It wasn't easy. Later, I confided my experience to another woman graduate student in our department. "I thought you knew he was like that," she said offhandedly. "I thought everybody knew."

I felt stupid. But I also felt crazy. I started to get panic attacks where I would blush uncontrollably for no reason. The blushing attacks became so severe that they dominated my life at college. I became so obsessed with them I sought counseling at the school's mental health clinic.

They assigned a male therapist to me who just wanted to talk about sex. He suggested my problems stemmed from not being as orgasmic as I could be, and suggested I order dildos from a mail order company in San Francisco. I wanted to talk about the panic, the obsessing, the fear, but somehow the conversation always turned to what my fiancee and I did in bed. Later, when I stopped in briefly after graduation, all he asked about was how the sex was now that I was married. He didn't even mention the panic attacks, which were still a factor in my life. It was only at that point that I realized what a quack he was.

Years later, I realized that the incident with my professor triggered my issues with my father and sexual abuse. Both were men I looked up to and trusted in my life, older, wiser, supposedly having my best interests in mind. Maybe that's why I'm so sensitive to the sexual harassment issue. It's the inequity of power, the implied threat, the confusion of being powerless before authority that I recognize like an old friend. It's so familiar that I used to not even question it when it was happening to me. It was a part of my upbringing as a child and still a part of my life as a woman.

I remember standing on the street corner one beautiful fall day in Plainfield, New Jersey. School was out for the day, and my mother drove us into town to do some shopping. I begged her to stop at the drugstore on the next corner so I could buy some candy. She pulled over to the curb across the street from the store, and cautioned me to watch traffic both ways before I crossed.

On the way back to the car, I stood at the curb in front of the drugstore and watched and waited until it was safe to cross. Out of the corner of my eye, I could see a boy coming towards me on the sidewalk. The next thing I knew, I felt a hand up my dress and a quick stroke across my private parts. I froze. The boy kept on walking, never breaking stride. I turned to look at him. He looked like he was about thirteen years old. I was around nine.

I looked across the street at my mother in the car. She didn't appear to notice anything wrong. It was a busy street, there were cars whizzing by and people all around. I didn't say a word. What could I do? The boy was bigger than me, and it all happened so fast, I wasn't even sure it happened.

There were so many people around me, yet no one who knew or seemed to care. It was like the whole world of grownups sanctioned the event. I felt so violated, so vulnerable in my pretty little dress with frilly slips that widened my skirt open to the world. It was so awful, so confusing to me that before I reached my mother's car, I just shoved it in the back of my mind and tried to forget it.

This is the first time I've ever said anything about it, the first time in 29 years. And they say if Anita Hill was telling the truth she wouldn't have waited ten years to say it. Most women wait a lifetime.

There have been so many more incidents since that time in my life, a progression of insults and invasions, large and small. The man at the newsstand who stood next to me reading a girlie mag as I rifled through the latest *Archie* comics. Shoving his elbow into my side to get my attention, he flung a beaver spread in front of my face. "Is yours like that?" he asked, stroking the raw slab of vaginal lips on the page. "Not quite," I said with disgust, hoping I sounded like a girl who could take care of herself, even though I was scared to death.

Then I sped out of there like nobody's business. I was twelve years old. I still remember that black and white photo, and my horror of being thought of in the same vein as that piece of meat on the page. Things like that weren't supposed to happen. But they did.

On the weekends, my parents would take us to New York City where we'd stroll around the streets taking in the sights. When I reached 14 years of age, I started to notice men making strange animal noises at me when I walked up ahead of my parents. It scared me, made me feel really weird—like a thing, not a person. I had no privacy rights anymore. Before, I could walk around in my own world, think my own thoughts, do what I wanted. Now, there were demands on me. Demands to respond, or not respond, to walk slow or run away. "Here, chickee chickee." Suddenly, I was entertainment and I hated it.

I came into bloom as a young woman just as "Female Libbers" started burning their bras. It was fine with me, I couldn't stand the things anyway. I was free, I was a hippie, more concerned with riding the wave of my newfound teen liberation than anything else. I had only a small sense of what these "feminists" were fighting for. I just stormed ahead and lived the benefits of their battles. Being a part of the counterculture was my first priority, and sure, equal rights and all that stuff were part of it, but drugs and free love and the war in Vietnam were far more important. Besides, that's where all the guys were—at concerts, at pot parties, at the anti-war rallies.

Still, something was not quite right. At a Santana concert at Xavier University in Cincinnati, about half the people in the audience joined hands together. We all danced around the auditorium, facing outward, in a crazy, wild dance of community as free children of the love generation. As I whirled around the circle, I felt hands reach out and grab my titties and genitals as I danced past. I knew we were all supposed to be into free love and all that, but it didn't feel right at all. In fact, it didn't even feel like love. It felt like a violation. But, like most girls my age, I shrugged it off as "my own hangups," once again repeating the age-old pattern of woman blaming herself.

My sister called me up last week-end and asked me if I remembered her telling me about the Jesuit priest at Xavier who surreptitiously felt her up while "counseling" her about her career choices. (She wanted to be a veterinarian; he tried to talk her into nursing.) "Do you remember?" she asked, still questioning whether it really happened to her or not. "What did I tell you about it?"

I assured her I remembered, and yes, she told me that she didn't know if it was on purpose or not, but when he leaned over her his hands and arms brushed her breasts. Several times. On several occasions. I remember very strongly that she wasn't sure what was going on, but that it made her feel "really weird," and that maybe there was something wrong with her to even think a priest would do something like that.

There is a very powerful voodoo at work here. To not acknowledge abuse as it occurs, and to blame ourselves for it, comes from centuries, not just generations, of the very subtlest and deepest kind of brainwashing. The kind that results in women defending their victimizers, and lashing out at their own kind. It has been incredibly effective, and still is.

My biggest lesson in sexual harassment came when I was raped on the streets of Berkeley, California. I was nineteen years old. I remember very clearly how I was dressed—jeans, old shirt, old thrift store jacket. I went over this point again and again for months afterward, because at the time (1974), the argument was that women "asked for it" by dressing provocatively. I had to defend myself, to convince myself that it wasn't my fault.

It was a cold, wet Northern California fall evening, and I was walking down a residential side street eating an ice cream cone in the rain and singing "Ain't nobody's business but my own." I wasn't quite sure of the address of the house I was visiting; I hesitated so I could read the street signs as I approached the intersection. On the other side of the street, I saw a man out of the corner of my eye, but I didn't care. The next thing I remember, someone was choking me from behind. "I've got a gun," the voice said.

For some reason, I didn't really believe the gun part, but it didn't matter. I knew this person could kill me with or without one. The attacker asked me for my money. I told him I didn't have any. He put his arm around me and told me to walk down the street with him "like we're boyfriend and girlfriend." At this point, I could tell he was a stocky black man, but I didn't want to look at his face. A young couple got out of their Volvo only a few feet ahead of us. I felt like a prisoner, paralyzed and hopeless, and thought there was nothing they could do to help me. I was literally in shock.

He took me to a garage where he raped and sodomized me. I went out of my body at that point and watched the whole thing from another place. I kept thinking this man knew nothing about me. All I represented to him was a couple of holes to get his rocks off in. He wouldn't let me cry or scream or say anything at all. I felt dehumanized. This time I didn't just *feel* like a "thing"—like I did when men would shout catcalls on the street—this time I *was* a thing, not a person. I think that was the worst part of all. It was like I didn't exist. After it was all over, he walked me back to the corner where he had jumped me. He checked my pockets and found around $2.00 in change and a small bag of pot. "Why didn't you tell me you had money?" he asked. His response really confused me. I didn't even consider it enough to qualify as "money," certainly not money you'd hurt someone to get. He kept the change and handed me back the pot. "Here baby," he said, "I don't want to take your stuff."

No, not my stuff, just everything else, everything that really mattered to me. He turned and walked away, and I ran as fast as I could to my friend's house.

I did not go to the police. I did not report it. I knew I had no way of identifying this man, and I didn't trust "the system" to help me. My girlfriend loaned me her douchbag, and I immediately took a shower and tried to flush all remains of this disgusting crime out of my body.

It still remained with me. For months afterward, I jumped every time someone on the street came toward me, even in broad daylight. At night, I had repeated nightmares of being attacked. I was so disconnected from my body that I felt like a zombie—literally a living dead person. In some ways, I wished I was dead, at least then I wouldn't feel so miserable. It took me a very long time to put the pieces back together.

The morning after I was raped, I remember passing the corner where the attack occurred and seeing the remains of my soggy, sad, ice cream cone on the street. My innocence, my belief that I was free to move about as I wanted, melted into the pavement with that cone. To this day, I cannot eat coffee ice cream or walk out on a dark street alone without thinking of that incident.

Making my way through this life as a "modern" woman, I have had many men friends, lovers, and mentors. I wouldn't want to live in a world without the beautiful balance that is possible between men and women. But I'm afraid my story hasn't really changed so very much from those of my ancient sisters.

I think of Persephone, condemned by a conspiracy of men to spend half her life in Hell in exchange for partial freedom. And like Psyche, I take my punishment for being a mere mortal woman who dares to break the rules and look in the dark at the things I'm not supposed to see in a man.

I am wiser now. I am learning to be a warrior in the battle for my own pride and freedom. Still, I say nothing when the man selling me a handbag stares lecherously at my braless chest. I kick myself for buying the damn purse from such a person. My actions betray my beliefs.

As I look up at Anita Hill on the screen, I swear that I will keep daring myself to speak up, and hope that someday I will. And just maybe, someday, someone will hear me.

Jana Gary is a writer from Savannah, Georgia, who is currently working on a novel about a woman's healing journey through the past.

CHEST X-RAY

Jill Ginghofer

In November, 1959, at the age of 22, I drove to Toronto General Hospital to have my tonsils out. I was with Bryan, a young writer with whom I was in love. In the gathering dusk, the five-story red brick building appeared menacing. "It's Debtor's Prison Gothic," I whispered as we ascended the deserted steps of the main entrance. Inside, under the bright lights of the reception area, we saw the intense activity, and withdrew emotionally, waiting for Joyce to arrive with a nightgown and robe for me. I'd brought my own toothbrush, but had assumed, probably from films I'd seen, that hospital patients were issued gowns. I was feeling particularly miserable. Three months of chronic tonsillitis and the ingestion of antibiotics had taken a toll.

We clung to one another trying to look inconspicuous, but my dyed black, inch-long hair and black garb and Bryan's 6'3" frame, shrouded in a duffle coat, made it obvious that we were more comfortable sitting in a coffee bar talking about the movie *Breathless* than dealing with the medical world. Nurses in blue dresses topped by white aprons, their bosoms strung with stop watches and safety pins, crackled to and fro. I slipped my hand into Bryan's pocket and entwined my fingers with his, the heat penetrating me, centrifuging warmly between my legs.

Heads turned when Joyce, her long hair flying, breezed in and handed me a bag. "That idjut George gave me these last Christmas," she said, before fleeing into the cold twilight. Sister McGrath, a large nurse with the face of a bruised potato, said in a brusk voice, "Change into your nightdress and gown in the cubicles over there and I'll take you up to the ward. Will your friend be taking your street clothes home for you?"

"Why would he do that?"

"This is a County hospital. We don't have locker facilities. Your friend should bring your clothes back when you are discharged."

Inside the badly lit cubicle I unearthed from Joyce's shopping bag a chiffon nightdress and matching peignoir, both black. When she saw me, Nurse McGrath gave a bark of despair. "Where are your slippers?" Then, softening a little, she said, "You'd better get your shoes back from your friend."

My white legs projected in a vulnerable way from the wide ankles of my scuffed desert boots. I felt entirely foolish. Nurse McGrath tried to push me into a wheelchair. "I can walk," I protested. If Bryan looked back I didn't want him to see me looking as if I were being delivered to Purgatory as did the other patients being wheeled around.

Nurse McGrath rushed me through crowded corridors, into a room-sized elevator where we were pressed against a gurney on which an old man sputtered with every breath. We finally arrived in a small office at the end of a long corridor. "Doctor will examine you. Then I'll show you to your bed."

A thick-set young man of medium height in white trousers and jacket flicked open a file. "You Jill?" He stared at me through white eyelashes, his skin so pale it appeared flaked. I nodded glumly. Without bothering to explain who he was, he asked about my health history, glowering with annoyance that I didn't have one. I had never been ill or in a hospital before.

"Come this way." I followed him into a windowless, dimly lit room, crowded with equipment. He sat me on a gurney and asked me to remove my robe. I was relieved he had not asked me to take off my nightgown. Although I always tried to appear sensibly calm when I'm examined by a doctor, I found it impossible not to feel vulnerable when my body was exposed. In an era that demanded that women remain virgins until married, any nudity could create tension. He pressed the cold stethoscope against my back. When he came to the front, he asked me to lower the top of my nightgown. I did as he asked. I weighed 108 lbs., and had large breasts. I held my breath, dreading a response. This unattractive man was only three or four years older than I. He leaned forward, his eyes coldly roving around the room as he pressed my breasts with first his hands, then the stethoscope.

"X-ray." He nodded toward a screen suspended waist-high on steel tubing running floor to ceiling. "Stand facing the screen." He pulled my arms behind me and looked over my shoulder at the way my chest and breasts were pressed against the screen. I felt an involuntary shudder jerk through his body. My whole body was alerted, but my mind fell into the familiar despair, the longing to be in my own safe world, the Bohemian world of artists and writers who, for the most part, managed to treat me, not just as a sexual challenge, but as a person capable of thought and feeling.

He disappeared into a door at the side of the room, reappeared and turned me, touching my shoulders, my back and upper chest to pose me sideways to the screen, and once more disappeared behind the door. He turned me to the other side, this time taking even longer to pose me. I felt wary and uncertain. He was acting as if he were performing a usual duty. I had no way of knowing if that were true. So I did what I normally did under threatening circumstances, I chatted wildly as if words would keep him at bay.

"Oh God, it's cold in here. How long will this take? Why do you need these x-rays—I'm perfectly healthy, apart from my rotten tonsils that is. I had a chest x-ray before reporting to the hospital. Are you the one who will operate on me?" The doctor silently and steadily took six "x-rays" of my chest from both sides before releasing me to the little office.

Nurse McGrath walked me into a large ward with barred windows on three sides. I was appalled. I had been paying a higher premium into the newly formed Canadian National Hospital Plan for private accommodation. When I expressed my horror to Nurse McGrath she gave a derisive laugh. "Do you know what our situation is like here? There isn't anywhere else. You want to go home?" She left me sitting dejectedly on the edge of my bed and, indicating a tray of food, said, "I expect your dinner is cold by now." On top of the aluminum warming cover a slip of paper stated, "Jellied veal." Underneath, a grey circle of fatty meat sat in a glaucous brown sauce. Next to me a woman with scraggly brown hair sat up in bed, smoking. Spittle ran down the side of her chin. "Hi," she smiled, revealing stained teeth. "I'm Miriam. Hole in the ticker." She tapped her chest.

An orderly asked me to change into a hospital gown which I did, only to find most of its back ties missing. A sweet, dark-haired nurse gave me a pill, explaining it would make me sleep through the night as I would be taken into surgery early the next morning. My eyes were already heavy when a squat, dark-haired man wearing white appeared and hastily circled my bed with a screen. "Examination," he muttered. He untied the top of my hospital gown and, pushing me down so that I was lying on my back, pressed my breasts with stubby fingers. I felt confused. Something was wrong here. I had already been examined. Somehow, because my breasts were involved, I felt as if whatever was happening was my fault. Since adolescence I had been trying to divert male attention away from my chest. The desire to sleep pulled at the bottom of my brain. I felt as if I were sliding backward, and only the monster clutching at my breasts was holding me in the lit world. "Oh, no," I groaned. As quickly and furtively as he had come, the dark gnome gathered up the screen and disappeared.

I don't remember being taken to surgery the next morning. The next thing I knew I was lying propped against a pile of pillows, mysteriously wearing the black chiffon again. A nurse pressed her face close to mine, "You must try to swallow." Obediently, I swallowed and nearly fainted from the pain. "Did you swallow?" I nodded, without intending to evoke that pain again and drifted away. When next I awoke Joyce was smiling at me, saying, "You look great in George's horror." Later, Bryan was there, patiently holding my hand as I drifted in and out of sleep.

Finally, I was fully awake and the ward was dimly lit. Sighs and groans filled the dark at the center of the ward. I turned my head and Miriam, the smoker with the dribble of saliva, winked at me.

"What day is it?" I could barely whisper.

"Ah, it's three in the morn of what will be Thursday. We've watched you sleep three days. You're known as Sleeping Beauty."

I did not see the doctor who had taken x-rays or the doctor who had "examined" me in my hospital bed. I was visited by my family doctor and the ward matron. "If you are swallowing nicely you can leave on Saturday," they both promised. Surreptitiously, I put my saliva into Kleenex, soggy mounds of which my friends smuggled from the ward in plain brown paper bags. On Saturday I was given permission to leave. "Won't be long, Nurse McGrath," I croaked cheerfully, awaiting Bryan and my clothes.

"Did doctor sign you off yet?" I frowned. No one had been near me all morning. I was perched on the edge of my bed when the pale doctor ushered me into the cluttered room again, muttering, "Final exam."

"Why do I have to go through with this? Can't I leave without it? I feel fine. Matron said I'm ready to leave." He listened to me breathe, briefly at my back and then for much longer at the front of my chest, his breath exhaling shakily. I turned my head to the side, hating the enforced intimacy, thinking, I'll be out of here soon.

"I'll need one more x-ray." He indicated a chair turned sideways in front of the screen. I sat down and, on guard as I was, obediently lowered my gown. Trembling slightly, he arranged my peignoir over one shoulder and behind my breast then disappeared into the dark of the room. I heard click after click after click, as if he were using an ordinary camera. I knew this had to be wrong. I felt helpless, afraid and confused. Surely a doctor wouldn't do anything that could be called to account? And wouldn't I be leaving any minute now? He came into the light and turned me the other way, his breath quivering, and carefully arranged my peignoir to reveal my breasts. Again there were many clicks from the dark at the end of the room. Then, his eyes behind his white lashes carefully avoiding mine, he came to turn me again. Although my mind had become numb, my body stiffened angrily. Taciturnly, he stepped back and said in a professional voice, "All right, you can leave now."

I did not tell Bryan about this incident. I didn't want to appear used, or to risk even a silent accusation that I might have brought this on myself. In fact, I don't recall telling anyone at the time of this incident, and if I had, I know I would have turned it into an amusing tale. I was always careful to seem tolerant, not to appear a prude. From time to time the thought flashed through my mind that photographs of me, bare-breasted and looking vulnerable, were passing through the pornography circuit (which then involved far more innocent depictions of women than now), or at least being ogled by medical students. I buried all memory of this violation of me by two young doctors until asked if I had an instance of sexual harassment for this book.

A requisite of my definition of sexual harassment is a disparity of power between participants, and certainly that went without saying in this instance. I'm sure these two young interns, as they became secure in their profession, moving on through prestigious careers, have become more confident and proficient at harassing women patients.

At the time this occurred there was a dangerous dichotomy for the romantic woman—and what woman wasn't romantic? Most male characters in the movies and books that educated and influenced us behaved decently toward women—did not press them unmercifully for sex in cars, in movie theaters, in their apartments, never gripped their necks and forced them to kiss them, nor pushed their hands and heads to their genitals, and yet this was how many men behaved in reality.

I had spent years talking with men whose eyes were never raised from my chest to meet mine. Many men, either silently or openly, accused me with anger in their eyes of deliberately provoking them, as if I were responsible for their reactions to my looks and figure. This accusation and accompanying anger was so commonplace, I had come to believe myself responsible for the sexually predatory behavior of males.

At the time, it was not safe to risk male displeasure or anger. To please was the only way to get by in the world. If you were rejected by the male, you were nothing. You could not succeed in school or in the working world, and no man would want to marry you, the one sure mark of female success. Because of this fear, many men did behave badly and rarely suffered unfavorable consequences.

In my need to protect myself, I chose men in the artistic community who fell in love, who were romantic and not as aggressive and competitive as those men who "scored" with women. It made my life happy, but made me inexperienced and vulnerable when circumstances out of the ordinary forced me outside of that world.

Jill Ginghofer works at Women's Crisis Support in Santa Cruz, California.

ONE LONG SEXUAL HARASSMENT EXPERIENCE

Cheyenne Goodman

My life is one big sexual harassment experience, from the time I leave my house to the time I come back home. A man exposed himself to me when I was five. I was molested by a stranger at age seven. I've been followed home. I've had to change my phone number due to strange phone calls. I've had men try to grab me and pull me into their cars. A man once grabbed my breast in broad daylight on a busy street. I've been yelled at, leered at, whistled and stared at. I've had strange men pucker up their lips in a sad attempt to blow me a kiss. I've been poked and prodded in the most personal places by strangers. I have had my space invaded, my boundaries disregarded and have been treated as a sex object by many, many men, and the worst part is I know that tomorrow will be no different.

There are two incidents of sexual harassment that I want to explain in depth. In the summer of 1988 I worked at the Democratic National Convention in Atlanta, Georgia, for ABC television. I was basically a courier, running video tapes here and there in the huge Atlanta Omni building. I came into contact with several middle-aged businessmen who didn't think twice about strongly coming on to me. A few even offered to pay me for sexual favors. I was sixteen. Even when I told them I was just a kid it didn't bother these men; in fact some seemed excited by this fact. I remember feeling incredibly unsafe when these incidents occurred, yet I knew I was supposed to respect, listen to, and obey adults, especially men. So instead of saying what I wanted to say, which was that they disgusted me and should be ashamed of themselves, I only mumbled no and walked quickly away.

I have grown up a lot since that summer almost four years ago. Sadly, society continues to teach men that it is acceptable to treat women as objects.

The other sexual harassment I want to mention occurs daily and is what I call "hit-n-run" harassment. I am a bicyclist. It is my transportation. Every day as I am riding, some man will stick his head out a car window and shout some offensive comment. "Wooo Baby! Hey Cutie, nice tits, oh yeah, pump it on that bike. Wooo Hooo, hey baby, wanna party? Nice ass, hey bitch, come here. Hey sweetheart come and sit on daddy's face. Check her out!" Sometimes they just stare as they lick their lips or tap their friend to "check me out." On two occasions I've had men grab me and almost knock me off my bike. Although I'm very often harassed by these hit-n-run offenders it hurts and angers me every time. None of these men ever treat me with the respect I deserve.

As a little girl, no one told me I would have to deal with this, or more importantly, how to deal with this. I was given no tools with which to handle these situations, no forewarning of what life is like in this world for women. But I learned, and am still learning.

Cheyenne Goodman, 19, is a cook and occasional waitperson at a vegetarian restaurant.

NUDES IN THE WORKPLACE

Marylou Hadditt

I've tried several times to write about sexual harassment, but it comes out garbled—no doubt because I'm not at all clear about my own thinking. I was raised a Southern Belle, which taught me at an early age how to use my sexuality to get what I wanted. I was dressed in pink silk underwear which always showed beneath my too-short skirts. As early as three years old, I knew that by sitting on laps belonging to Daddy, Grandpa, uncles, or male family friends, good things would happen to me: a ride when Mother said I must stay home; an ice cream cone; or an extra bedtime story.

By age ten, the art of the coquette was well ingrained, as evidenced by this oft-told family story. We were vacationing, visiting a submarine base in Connecticut—it was past the hours for touring inside the subs. I became emissary for my entire family, sashaying over to the sailor in charge, blinking my eyes, "Y'all know, Ah came all the way from Jawja jes' to git on a submarine" (which was not at all the case—we'd come for the New York World's Fair), "and now y'all won't lemme in," followed by many smiles and a few tears. We had our own personally conducted tour.

During World War II, as teenagers, my girl friends and I promenaded on downtown Peachtree Street, where great gusts of wind blew our skirts panty-high—we were flattered and giggled when sailors and soldiers gave loud wolf-whistles, and when actually dating, if a boy didn't make a pass at me, I was insulted; if he made too much of a pass, I feigned insult but secretly was pleased. We kept inventory on how many boy friends, how many prom dresses, how many corsages, how many fraternity pins we had—always competing with each other. We were taught that we must never be rude to men under any circumstances, and that "you catch more flies with sugar than you do with vinegar." (No one ever told us what you did after you caught the flies.)

In my early twenties I moved North, discarded my Southern accent, substituted veal scallopini for fried chicken—yet held on to my Southern Belle upbringing, carrying manipulative uses of sexuality into my professional adult life as a reporter and ad rep for a small weekly newspaper. To get a news story, I put so much sugar in an interview that male informants were figuratively seduced into giving information they probably had not intended. To sell ads, less subtle methods were applied: When Dick A., a bank vice president, flirted with me, I brazenly flirted back. When George R., a men's clothier, discussed his advertising schedule, his office walls were covered with nude calendars and his conversation spiced with off-color jokes. I admired the calendars and laughed at his jokes. When Mr. B., an aging realtor, wanted a modest pinch on my bottom, I let it happen.

This is what I was taught to do—it's not surprising it became an acceptable and a preferred manner of interacting in the business world. I never thought of these as acts of sexual harassment in the workplace. If I thought about them at all, it was later, when as a feminist, I wanted to forgive myself for the way in which I was raised and my inability to cast off my background. Were George's nude calendars a form of sexual harassment? Certainly, Mr. B.'s stolen pinches were.

Only once in my forty years of working did I fight back. I had started a new job, in the creative department of an ad agency, sharing office space with three men, each of whom had decorated the walls above their desks with two-sheet posters of near-naked women, on Harley Davidsons, wearing G-strings and pasties. I carefully placed my post card of Michelangelo's "David" above my desk. When my thirty days' probation was over, I was terminated.

I don't know what sexual harassment is, not really. I don't know if it's harassment when a clinical file reads, "A large breasted, 24-year-old Caucasian woman," or when my present boss identifies a Down's syndrome female client as "that girl with the big hips," or, recently, when I was called into my boss' office to be told I ought to wear a bra. I responded defensively, "But I do wear a bra." (Feeling guilty because I was wearing the lightest possible bra, and no doubt my nipples showed.) "Well, it doesn't look like it," he snapped at me. When I told my lawyer-daughter, her reply was, "Mom, that was sexual harassment. You should have told him he has no business looking at your chest."

On the Monday after the Hill-Thomas hearings, I listened while this self-same boss expounded on how careful he was about never saying anything which might be construed as sexual harassment.

I listened, without interruption, without questioning. I realized this was collusion on my part. Am I still a Southern Belle?

I need my job.

Marylou Hadditt, 64, is a writer who has also been a newspaper woman, mother, wife, recovering mental patient, lesbian, and social worker.

ATTITUDES

Catherine Hanson

Yeah yeah I've heard sexual harassment is part of everyday life for women. I hear it all the time. It's just a fact of life. So what's the big deal? So what if a man makes sexual comments or insinuations? Words can't hurt you, can they? You should take it as a compliment. Don't women have the advantage of using that attention to advance their own goals? What are you so upset about? It was just a joke. Where's your sense of humor? He touched you? Well, it's not as if you were raped, right? Lighten up, boys will be boys. Why are you making such a big deal about this? Just go find another job. If you stay there you're just asking for it. Oh, it didn't happen at work? Your landlord was doing this? Well that's a whole different thing. I mean you're a pretty woman. He probably just wanted a date with you. He's married? Oh, well it sounds like he's just looking for a little excitement on the side, maybe he's in a bad marriage. His wife is probably frigid, poor man. You know there's nothing worse than being trapped in a bad marriage. He asked you to watch pornographic movies with him? Well, maybe he's just trying to figure out what turns you on. I still don't see how he's harassing you. He called you Miss Boobs? Well, you know a woman of your...uh...endowment should be used to that sort of thing. You're probably just being overly sensitive. He puts notes on your door and says they're from a secret admirer? See, I was right, he just wants a date. Maybe you shouldn't dress the way you do. What do I mean? Well let's face it, you look pretty good when you're all dressed up. I mean, maybe you could wear your skirts a little longer or wear flat shoes instead of those high heels, and you know you could always wear looser tops so that your figure is not so noticeable. Oh, I'm not trying to say it's your fault. But, maybe you're giving out the wrong kind of signals. Well, have you tried to tell him that you're not interested in him? What do you mean he threatened to evict you? Well he can't do that can he? He has to have just cause to evict you, right? He doesn't? Well in that case I think that the solution to your problem is simple—just move. Oh, I didn't realize that you're in low-income housing. You waited how long to get in? A two-year waiting list huh...? Well you made it before you had low-income housing right? Oh, I didn't know that you had been homeless...and with your children? That's really a shame. But, can't you move to another apartment complex that has low-income housing? Oh sure, I understand that you have to think about what's best for your family, I know you're trying to make a better life for you and your kids. Of course you're right, you probably shouldn't have to give up your right to a safe home. Oh, you don't think that you should have to run away from this situation. So like I said, maybe you shouldn't make a big deal about this, you know, just try to ignore it. Oh, he's doing the same thing to other women in the complex? She woke up in the middle of the night, and he was standing over her bed taking his clothes off? Are you sure she didn't invite him in? He uses his key to go into women's apartments without permission? She was walking out of the shower and he was standing there? Well maybe he thought no one was home and he just needed to repair something. He asked women to pose in lingerie so he could take pictures if they were short on their rent? Said he had to check her body for stretch marks first? Boy, this guy's really got some clever lines. He grabbed her breast? In front of other people? Well, it could have been accidental. I mean I can't believe a man would just walk up and grab a woman like that. He has a curfew for single women at the complex? That sounds ridiculous, and what would be the point of that? Oh, you think he's trying to intimidate the women. And you say he threatens the children of these women with a gun, and tells them that he will make sure that they are sleeping in a park at Christmas if their moms don't do what he says? Well, you know how children are. They probably exaggerated the whole thing because they got caught doing something wrong. He was probably just trying to get them to behave. So, what happens if a woman refuses his advances? He towed their cars away? What does that have to do with sexual harassment? Oh, you think he is retaliating because he didn't get what he wanted. So, he turned women into the welfare department and child protective services on false charges? But that's not sexual harassment. He started rumors about having affairs with women at the complex? That doesn't sound like sexual harassment either. Maybe he's just bragging to make himself seem more appealing to women, you know, trying to portray himself as a ladies' man. We men do that all the time. He takes their property and keeps it and goes into their apartments and goes through their lingerie and personal belongings and then tells them what he saw? I don't think that is sexual harassment. I really find all of this hard to believe. What are these women's husbands doing about it? Oh, he only goes after the single women who are low-income. What do you mean he's on some kind of power trip? Oh, you think he's abusing his authority? Well, what kind of authority does he have over you? Oh, yeah, right, he can evict you. All of the women are low-income? And you think he just goes after the most vulnerable tenants who he can intimidate? A woman came in to pay her first month's rent and he put his hand between her legs? Why didn't she change her mind about moving in there? Oh, I see, she had just come from a battered women's shelter, and she didn't have anywhere else to turn. This whole thing is really far-out, I mean, I've never heard of a situation like this before. Are you sure that all these women aren't just overreacting? You know it is common knowledge that women tend to get a little hysterical. Isn't all this against the law? I mean if he's really doing all of these things, why don't you do something to stop it? Well, I don't know, maybe you should have a boyfriend or your brother beat him up. That would put a stop to it. Well, yeah, I guess he probably would press charges, and it might make things worse for you and your kids since you insist on keeping your apartment. No, no, I'm not saying that you're wrong for wanting stability for your kids' sake. But, you know nobody's forcing you to live there, it does kind of sound like you're letting this happen to you by staying there. If you don't want to lose your home, maybe you should just consider yourself lucky, since you're not homeless anymore. Maybe you should just grin and bear it. Fear? You're afraid because it's getting worse and worse? Well, how long has this been going on? Two years? Now I really don't understand, why are you allowing this to happen? Oh, I didn't realize that you had tried to do something. You wrote a letter to the owner of the apartments, and he did nothing about it for two years? He didn't even meet with any of you? All of you called the property management company repeatedly during the last two years? And you reported this to housing agencies, lawyers, and organizations, and they said they couldn't help you? And you called the police and legal aid, and there was nothing that they could do? The police told you that you would have to confront the manager yourself and make a citizen's arrest? Well, maybe that should tell you something. If there's nothing they can do, maybe you should just learn to accept it and stop trying to fight it. I mean, if the law isn't even on your side, then he must be within his legal rights as a property manager. What do you mean I'm ignorant? Well, yeah I can see how this guy might be making your life miserable, but if it's not against the law then he's not doing anything wrong. No, I guess I don't understand. It makes you feel degraded and victimized? Well, you women always get so caught up in your emotions and the way you feel. You should just learn to ignore your feelings the way that we men do. Then this wouldn't seem so bad to you. Emotional rape? Now you're really going too far! I think you're taking this whole thing much too seriously. You're afraid to leave your apartment and you're afraid to stay there? What is it that you're afraid of? Oh, because he's already done things to other women and so you think he might do them to you? Like what? He's already sexually assaulted other women...he tells people that he is going to get anybody that tries to stop him and he knows that you have made complaints...he's threatened other tenants about associating with you...he tells people that he is the gatekeeper of information and that he decides who stays and who goes...and you've seen the gun that he carries with him? Well that is sort of outrageous behavior, and I can see how a woman might be intimidated by all of that, but I bet if you really confronted him he would back down. I mean if anything, it sounds like this guy just has an ego problem. You know, a tough guy on the outside, but a marshmallow inside. No, no, I'm not trying to trivialize what he's done. What do you mean, you're going to sue him and the owner and publicize what's been going on there? What good would that do? You're just going to make a big stink about this and all it's going to do is embarrass your family and friends. After all, it's probably going to be your word against his. Oh, you've been documenting everything and you say there are over twenty women who have had the same kind of problems with him. Well, yeah, I know that you have the right to speak out, but why would you want to? I mean it's not going to be easy and think how it will affect your kids. Oh, of course I'm sure that it has already affected them. You say your children have witnessed many of these circum-stances, and some of them have been having severe emotional problems and are afraid of this manager? Yeah sure, I can understand that you don't want them to see you as a victim who is helpless. Oh, you want them to learn that you should stand up and do something for yourself and for other people when you know something is very wrong. Well, I guess I should wish you good luck. I think you're going to need it. I'm not sure I really understand why this is so important to you, but I guess there's one good thing that's already come out of this...it's probably already taught your daughter a hard lesson on the facts of life.

Yes, it most certainly has.

We did finally persuade the owners to meet with us with the threat of pickets and publicity. That meeting resulted in the manager being fired. How-ever, he was given three months' salary and a letter of recommendation by the owner. We did find feminist attorneys who were more than willing to take the case. The case of *Fiedler vs. Dana Properties* was settled out of court in June, 1991, for thirteen women and their children for under a million dollars. Eight other women are being represented by the United States Justice Department. We also followed through with our plans to publicize what we had experienced. As a result of that publicity, two other women came forth and pressed charges of rape by the resident manager. He was arrested while working at another apartment complex in another town, and he is presently in jail awaiting his trial for five counts of rape, to be held in January, 1992. Molly McElrath and myself have formed an organization called W.R.A.T.H. (Women Refusing to Accept Tenant Harassment). W.R.A.T.H. is dedicated to promoting awareness of sexual harass-ment in housing. We provide information and resources to women concerning their civil rights under the Fair Housing Act, their rights to legal recourse, and referrals to the proper agencies whose responsibility it is to provide assistance in these situations. After fighting back through an unresponsive system and eventually winning an unprecedented legal victory, we now offer our experience and support to other women who may find themselves in such a situation. Sexual harassment in housing is not widely talked about. It demonstrates the extent to which our society is willing to allow women to be victimized. We feel that it is our responsibility as women to speak out about this issue and provide other women with the information they need to fight back. It is our goal to bring this issue out publicly, as we cannot be quiet, nor should we have to endure this type of harassment.

Catherine Hanson, *co-founder of W.R.A.T.H., is 34, with two children, and is happily married to a man who has a great "attitude" and who has given Catherine and the other women involved 100% support throughout all this.*

DIANNE REUM

WHAT TO DO?

Rowena Harries

I want to write something about sexual harassment at work because I'm thinking about whether I want to keep working in my job. It's been a big issue for me, especially in the last year. In fact I recently had the anniversary of one of the worst experiences in my life and I was surprised to feel so upset and anxious.

I drive electric trains from Sydney to adjacent cities. I've been employed as a driver and trainee driver for nearly four years. There are very few women in my occupation. The two in my depot I don't get on with, though I've tried and given up. I don't know if it is because I'm the only lesbian that I get on so badly with the other two women.

I work day in and out with men. When I was still training I would usually spend my shift on an engine with one bloke for eight hours. Now that I'm qualified I drive alone on inter-urban trains and have to spend my time around men only in the meal room when I am on standby and in barracks where we stay overnight in foreign depots. Other drivers chat with me in my cab on their way to work and I sit in their cabs when I'm getting let off somewhere apart from a station, like the maintenance sheds.

There are pictures of naked women and obscene cartoons in the meal room and sign-on room, and occasionally in the engines and driving cabs. One meal room I used to have to sit in for hours while waiting was covered on every wall and locker with Playboy/Penthouse pictures.

The meal room I used most often in training had some pornography which I'd pull down when alone in there, so as not to have to face the men's anger. One time they figured out who did it and complained to the supervisor who told me off. I told him I was putting in an official complaint about the pornography in his office. He ordered me out and never mentioned it again.

Most of the men I work with see these pictures as non-pornographic and have no concept of why I'm disturbed by them. There was a legal case recently where pictures of naked women displayed in mixed sex workplaces were deemed to be sexual harassment. It was well publicized, so the men knew about it.

Sexual jokes are very common. Sometimes I just play deaf. Sometimes I complain. Sometimes I walk away. It depends how I feel.

When I was still in training I worked on a shift with a man known in the depot to be (more than usually) misogynist. We worked a long haul to the South Coast and were arguing by the time we got there. When we were getting off the engine, he got off first and poked the radio up between my legs as I was climbing down backwards.

I wished I'd kicked his face in. I could have from where I was. But being who I am, or was, I didn't and tried to pretend it never happened. A few days later I was very upset and in talking to a friend I realized how upset I was and that I needed to do something.

I went to a counselor, paid for by the railways, for a few months and reported the bloke to my chief Rostering Officer and said I refused to work with him again. His attitude was "Yes, we know he's a prick and there's nothing we can do about him—why didn't you belt him one?" He accepted that I wouldn't work with him anymore. I took the Equal Opportunity Officer along with me for support, though it wasn't easy to convince her to come.

I had some days off, due to stress. I felt quite split inside—part of me wanting to deny anything and everything, and the other part screaming for attention, to be listened to. I felt quite mad. I'm in the 12-step programs and found going to meetings and sharing what was happening to be very good. I got a lot of support at women's and lesbian meetings.

When I went back to work I was afraid of the reaction from the other men and the man concerned. He in fact behaved much better for a long time and became quite respectful. Not many others knew about it. A couple did and asked me about it. I told them what happened and that was that. They seemed to think I'd done the right thing.

I attended a three-day training school and on the first day the instructor made remarks like, "That's the trouble with this job—women," and other sexist statements that I've forgotten. I took the next day off because I was so angry I couldn't bear to go back. On the third day I went and saw him before the class and told him how I'd felt about his comments. He apologized and was on best behavior for the rest of the course.

The harassment a year ago was the worst in its long-term effect. I was in the meal room on standby. I'd been there for a few hours reading a book. Two male drivers were standing by the sink in the meal room when I got up to wash my tea mug out. One of them said, "Why don't you take your top off, Rowena?" I tried to joke about the remark. But when I washed my mug out under the hot water urn he wrapped his arms around me from behind and I flung the boiling water at him.

Unfortunately, as well as burning him I got burnt too. I yelled at him and told him off. The other man then got angry with me, telling me I had no right to complain, it was "just a joke." I was burnt on the face and went down to the women's toilet to cry and put cold water on it.

Away from the men, I realized I was too upset to ignore it. I reported it to the supervisor who said, "I don't want to know. Go tell someone else." I filled out an injury report and went to get medical attention for the burn, then went home, rang a friend to come over and went to bed.

This time I made a written statement of complaint and reported it to the manager of train crews. He was a real prick to deal with and got angry and told me off. I took nearly two weeks off work.

The upshot of my complaint was that the bloke got a gentle telling off and I was asked to shake his hand and make up, which I refused to do. When I got back to work the two men had told most of the depot all about their version of what happened. I heard quite a few of them. The main line was: the poor bloke had done nothing and I was a bitch for dobbing him in.

The vast majority of the depot wouldn't talk to me and didn't for months. I had eight-hour shifts, sitting on an engine with a silent malevolent man in charge. It's usual to share the driving, but this stopped. It was hell going to work.

I'd just finished my training but wasn't given my own trains to drive yet. I felt like quitting. But it seemed like such a pity to do three years training and then give it up because of the bastards. The advantage of the ostracism was that I didn't have to talk to the worst creeps anymore.

I got trained in single-person operation trains and so had some shifts where I didn't have to deal with men. And I did start to get support from some of the men at work. Often their comments were a bit confusing, but I was glad of any support. It was so difficult to cope with so much bad feeling. The other women in the depot ostracized me along with the men.

I went to a counselor but didn't find her much help. The one I'd seen before wasn't there anymore. The railways refused to pay for the four days I'd been off right after it happened. I had to go through many months of meetings with a very supportive woman from Employee Complaints to get them to pay.

The manager I'd reported it to had decided that the injury was as much my fault as the man's—so the railway wasn't liable to pay. The pettiness of this decision—not to mention the underhandedness of never telling me this directly to my face, or in writing—gave me a focus for all the anger I was feeling. It's hard to confront people who aren't talking to you. I did eventually get the four days' pay, but that sure didn't feel like enough. I guess I wanted them to admit they were lying bastards. And I didn't have much hope of that. I kept on working there despite many negative feelings about it.

I'm just coming to the end of a two-month break from work. I had a month's paid holiday and took a month unpaid leave because I was feeling so bad during the last month at work. I was hoping to decide something in this time off. But it's

Saturday night and I start back at work on Monday morning. I don't know what I'm going to do. The sexual harassment has made my last year at work hell. There is high unemployment in Australia now and finding another job would be difficult. Besides I don't know what I want to do. I was hoping writing this would help.

Rowena Harries is a 32-year-old train driver living in Sydney, Australia.

Cath Jackson

BEGINNING TO MAKE SENSE

Kate Huard

Have I ever been sexually harassed? "Ain't I a woman?"

It started in 1969 with my very first job, at the age of 16. I was a counter-girl in a small bakery-coffee shop within walking distance of my home. I enjoyed the work, and the attention of the customers. I was at the very beginning of my career path; I had no goals, no idea what I wanted to be when I "grew up," no idea what it was to be a "professional," and I had no particular investment in school. I was learning on the job, however, and I was learning that I got bigger tips for flirting. Since I was only getting paid minimum wage, those tips, the money in my pocket every day, was very motivational.

Except for what it taught me about my self-worth, the flirting was harmless. The customers were on one side of the counter, I on the other. Today, I know I was lucky, at least on that count.

Louis, the man who owned the bakery, worked with his brother and his brother-in-law. His brother-in-law used to rub up against me whenever he had to pass me in the bakery where I would have to go to get supplies for the coffee shop. He was always trying to get me to confide in him about my sex life. My personal life was pretty much a mess, and this wasn't helping.

Eventually, I spoke to someone about it who suggested I talk to the boss. I was scared. I was young, inexperienced, and, after all, this was the man's brother-in-law. What if the brother-in-law got mad at me? And decided to be mean, and didn't like me anymore? Or got me fired? I was only sixteen years old, what did I know?

Eventually, on my way out one day, I brought the subject up with my boss.

"Do you have any idea what you're saying?" he shouted, "This is *serious*! You had better make sure what you're saying before you make accusations that could ruin a man's life!"

Well, I thought, maybe it wasn't *that* bad, maybe it's part of having a job, maybe...

"You know, if you don't want this job, just let me know! There are lots of kids out there who *do!*"

Oh, I thought, never mind, it's not that big a deal, I'll never mention it again, just *forget* it!

Not long after that, I started my juvenile career as a chronic runaway. I saw no future for myself—at home, at school or at work. I headed for Manhattan, the big city.

At Port Authority bus terminal, I met what many young people meet...my first, last, and only pimp. He taught me how to walk, who to talk to, where to go, and managed my money for me. After all, he convinced me, if you have to give it away anyway, you might as well get paid for it.

He wanted too much control, however. When he started talking about building up a "stable," I drew the line. He slapped my face. Oh! Such pride I had then!

"No man has *ever* slapped me before, and you will *not* get a chance to do it again! I'm leaving!"

The Goddess was watching over me; that white man let this little fool go. He kept all the money I had given him, but he had given me the tools to make more. I didn't want to make this my life's work, I did not intend to get rich—just to get by.

I went to a coffee shop I had frequented and told my trouble to the owner, Amir. "What's a nice girl like you doing this trash for? Make an *honest* living," he said. "I'll give you a job! You don't need to peddle yourself on the street!"

I took a lot of convincing. Did I want to be a waitress again? I made $15-$20 a trick as a streetwalker. This man was offering me a dollar an hour. But he continued to pressure me, appealing to my sense of shame/pride. When I finally agreed, he took me downstairs to the store room to get me a uniform—and raped me.

ANGER! Rage! Resentment! Despair! *This* was an *honest* job? I tried, even after the rape, I tried—but I had no place to live, no place to launder or iron my uniform, and one night I just didn't show up. I laughed from outside the coffeeshop as I watched him racing to fill the gap I had left. Would I *ever* trust a man again? Or those values the patriarchy creates for women only? But I knew nothing of patriarchy then.

Life on the streets for a kid was hard. I had gonorrhea four times before I was 18. When I went home, I was placed in a state hospital. That's another story. I signed myself out at the age of 18, without staff support. They told my mother I was a nymphomaniac with latent homosexual tendencies. They never asked if I had ever been raped. I was there for six months, and the subject of rape was never discussed in my therapy, or, to my knowledge, anyone else's.

I became a waitress again. I got a job in a lunch counter with the help of a wonderful Sister of Mercy who continues to hold a special place in my heart. Two men ran the coffee shop. One of them was already "dating" the other waitress I worked with. The other guy was pressuring me.

"I feel like if I don't give in, I'll lose my job," I said to the Sister. I did not want to go back to working the streets, and didn't want to have sex to keep a less-than-minimum wage job. The moral issues were more than I could struggle with.

"They can't fire you for that!" she said emphatically. I didn't believe her. I quit.

I did find another job, as an apprentice in a dental lab. A husband and wife team ran the place; it was a small operation. I was safe at last. Until I got pregnant.

I lost my job. My husband walked out. And I ended up on welfare, which became my mainstay, off and on, for 13 years. I worked when I could, and my daughter, at the age of three, was raped at home, and continuously sexually abused thereafter, until she started acting out at 15.

I married and divorced three times; was physically, mentally and spiritually abused in all my marriages and abused by a welfare system that holds you accountable for not finding a man—boss or husband—to support you. When my daughter was eleven, and my son seven, I began to seriously look at what I was going to do to earn a living—my prince just wasn't coming.

Marriage wasn't cutting it, I have never received child support, and welfare has its limits—especially dealing with cutback after cutback, rent increases, the children's needs, not to mention therapy for the stress that poverty incurs. I went back to school, and though I was spared the humiliating experience of being sexually harassed by a professor, I watched it happen to many of my classmates. I was becoming more and more enamored of books and paper, which were fairly safe and predictable.

In struggling to extricate myself from my second marriage, I discovered the Battered Women's Movement, and developed my sense of feminism with Phyllis Chesler's *Women and Madness* and Kate Millett's *Sexual Politics*. It was all beginning to make sense. In school, in my term papers, I pulled together the violence of patriarchal religion and the victimization of women—while my daughter's need for help was ignored in a school system where "boys will be boys" and "girls are nothing but trouble."

I got temporary work that created havoc with my welfare budget, and eventually got a steady job in the circulation department of the local newspaper. I worked 9 to 2 Monday through Friday with no benefits, brought home $100 a week, paying $300 a month rent and losing *all* my AFDC benefits because I was not *gainfully* employed.

I became more active in the community, doing volunteer work. The newspaper promoted me in an effort to control me, and I was fired shortly thereafter when the city council candidate whose campaign I was working on lost the race.

I was devastated. I had done nothing to deserve this kind of treatment. I had held a job for a year and a half, and couldn't seem to do anything right. I didn't understand the rules, I guess; but I had two children to support, with birthdays and Christmas coming up. I began to despair of ever getting off welfare.

While I put my name in with temporary agencies I got involved with community radio. On a volunteer basis, I developed my own public affairs show, and discovered a *new* level of sexual harassment. Up until then, all my volunteer work had been with women and was fairly safe. Here was a male dominated "community" radio station where women were passed around like community property—and none of their work taken seriously. When my work got to be too threatening for the Chief Engineer who felt he could no longer use our relationship to control my work, he sabotaged my efforts. If I hadn't shared my experience with other women there, I would never have known what a common experience it was.

Today, I work in a woman-centered, supportive, safe environment, and I am truly blessed. I volunteer for W.E.A.V.E.—Women's Energy Against Violence—and have helped to organize an annual Take Back the Night march and rally since 1985. I am in incest recovery. And I am a lesbian—out, loud, and proud.

Have I ever been sexually harassed? Ain't I a woman?

No, I never pressed charges. I have no respect for our laws, or our legal system. Laws are created and enforced by the powerful to control the powerless. I don't believe court is the answer.

What is the answer? Education. From daycare up, we can create a new world if we take personal responsibility for our own power and the messages we give our children. We need to challenge ourselves and each other. Each day I grow in the wisdom of a spirituality that respects the sacred in all life, and I can only hope to be a model for a way of being that touches people around me and makes a difference in my small circle of friends.

And I want to share my recovery from the violence that is our heritage in America, a country founded on invasive, power-over dynamics. With my ability to use words, I will challenge the media in all its forms, particularly advertising, to change its violent and destructive images of women.

It's not about justice. It's about life. It's about caring. It's about hope. We may not see the effects of our work in our lifetime. That's OK. It's about making a difference. As much as we can. One day at a time.

Kate Huard, 38, of a multi-ethnic background, is an Education Secretary for Planned Parenthood of Central Massachusetts.

I look for a way of living with my head held high.

—Jay Cherian

Is it their problem or mine that men tend to go into a reflex action similar to Pavlov's dog at the ringing of a bell when a female enters their work domain?

—Chris Karras

I thought that men had the privilege to touch a woman without her consent.

—Barbara Paller

How many times does it take for you to feel that it's not your fault?

—Doreen Stock

When I remember the many moments during which I was sexually harassed, I wonder how any woman over the age of thirty could possibly be so protected or so naive to say she has never had similar moments.

—Terri L. Jewell

Hell, yes, I've been sexually harassed. What woman who's been alive more than five minutes on this earth hasn't?

—Laurel Speer

Mandatory Doctor's Visit

Diane Hugs

Being a disabled woman with a progressive disability requires that I document some of that disability through social security. Knowing that my primary physician documented what she saw on my visits, it surprised me a little when Social Security sent me a letter stating that I must see their doctor or I might no longer be considered disabled. This was funny because the small progression of my disability was not even the reason I was on Social Security and could no longer work. But they set up an appointment for me with a doctor I had never heard of and assigned the day and time of this appointment, and they stipulated that I had to go to that appointment.

As usual I took along a friend to the doctor's office; I've found it useful to have someone with me as a patient advocate and to help me remember what I wanted to ask. The doctor's office was in an old building with many rooms in his suite. When we got there it was unusually quiet for an office. We checked around and could not find anyone there. So we picked out what we thought might be the waiting room and waited for the doctor to show up.

The exam was routine and did not require that I remove my clothing. During the exam the doctor started by stroking my thigh as he looked over my chart sent by Social Security. He then asked me about my level of sensation since I am a paraplegic and cannot feel below the point of my paralysis. I held out my hands in front of me indicating that my sensation ended about the same level as my breasts. The doctor stroked my breast and asked me if I could feel that. Since he was below where I can feel I told him no, biting my lip so I wouldn't scream at him. Then he moved up to my level of sensation and touched my breast again with a stroking motion. I said, "Yes I can feel that. But is this necessary?" The reason I wondered was because he was checking neurological data and he was not a neurologist. He answered, "Actually it isn't, I was just curious."

During the exam he rubbed my shoulders and even kissed me; in fact he tried to kiss me on the lips but I turned away. There was no safe way I could think of to stop him; after all, his report would affect my Social Security status, and that is all the income I have in the world. Even though he could not deny I was disabled, he could have messed with my case to stop my checks at least temporarily. This was a psychological weapon which I felt was held over me the entire time I was there. So I kept my mouth shut and held myself back from hitting him during the exam.

As soon as I made it out of the office I burst into tears. My friend felt terrible for not having stood up for me but she was afraid of making more trouble for me. I was numb as I waited for the accessible van to pick me up and drive me home. Once inside the van I broke into tears again and told the driver what had happened. She was furious and told me to call the Center for Independent Living to get some advice. That was very helpful because at that time I could barely think at all.

Upon returning home I called the Center and the first person I talked to told me to call the rape crisis line. At first I was surprised at this suggestion; I had not been raped, just molested. But then I remembered that the local rape crisis center did more than counsel women who had been raped. They also gave information about what you can do or who you can contact in situations like this. So I called the crisis line and talked to one of their counselors. She told me to file a complaint with the police, that this was a crime and I should prosecute. It took me by surprise to have my feelings validated so strongly. Keeping the momentum up I called the police immediately after speaking with the counselor. During the hour and a half that it took before the officer arrived I went through a tornado of feelings. Was I taking this all too seriously? Would the officer think I was paranoid to be making such a charge? Were my perceptions accurate or was I blowing this out of proportion?

While the officer was not the most understanding or sensitive person, he did take what I was saying seriously. He wrote out the complaint and told me they would be back in touch with me for more information and that the medical ethics board would be notified. A few days later my friend was asked to meet with the police and an investigator from the Board of Medical Quality Assurance. She told me the investigator was a really nice guy who seemed seriously interested in seeing this case prosecuted. The next day the investigator came by to take my statement. He was disgusted by the story and hoped they would be able to do something to stop this doctor. It made me feel stronger to be taken so seriously and the investigator thanked me for filing the charges. He had two similar cases with physicians he was working on but it had taken the women years to come forward, making it a lot more difficult to prosecute. Because I had reported the event so quickly, there was a better chance of the investigator being able to prosecute. He first contacted Social Security to obtain a list of others who had been sent to this particular doctor. He needed to know if there were other women who had been similarly mistreated but who had not had the courage to report it. Although he went through every channel including the police, Social Security would not release any information. They claimed it would violate rights to privacy of Social Security recipients. He even asked if they would have their own people contact other patients they had sent to this doctor to see if anyone else had been abused, but they simply refused his requests. I was so angry—it was a lame excuse for Social Security to say it was a violation of our rights to privacy when they were the ones that made me (and how many other women) go to see this doctor.

Finally the investigator came up with a plan that Social Security would go along with. An undercover policewoman was to be sent in to see the doctor as if she were a disabled woman being sent in by Social Security. She sat in a wheelchair and had all the same forms as I had from Social Security. The exam went the same, the doctor did almost exactly the same things to her. When I learned of this, I realized this must be routine for him to mistreat and abuse Social Security or disabled patients during the exam. And although the undercover policewoman felt horrible and powerless when he kissed her and fondled her breasts, she wrote in her report that she wasn't sure if his actions were criminal. What I think she and the system did not understand was that he had power over my life through what he could do to my Social Security payments. I know it wasn't a weapon he could hold over the undercover policewoman, but I wished she had understood that he had no way of stopping her income. She could have fought back without risking her livelihood.

The district attorney did not see grounds to prosecute. This same D.A. was known for not prosecuting sex-related crimes; in fact later that year he was required by the City Council to prosecute over seventy rape cases he had passed by. Knowing that he did not take sex crimes very seriously, I checked to see if there was any other way to get this into court. But the sad fact is that the D.A. has the final call on whether or not to prosecute a case, and nothing I could do or say could change that fact. My next hope was the Board of Medical Quality Assurance. They brought him up before the discipline board and asked him to explain himself. The doctor admitted to everything that had happened; he just didn't think there was anything wrong with it. The Board warned him to keep his hands to himself and left it at that. Even though I wrote the Board an impassioned plea to reconsider on the grounds that his position of working for Social Security was a weapon against disabled women, they would not hear me.

This was more than I could take. On one hand I was told that I was right, that he had no right to fondle and kiss me, that in fact it was criminal; on the other hand no one would do anything to stop him from doing it to every woman he came into contact with. It really bothered me that he was not only going to get away with what he had done, but there was also no way for my testimony to keep other women safe. I told Social Security that his report on me was invalid since I was a victim, not a client; they told me they didn't want to hear about my personal problems. No way could I make them stop sending people to this doctor. It was driving me crazy to feel so helpless.

Having exhausted all means of legal prosecution, I decided to take him into civil court. There was a lawyer, Leslie Levy, with an outstanding reputation, so I decided to call her. She took the case even though I didn't have a dime and went right to work on it. The malpractice insurance company jumped into defending him even though they said they were in no way liable, because there is an exclusion for the insurance companies for any act that may be deemed criminal rather than a malpractice claim. So we had to battle these high-priced lawyers even though their company assumed no responsibility. There were two years of foot dragging and legal manipulation which my lawyer had to fight while the doctor continued to practice. He said he would settle for five hundred dollars. I rejected this because I could see no indication that he had the slightest clue that he had done something wrong.

Two years after filing this case and having every legal trick in the book thrown at us, we finally got around to doing court depositions. I was unable to sit upright at the time so not only was I unable to go to his deposition, I had to give mine from my bed. Instead of having all these strangers in my bedroom I used the bed in the living room. That was a very good thing because the doctor decided to show up and listen to my statement. A deposition requires the presence of lawyers from both sides along with a court reporter, and that felt like a huge invasion in itself. The deposition lasted about three hours and I was very lucky to have such a brilliant lawyer on my side. She did not let them get away with asking anything that was not relevant. She jumped up and down a lot, screaming at the other lawyer to back off. Since Leslie was familiar with abusive lawyers and litigants, she protected me from unnecessary harassment and abuse, for which I am eternally grateful to her.

That deposition did the job. The doctor seemed to realize I had been hurt. For the first time he understood that he had done damage, though he was not willing to pay for it. So onwards towards court we went. It was finished four months later and while I cannot divulge the outcome, I can say that the judge was understanding and resolved the case so I didn't have to go before a whole courtroom with it. The terms of the settlement prohibit me from saying anything.

I am still left with feelings of rage and sadness about what he did to me and how the system let him get away with it. If it had not been for the interest of Leslie Levy I would have been left out in the cold. There are not enough lawyers like her.

The legal system is still predominately male and does not take women seriously. It is not a lucrative business for lawyers to take on such cases since there's not that much money in these cases even if you get the court system to see the damage done. For me that was the hardest part, being asked, "Describe how this hurt you" in front of strangers who were not sensitive to my feelings. How to explain what having this uncaring authority figure run his hands all over me did to me, how he made me feel like a whore.

I used to trust doctors, but not anymore. I lost trust not only in the system which ignored my pain, but also I lost trust in people in general. It took over four years for me to let a stranger touch me at all. I had to explain to the doctor's lawyer that this lack of trust, not wanting to be touched, was damage in itself. He tried to downplay it by asking me if I would ever let anyone touch me again. I told him I had every intention of healing from this and hoped to be able to regain my trust. I fought hard. I fought long. It was worth the effort. The doctor knows he was wrong now. I just wish I had been able to stop him from continuing to practice. But I did everything I could and I can live with that.

What I would like to say to other women, disabled or not, is that a doctor does not have the right to touch you in any inappropriate way. We all have the right to fight back. More women need to fight the doctors who don't know the limits of conduct. If you are not sure whether your doctor went too far, but you do not feel good about what happened, follow it through. Contact the Board of Medical Quality Assurance, rape crisis centers and please, if you think there is even a possibility of a criminal case, call the police. The more women who call doctors on misconduct, the fewer doctors will continue to do harm to their women patients. If you cannot do this for yourself, please consider doing it for the next woman. Even though your doctor may not have taken you seriously, having to answer to all the different authorities will make him think twice before he treats another patient the same way again.

Diane Hugs is a working-class woman with severe multiple sclerosis who is a writer and disabled activist.

118

Jennifer Camper

THUMBS UP ANYONE?

Alyce Ingram

Back in the early thirties, during the depression, just out of high school with holes in my soles and the salutatorian speech fresh off my tongue, I was fortunate enough to get myself hired as a housemaid in a WASP-y somewhat gothic household for which I was paid three dollars a week plus room and board. Most young women those days who worked as domestics received no cash whatsoever for their services, only room and board. I was quite jubilant to have hit the jackpot, even though I knew perfectly well from past experience there was no possibility of my getting either a raise or a promotion while working there. In fact, I learned quickly enough that the only move upward would be to wash the ceilings and walls of this smoke-damaged house my employers had just recently inherited from a relative.

But wall-washing was not all there was on the agenda. In addition I cooked, scrubbed, dusted, Hoovered and did the laundry for the family, a family that consisted of the man of the house, his wife (she had a wooden leg), and their ten-year-old daughter whom I seldom saw for she kept to herself most of the time and frequently stayed over with friends. When she was at home, she slept in a bedroom on the second floor of the house down the hall from my own room. The man and his wife retired to their sleeping quarters downstairs in a room with curtained French doors that connected to a small sitting room where I spent my evenings reading on a love seat after I had washed the dishes and cleaned up the kitchen.

The reading supply in the house was meager and I no longer remember the title of the book I was reading on one particular evening as the lady of the house and lord of the manor slept behind closed doors. I do recall, however, occasionally wondering about the two of them for the woman seldom ventured out, yet made no attempt to get better acquainted with me, and I saw her husband only at the supper table where he kept his head bent over his plate and never spoke a word. His wife once told me that he became absolutely sick upon learning that young girls my age attended the Winter Garden Ballroom downtown which he considered a den of iniquity "with all the shimmying and shaking," a statement I could not dispute since I had never been to the place. I wondered how he had acquired his knowledge, whether firsthand or by hearsay.

So there I am on this night with book in hand and quiet all around (I had never seen a radio in the house) when suddenly, from behind, comes a man's hand cupping my right breast, with thumb flexed upright stiff as a poker, a thumb that I instantly bit like a crocodile.

There was no outcry. No hysterics. No threats of exposure as the man fled from my presence into nether parts of the house. Nor did money ever change hands over the incident. As I recall, the larger part of my disgruntlement that followed stemmed from the fact that I was "let go" at week's end without sufficient notice. Or reason.

Alyce Ingram is a 77-year-old writer from St. Paul, Minnesota.

Fairy Summer—
Or How I Learned to Wash Dishes

Ruth Innes

I didn't want to take the man up the hill with me. I didn't want to show him where I played. But he asked very nicely and I was afraid to be rude. No one had ever taught me that a child could say no when a grownup asked for something.

My grandparents had a restaurant and lived in the apartment above it. One summer, when I was five years old, grandma and grandpa took a trip to Sweden so my mother ran the restaurant for them. To make it easier, my parents moved from our house to the living quarters above the restaurant.

There wasn't anyone for me to play with around the restaurant, but I had always been a solitary child and liked playing alone. My favorite place to play was up on the hill behind the restaurant. There was a little spring up there which made even the hottest day seem cool. I was sure the fairies came there to drink and I spent hours making fairy houses with the softest of mosses for their carpets and beds, pretty pebbles for their chairs and tables, and flower petals for bedclothes and tablecloths. The nooks at the roots of the big hemlock trees were wonderful spots for fairy houses, and damp earth from around the spring made good stout walls to keep the fairies safe while they slept. Sometimes, when I inspected the houses early in the morning, there were definite signs that the fairies had been there—a tantalizing footstep in the moss or a bit of dust from the fairy wings left on the furniture. I shivered with delight and carefully smoothed out the moss and dusted the furniture.

I hated the days when it rained and I had to stay inside to play. Those days I spent a lot of time at the kitchen table cutting out paper dolls and peeking into the bar that stretched across the restaurant, watching the men who sat there drinking beer. Most of those men worked for the lumber company that was sporadically cutting timber around town. When they weren't actually in the woods working, those men seemed to be sitting at our bar drinking beer. They worked in the woods and they drank beer, which made them hiccup a lot, so it seemed very logical to me that they were called woodhicks.

122

Some of the woodhicks fussed over me, asking dumb questions about how old I was and where I got my rosy cheeks. I didn't want to talk to them but mother and dad always told me to be polite. So when one of the woodhicks stopped me as I was about to start up the hill and asked me to take him along, I didn't know what to say. I didn't want to, but I didn't want to offend him either. I can still remember his beery breath in my face as he coaxed, "Come on, show me where you play, pretty please."

"You wouldn't like it up there," I finally told him. "And besides, your feet are too big and you might step on a fairy."

"I'll be very careful where I put my feet...I'll walk softly," he persisted.

Reluctantly I started up the path with the man close behind me. I went as fast as I could, hoping that after I showed him he'd go back down to the bar. We hadn't gone very far when he suggested we sit down. "No," I protested, "this is not up the hill yet. This is just the path. You said you wanted to see."

"What's the hurry? I need to rest a little," the man said, sitting down by a fallen log. "Come sit with me...we both need to rest."

I was puzzled. This man worked in the woods all day. Surely he could walk further than that without being tired. Still at a loss as to the proper thing to do, I finally sat down beside him. He immediately put one arm around my waist and pulled me close to him. He put his other hand on my knee and pretended to brush off a bit of dirt. "Oops," he said, as the dirt turned out to be a scab, and then he quickly moved his hand up my leg and under my shorts to stroke the crotch of my panties. His sour breath was in my face again and he began to lean over me even closer. I didn't know why, but I knew something was wrong and I broke away from him and ran down the hill as fast as I could.

"Here now, come back girlie, I won't hurt you," he called after me, but I kept running.

Down at the restaurant I rushed into the kitchen bathroom and hid behind the door. I didn't dare shut the door because that meant the bathroom was in use and I didn't want anyone to know I was in there. I was afraid that the man might come looking for me and someone would tell him where I was. I hid behind that door for what seemed like a long time; I kept peeking through the crack the door made where it was hinged to the wall, but I couldn't see very much. I thought that if he appeared in the narrow view I'd slam and lock the door.

Mother finally came in to use the bathroom and discovered me cowering behind the door.

"What are you doing in here?" she asked, looking at me curiously.

"Nothing," I answered, "just hiding."

"Who are you hiding from?" Mother demanded.

"That man," I said.

"What man?"

"That woodhick I ran away from."

"Tell me exactly what you're talking about."

So I told mother about the woodhick who asked so politely for me to take him up the hill and how I was afraid to be rude so I'd started up the hill with him but then ran away from him.

"What did he do to you?" Mother insisted on knowing.

"He felt my panties," I admitted, feeling ashamed.

Mother rushed out of the bathroom and into the restaurant searching for that man, but he wasn't there. When she came back to the bathroom I knew she was very angry and she said to me, "Don't you ever do that again!"

I started to cry. Mother dropped to her knees and put her arms around me. She explained that she wasn't angry at me, but at the man, that she only meant I should never go anywhere with anyone again but come and tell her if anyone even suggested it. In spite of her reassurances I felt that I had done something wrong.

The rest of the summer was ruined for me. Up the hill was a dangerous place to go. What if the man was up there waiting for me? Or what if he came up while I was there and wanted to touch me again? I stayed away from the hill and, because I hung around the kitchen at the restaurant so much, mother decided I might as well learn how to wash dishes. By the next summer I didn't believe in fairies any more.

Ruth Innes is a divorced legal secretary in her 60s living in Florida.

124

WE CAN MAKE A DIFFERENCE

Alice Irving

The first thing I noticed when I walked into Professor Kraig's office was the Farrah Fawcett poster on the wall. It was the poster that made Farrah famous: lots of shiny blonde hair tossed back, big white smile, nipples pointing through her wet red bathing suit. She shared a wall with a diploma announcing that Frederick Kraig earned his doctorate from the University of Chicago in 1953.

I was surprised by the poster. Sitting at his desk with my freshman schedule and academic file in front of him, Dr. Kraig didn't look like the kind of man I associated with pin-up posters—the pudgy man who ran the local gas station in the small rural town where I grew up or the gangly, pimpled boys I went to high school with who kept pictures of naked women taped to their locker doors. Instead, Dr. Kraig looked like everything I imagined a professor to be—almost gray, balding, round gold wire-rim glasses, wrinkled khaki pants.

During our first hour together, any doubts I had about my new academic advisor vanished. I thought he was wonderful. The chair of the History Department of a small private liberal arts college, Dr. Kraig had been chosen as the advisor to a small number of incoming freshmen, all scholarship recipients. He gave me his complete attention. We went over my fall class schedule. We talked about current news events, the political environment on campus, my goals for the future. Dr. Kraig was impressed with my college entrance exam scores and when we were through talking, he said he was impressed with me. I left his office feeling smart and, more importantly, like an adult. His attention confirmed what I was beginning to doubt—that I belonged at this college. I understood his interest and enthusiasm to be a reflection on my talent and maturity, both about which I had wild doubts.

College was a foreign and frightening world. My identity was solidly rooted in the poverty of my childhood. We had lived in low-income housing and survived on welfare until my single mother finished her education and began working. Education meant escape to a better world; it meant that I would never have to count out food stamps in front of a disdainful clerk. A good education meant I would never live in government housing and there would be money for new shoes when I needed them. I wanted this security for myself and my mother wanted this success for her children. The oldest child, I was breaking new ground by attending a private college on a combination of scholarships, loans, and grants.

Initially, I felt out of place at college. I washed dishes for my work study job; most of the students I knew didn't work. The people around me were comfortable, confident, older. Having skipped a grade, I was younger than anyone I knew. I felt a little like a child sneaking out of bed to peek into an adult party. Someone might discover I was somewhere I didn't belong. Slowly, my self-image changed. I found a few good friends and began to see myself as a confident, capable adult. My success in school convinced me that college was where I belonged. But this took time and Dr. Kraig's early enthusiasm was important to me in my first few weeks of college. In fact, his support was so influential that I chose History as my major. I was sure that Dr. Kraig could teach me a lot.

Over the next two years, my experiences with Dr. Kraig did indeed teach me a lot. I learned about sexism, sexual harassment, and the institutionalized abuse of power. I learned that sexism knows no class boundaries; that sexual harassment exists among the most educated men; and it is barely acknowledged and frantically hidden by the most enlightened liberal institutions. Most significantly, I learned that I was a strong, resourceful woman and that standing up for principles I believed in made me even stronger.

I took two classes from Dr. Kraig during my freshman year and visited his office regularly for academic advising until the middle of my sophomore year. I discovered that he had a reputation on campus for being a "dirty old man." Women laughed about his Farrah poster and senior women whispered more serious warnings about what might happen if they let him close his office door. Students joked that his History classes were thinly disguised sex lectures. Generally, people I knew accepted these incongruities between the dignified research scholar and the classroom teacher. I did too. Laughing away Dr. Kraig's antics were more difficult for me, as I relied upon his academic advice and personal support.

However, a number of things that occurred during the classes I took were too disturbing to forget, too inappropriate to simply laugh away. In one of the classes, he frequently made a point of inviting me and another young woman to take seats in the front of the room. He told the class that he liked to see pretty faces and nice legs while he lectured. Everyone laughed and my friend and I took our places in the front.

I was always embarrassed. Was my skirt too short? Blouse too low? I became increasingly aware of what I wore and how I looked. Trying to listen to

Dr. Kraig lecture, I found myself focusing on how I was sitting, which way my legs were crossed. I was frozen between my desire not to fall from Dr. Kraig's favor and my equally strong desire not to draw more attention to myself.

Class lectures were dotted with comments on sex and women's bodies. For every historical figure we studied, Dr. Kraig had a series of lengthy speculations on that person's sex life. These tangential remarks were followed by small jokes about the good times Alexander the Great or Winston Churchill must have had—what Dr. Kraig wouldn't give to be in their shoes—or pants. The class gave the obligatory giggle. There were frequent and obvious sexual innuendos made directly to select women in the room. These comments extended to his exams. One question on a multiple choice test read: "Putting out is (a) term for cottage industry in the 1900s; (b) reference to militia blitzes in WWI; or (c) what naughty girls do in the dorm at night."

In the middle of one lecture he paused to ask why he even bothered to talk about history when "over 80% of you are having sexual fantasies and not even listening to what I say." I looked furtively around the room. Was Dr. Kraig right? Was I the only person who wasn't fantasizing, who actually cared about the class? I began speculating about what my classmates were thinking and wondering if any of them thought I was fantasizing! Again, I worried about how to act, how I appeared. My face remained purposefully frozen. I was afraid that any smile or glance might indicate that my mind was on sex, as Dr. Kraig suggested.

The classroom became a highly sexualized environment. Just beginning to be comfortable with school and still uncovering the sexual mores which worked for me in my personal life, I was unhappy to discover sex in the classroom. Classes had been one area where I felt secure, where I knew what was expected of me and how to respond. Suddenly, what was expected of me seemed vague and somewhat insidious; there were new rules to the game.

Despite this, I did well in the two classes I took from Dr. Kraig. But I was also taking other classes, learning a lot there and more from my new friends. Politics began to interest me. My ideas about how the world worked changed. By the middle of my sophomore year, I thought of myself as a feminist and was part of a small group of politically progressive students on our conservative southern campus.

History remained my major, however, and Dr. Kraig was my advisor and the chair of that department. During my freshman and sophomore years, while I was still developing my new political beliefs, I had frequent appointments with Dr. Kraig in his office. During these appointments he had nothing but praise for my academic work. We went over my essays, class assignments, exams, and he pointed out particularly good observations or analyses I had made. He was enthusiastic and listened to me talk about my work. I wanted to go to graduate school. He encouraged this goal and promised to help me. These conversations left me feeling hopeful and confident about my career.

However, there was always another side to our conversations that left me confused and uncomfortable. Early in my freshman year, Dr. Kraig asked me if I had a boyfriend. Did he live on campus? How tall was he? My advisor also wanted to know if I would consider going out for "coffee or something" sometime. I gave polite honest answers and managed to defer the request for coffee. Time passed and my discomfort increased. Dr. Kraig began commenting on my body and my clothes. Right after giving me advice about graduate school, he told me that if I kept "that fantastic body" I wouldn't ever have any problems in life. He wondered out loud about all the men that must follow me around campus because of the "cute little patch" in the seat of my jeans. Another time, he leaned over his desk and stuck his finger in a small hole gaping through the knees of my jeans. "What's this for?" he asked, wiggling his finger and laughing. He began greeting me with remarks about how a pretty woman in his office made his whole day brighter. He told me that I had the mind of a thirty-year-old in a twenty-year-old body. Twice, he called me a "good hunk of woman."

I had no idea how to respond. Usually I laughed or smiled, ignoring the content of the remark and hastily changing the subject. My heart would begin to beat faster, my face flush. The closed door and tiny office made me feel trapped. I was inordinately conscious of my body and felt that it was somehow out of control, that it was doing something quite on its own to draw so much attention. By the end of our visits, my legs would be tightly crossed, my arms folded across my chest. I felt like two different people—an awkward child with Dr. Kraig and the self-assured young woman who was everywhere else in my life.

Eventually, I understood that Dr. Kraig's behavior was inappropriate. Not knowing what to do about it, I decided to avoid him. I had developed a strong and uncomplicated relationship with another professor and he became my advisor. However, Dr. Kraig was still the department chair and thought highly of my work. I wanted that strong letter of recommendation to graduate school some day. Telling myself he was annoying but harmless, I decided to keep smiling at his jokes. This was just one of life's necessary evils, like looking straight ahead while someone whistled at me on the street.

Then Dr. Kraig asked me to be his teaching assistant. I hesitated. On the one hand, I desperately needed the money. College was expensive, and as Dr. Kraig knew, I supported myself and was barely getting by. Also, the job experience might help my graduate school application. On the other hand, taking the job meant working closely with Dr. Kraig, whose very presence made me nervous and jumpy.

Seeing my hesitation, the professor leaned over his desk. "I can make or break History majors, you know." He may have said more, but those words were all I heard. Images of all my hard work crumbling at his hands crowded out all other thoughts. I accepted the job. He said he was delighted and fished a small black leather book out from the piles of paper on his desk.

"Now I can add your name to my list of wild women. What memories this little black book holds." He tapped the book and smiled. "My last teaching assistant was truly incredible. Beautiful woman. Yes, she was something else." More smiles and laughs, shaking his head as if the memory was too good to believe.

I didn't want to be on a list of wild women. He wrote down my name and number and asked if I ever went cruising. It wasn't really a question, but an opening for him to talk. Trying to look polite, I listened to him tell me that he liked to pick up women in his car. He pinpointed the area he drove through—usually the local red light district—and laughed about how surprised the women were when they learned he was a professor. When he was done talking about his late night escapades, I fled, completely unnerved and unsure about what had just taken place.

That night I agonized over my decision, or lack of one. I felt completely railroaded, manipulated. Being his teaching assistant implied that I would also be something else, something sexual. My name in that book seemed to mean I had agreed to be one of his wild women. I stayed up, trying to think like Dr. Kraig might, so I could understand what he was saying to me. Finally, I decided that this was probably just his inappropriate and awkward way of talking to women. If he was actually toying with the idea of having some sort of sexual relationship with me, I would simply have to make sure I gave him no encouragement, provided no opportunity for misinterpretation.

I decided to keep the job. The money would mean a real difference in my life and I would avoid Dr. Kraig as much as possible. I would act removed but polite when we were together.

Almost a month passed without any significant incident. I saw little of Dr. Kraig. Work was slipped under the office door when he wasn't there. Things seemed to be running smoothly until one afternoon when he asked me to sit down in the chair next to his desk. We talked a little. Suddenly, Dr. Kraig reached over and pulled my shirt open in the chest. I was wearing a blouse with a T-shirt underneath. "My, aren't we looking sexy today," he said, holding my shirt open and looking at my breasts like he was pulling apart drapes to survey the scenery.

I started to cry. I felt absolutely humiliated. Dr. Kraig leaned back into his chair again and I stood up. Still crying, I said that I had to leave. For the first time, I saw Dr. Kraig look unsettled. He asked if I was coming into work the next day and I said I didn't know.

Walking back to my dorm room, my confusion and shame lifted just enough for me to actually feel the anger that had been brewing for almost two years. Long months of silent humiliation pressed into me and I was moving on anger and the need to speak. The friend I told was horrified by my story and urged me to talk to an administrator, to do something. I needed little convincing. The person I spoke to had to be someone with authority over Dr. Kraig. Having no idea how university systems of supervision worked, I went to the president.

Probably swayed more by my visible distress than by my assertion that I came about something tremendously important, the secretary let me in to his office. By the time I finished telling him what had happened, his initial surprise at seeing a distraught student in his office shifted to concern. Without questioning what I'd said, he carefully outlined the options available to me. Two were informal routes involving Dr. Kraig's supervising dean and meant no record would be kept. The other option was to pursue the matter formally using the university's brand new sexual harassment policy.

President Greene strongly suggested that I go to the University's ombudsperson and work with her. She had helped write the sexual harassment policy and could help me, no matter what route I chose. He advised me not to speak with Dr. Kraig alone again. With real concern for me, and most likely, for the possible liability of the university, he told me the decision about which step to take was entirely mine.

Familiar with the issue of sexual harassment and aware of the appropriate institutional responses to a complaint, President Greene was able to give me exactly what I needed: specific options, concrete steps I could take.

The next day, I typed a letter outlining my formal complaint. It was a difficult decision. I was 19 years old and it was spring. People all around me were shaking off the winter months with long walks, bike rides, picnics. I wanted to feel as carefree as they looked. The decision I was making felt burdensome— what was I getting myself into? Repeating what Dr. Kraig had said and done would be embarrassing. He might deny it. Who would believe me? People could find out. What would they think of me? More than these things, I was afraid of Dr. Kraig. The stakes were high. Who knew what he would do or say?

But I knew an injustice had been done. I now had the power to make sure it never happened again. How many more women would he intimidate in the years to come if I did nothing? How many had he harassed in the past? He needed to know that what he did to me was not only morally wrong, but illegal. Filing a complaint seemed clearly the just, responsible action.

My letter of resignation to Dr. Kraig explained that I would be too uncomfortable to work with him again. The reasons for my discomfort: I described what happened yesterday and chronicled specific details of the past two years. In conclusion, I informed him that I was pursuing the matter formally and listed the people who would be receiving copies of this letter.

The ombudsperson, Professor Christine Harris, was racing to a meeting when I arrived. Telling me she didn't have time to talk until the next day, she started skimming the letter I gave her and then began reading slowly. She picked up the phone, cancelled her meeting, and closed the office door. In her office, on that afternoon and many to come, I found the support, empathy, and guidance I needed.

After I was through talking and crying, Professor Harris assured me that the incidents listed in my letter constituted sexual harassment. She couldn't tell me what to do but it was her job to stand by me and mediate with the institution. We talked about how the sexual harassment policy worked and what would happen next. There were more decisions to make and I was suddenly overwhelmed and exhausted. Anxiety tugged at the edges of conviction; maybe I should just let it go.

Then Professor Harris told me I was not the first person to come to her office about Dr. Kraig. She had several other complaints listed in her files, but no one had ever been willing to take the next step. Dr. Kraig had never been confronted and the institution remained unaware of the problem. Hearing this, I knew I would never turn back. Dr. Kraig had to be stopped.

The suit took three months to settle. The process started off with an emotional, manipulative letter from Dr. Kraig. He wrote that he was stunned, had never been so betrayed in his life. He had thought of me as a daughter. Couldn't we work things out? Not only could a suit prove legally and emotionally destructive to him, but to me as well. He ended with a poignant description of his anguish. It was an eloquent, powerful letter.

I was devastated. How could I do such a thing, hurt someone so deeply? This kind of pain—I was responsible for causing it. Overwhelmed with guilt and sorrow, I cried for a long time, reading the letter over and over. Maybe I was making a mistake. It wasn't until I showed it to Professor Harris that the veiled, threatening nature of the letter became apparent.

She pointed out statements about possible legal harm to me and how he didn't want to be "forced" into making damaging revelations. Hoping to influence my behavior by being both a betrayed, caring friend and a powerful intimidator was similar to his form of harassment—interweaving academic praise with sexual appraisal. In both cases, it becomes hard to separate the two Dr. Kraigs, friend or foe. In Christine Harris' opinion, this letter constituted additional harassment. While the suit was being settled, my life was driven by anxiety. Walking across campus was frightening. The university sat on one large city block, a space small enough that Dr. Kraig and I saw each other fairly often. Once we came face to face in a cafeteria. He looked directly at me with long, raw hatred laced across his face. No one had ever looked at me like that.

Not only did I alter my movements to avoid Dr. Kraig, I tried to escape the rumors and gossip flying around campus. Everyone—the institution, Dr. Kraig, myself—wanted to keep this issue private while it was being settled. Of course, I told my friends; I needed them for support. There were memos, letters. Perhaps Dr. Kraig told colleagues. In such a small community, even the most private secrets spread.

A professor I respected immensely found out and called me to his office to convince me that my actions were misguided. What I claimed as truth was unbelievable. Did I realize what this was doing to his longtime friend and colleague? I heard people talking about Dr. Kraig and the female student he slept with who was now suing him. Who was she? they wondered. The editor of the college paper worked hard, questioned everyone and found out "she" was me. Talk, he pleaded over and over, one interview. It's too important to remain silent. I was angry. If the editor knew my identity, how many of these other people I saw every day did? What were they thinking? Were there more wild stories circulating? I survived this time with the strength of my friends.

In addition to these more social concerns, I worried constantly about how the suit was progressing and the possibility of Dr. Kraig taking some legal action against me. For Dr. Kraig adamantly maintained that he was completely innocent. He hated to use the word "lie" about a formerly beloved student, but these charges were untrue. Never, ever, would he say anything remotely sexual to a student. He wouldn't dream of discussing his personal life to a teaching assistant. The final "shirt incident" was most unbelievable. All he did was tell me that my shirt was missing a button and he touched the shirt to guide me to the empty spot. Why was I doing this to him? Over and over, he claimed I was ruining his life, destroying a reputation.

My complaint was being pursued along the "informal" path of the policy, meaning Professor Harris and the college lawyers would work out a settlement between Dr. Kraig and myself. The college would have a written record of the complaint and its outcome. The "formal" route involved both parties testifying before a panel of students, faculty, and legal administrators. The thought of sitting in the same room with Dr. Kraig and telling my story to all those people filled me with dread. If Professor Kraig and I couldn't come to any sort of agreement using the "informal" path, the case would automatically move to the formal procedure. This was the last thing I wanted. Who would believe me? It was my word against his.

In order to settle the case informally, I was to present the terms of "justice" to Dr. Kraig, who would reject, accept, or alter them. Then, the terms came back to me. Christine Harris told me that this was my opportunity to make a difference, find justice. Dr. Kraig was thoroughly frightened and wildly defensive, she said. There's too much evidence—the test question, comments made to classrooms filled with people. He'll agree to anything reasonable.

Defining justice felt burdensome. Why should I have to do this, too? I thought victims just told their stories; someone else was the judge. These were circumstances I didn't instigate; now I was responsible for their resolution. Intellectually, I knew that this process gave me a voice, control. Emotionally, I felt another guilty responsibility emerge.

Despite his vehement declaration of innocence, Professor Kraig agreed to the first set of terms that Christine Harris helped me work out. I would receive a written apology and be paid the salary I had planned on earning. Dr. Kraig would no longer be assigned freshman advisees. He would complete at least six counseling sessions regarding his sexualized behavior toward female students, with a statement from the therapist verifying his attendance. Finally, at Professor Harris' suggestion, a sexual harassment evaluation would be required indefinitely at the end of his classes—an evaluation with very specific questions asking if students noticed inappropriate sexual comments in class, questions on tests, or conduct in his office.

For my part, the university and Dr. Kraig asked silence. I was not to discuss this issue publicly. This felt like a victory. Although he was protected by tenure, Dr. Kraig would be monitored. Safeguards were established to prevent him from doing this again. I happily agreed. Putting this whole nightmare behind me felt wonderful.

It was over. My friends and Professor Harris were proud of me, congratulated me on my victory and my courage. Professor Harris and the university were delighted that the new harassment policy worked. I felt proud, too. I stood up for what I believed in breaking new ground, using a system of justice never tried, and winning. If I could face this I could do anything.

Despite my newfound confidence and relief, the anger remained. Dr. Kraig's apology letter had been two short sentences, noting that each person interprets events differently and he was sorry if my interpretation had caused me pain. Never once did he acknowledge the truth. We still ran into one another. I was still afraid of him. Somehow, I wanted more.

I talked at length to my friends about this. Told them how alone I felt during the complaint process. About the uncertainties and anxieties that had plagued me. How if only I had known what harassment was before it had happened. There should be a specific place on campus where women could go for support. A place that wasn't concerned with the legal process or university liability, a place just to support women.

Two weeks later, my friend Beth and I stood in front of the university's Board of Trustees to present our proposal for a women's center. We would research women's centers on college campuses across the country, create a structure for our own, set it up, run it. We would be paid for our efforts. The college needed this service, we maintained, and we presented statistics about sexual violence and harassment. The Board, well aware of the recent harassment settlement (but not knowing the student's name), agreed.

By the time I graduated, the University Women's Center had been up and running for a year. The administration had paid Beth and me to act as co-directors for the first year. We had an office in the student center with lots of space and a wealth of information for women. Volunteers helped staff the center. The women's center was structured as a university service, not a student group, so we received operating funds and had a board of advisors. One of our board members was establishing a curriculum committee to establish a Women's Studies major at the school.

At graduation ceremonies, Beth and I received the newly established Human Services Award. Created to acknowledge our work, the award would be given each year to a student whose human rights activism challenged and changed the college community. I said good-bye to my school, proud that I had made a difference. Women's issues would never again slip between the cracks of bureaucracy. I had been part of a group of women who changed the University. I felt that I had helped turn my experience with Dr. Kraig into something positive, powerful and permanent. I was no longer afraid.

I still feel that way today. Now I teach sociology and women's studies at a large university. Those years in college changed the course of my life and I like where I am, where I'm going. The only lingering regret is the silence I promised. Did I sign something? I don't remember, don't think so. Was this silence limited to when I was a student, or did it extend to me now?

Talking about this with Christine Harris, a decade later, I learn that Dr. Kraig is still angry. He insists that I ruined his life, cost him the chairmanship of his department and destroyed his reputation. She says he is an angry and vindictive man; he might sue me if the opportunity arose. Checking with the university lawyers, she phones me to report that they advise me to stay silent. When I ask, she thinks that writing about my experience under a pseudonym would be all right. Just as long as Dr. Kraig can't be identified.

I remember my silence during those first years in college. I remember the urgent need to talk about the harassment suit, over and over, to my friends. When I watch Anita Hill testify before a congressional committee, the urgency returns. I am completely demoralized to see this woman attacked, her words brushed off as fantasy and to find Clarence Thomas triumphant on the cover of People magazine. Our new Supreme Court makes me frightened for my future and the future of my daughter.

If I don't speak now, it is because of fear. Fear of again angering Dr. Kraig, fear of what he might do to me. I refuse to live with that fear any longer. There are ways I can speak out within the constraints of our legal agreement, without revealing his identity. I believe it's important that our accounts be made public, to provide the history, the evidence, even the models, for women who will fight harassment in the future. We can make a difference. The strength of so many voices cannot be ignored.

I decide to write.

Alice Irving is a midwestern writer.

Jackie Urbanovic

HOW TO TEACH ONE DOG A NEW TRICK

Terri L. Jewell

Harass—from the French "harasser, to set a dog on." To disturb or irritate persistently, to enervate an enemy by repeated attacks or raids.
                                    —The American Heritage Dictionary

Am I a piece of meat? Am I an enemy? I am a 37-year-old Black lesbian feminist born to working-poor parents in Louisville, Kentucky. When I remember the many moments—and they were only moments—during which I was sexually harassed, I wonder how any woman over the age of 30 could possibly be so protected or so naive to say she has never had similar moments.

I can remember the boys who would swim up behind me and grab my butt when I was a swimmer, then a lifeguard at the public pool. I remember how my being the first Black female guard in Louisville aggravated the boy guards. As an initiation, they took me into the deepest end of the pool and attempted to tear my swimsuit off. When I nearly drowned one of them, I gained their respect.

My best friend, Theresa, lived a few houses away when we were in junior high school. Not only was she physically abused by adoptive parents, but every time I visited her, her father would ask me for a kiss, sometimes attempting to pull me to him. I would always talk my way out of it. He died in a fire many years ago. Theresa died in a car accident a few years after that.

I can remember a college boyfriend, Jerome, whose alcoholic father and two brothers would constantly make plays for my attention, sometimes to the point of beating up Jerome and sending us both running from the house into the street.

And there was the male student who exposed himself to me in a Music Room at Montclair State College in New Jersey. He begged me to suck his penis. After I told him I "did only Black men," he left.

Then, there were the retirees who volunteered for the Meals-On-Wheels program I coordinated part-time in Louisville. These men, knowing I was unattached to (and thus unprotected by) a man, made constant requests to visit my apartment, take me out "for a good time," buy me things in exchange for "a little kiss, honey." Or they would speak of their younger, stronger days, then ask me to look at the bulge in their pants as proof of their virility still. I would say something glib, then smile and walk away, always aware that a negative or harsh response might cost the program a much-needed volunteer.

In the early 1980s, my apartment in Irvington, New Jersey, was burglarized by a convicted rapist(!) next door. When the police arrived, a detective tried to ascertain if the burglar had been a boyfriend, since the burglar left a note that he would return. When I told the police I lived alone and had no boyfriend, the detective volunteered to become my boyfriend and asked for a date. I asked them to leave and have not trusted the police since then. I moved back to Kentucky.

While working as a claims examiner for the Unemployment Office in Newark, New Jersey, I assisted a man who wanted his benefits reinstated. This Vietnam veteran showed his gratitude by bringing me flowers and small gifts, all politely refused. He persisted; I went out to lunch with him once. He began to call me at home and his conversations, except for those "moments" when he would tell me how he would love to kiss my breasts and impregnate me, were congenial. I finally "came out" by saying I wanted no sexual relations with men. Since then, he has tracked me from New Jersey to Kentucky to Michigan, where I now live. I get occasional letters, either on paper or on cassette, but no phone calls. I have kept my phone unlisted since then and I have never answered a letter since such a response would surely verify my residence. He has threatened to appear on my doorstep if I do not respond. He has even called my parents in Kentucky to ask if he could marry me. The police have consistently said that there is nothing to be done unless he shows up in person and/or assaults me. I have been advised to keep running from this fool. His name is D. Newsome.

Men have approached me for sex while I stood at bus stops or in the stacks of large libraries—anywhere and any time I am out of my house and alone—the above-mentioned are but a few. Am I a piece of meat? Am I an enemy?

Up to this point, I learned that the way to deal with men who sexually harassed me was to play it off—smile, joke, go numb and walk away, turn away. In any case, do not create a disturbance. "Be an adult." My Momma would say, "It is no big deal. Just carry yourself like a lady." My womenfriends who were heterosexual would say, "Well, did you do such-and-such" to provoke such behavior and bring "attention" to myself? I learned to deal with it quietly. But I was still a woman alone...on the streets, at work....

Then something changed in me. I watched Anita Hill.

On Monday, November 18, 1991, I made the first step in beginning a sexual harassment investigation against a male co-worker. Here is the information I have written to the sexual harassment counselor at work:

First incident of note—Sometime mid-February or early March, 1991, when I first entered the Central Records Department, Miguel and Ron stood in the workers' area after 8:00 a.m. and spoke to one another (but loud enough for all to hear) about the breast size, thighs, and physical desirability of women they had seen at a bar up the street from the job. I asked them both to show respect and to take their comments elsewhere. I was loud and direct. They walked away. Ron has had little to say to me at all since then. Miguel made references for two to three weeks afterwards about people not saying gender specific or sexual jokes and comments around me because I may react negatively.

Second incident of note—A few months later, Miguel was speaking to anyone around him about picking up women. As he was walking away from his desk (I was seated at my own desk and not participating), he told anyone who was listening, "I bet Terri could give me some tips on picking up women." I was angry, but did not respond at all since he did not speak to me directly. I am not officially "out" at work, but I do nothing to give the impression I am heterosexual or at all interested in capturing male attention. I was furious that I had not been quick enough to retort: "Yeah, I bet I could. Sounds to me you need them." Nevertheless, I did not appreciate his offering up my business as a target for ridicule.

Third incident of note—Several times, Miguel called out to me (to receive a phone call, for instance) as "Terrence." I ignored him initially. The conduct continued. Once I asked him not to call me Terrence. No response from him; the conduct continued once or twice more, then it stopped.

Fourth incident of note—In late August or early September 1991, I received a phone call from a male friend. Miguel, upon hearing from a co-worker that my caller was a man with a nice voice, responded loudly, "Terri? A call from a man? Really? I wonder what that could be about?" I ignored him and took my call unperturbed.

Final incident of note—On Friday, November 15, 1991, Miguel sat at the office phones shortly after lunchtime. I was standing nearby, checking files I had pulled for an employee upstairs. Miguel was trying to engage me in casual conversation. I was not interested; I asked him to be quiet. He continued; I asked him to shut up, all this time not making eye contact. In fact, I was standing with my back to him. No one else was in the area. He had been talking about buying men's clothing. When I asked him to shut up, he muttered that perhaps I would be interested in men's shoes. I then said to him, still not facing him, "I'll remember that. I won't forget. You've stepped over the line now, Miguel." About a half hour later, my supervisor and a few of her associates walked into the area and Miguel was behind them. I said, "Miguel, I want an apology!" He looked embarrassed, but said nothing. I said, "Formal complaint! I'm filing one." My supervisor asked out loud, "What happened? What did Miguel say to you?" I retorted, "You ask him. And if he can't figure it out, he *is* in trouble." I asked my supervisor then and there where I had to go to file a sexual harassment complaint and she immediately directed me across the hall from our office. Miguel left for the day and I will never forget the astonished look he had on his face. Utterly astonished! I talked to the sexual harassment counselor and she gave me the necessary forms. I filled them out over the weekend and returned them to the counselor Monday morning.

Miguel is the only male in an office of seven. Throughout my stay in this office (less than a year), Miguel has rendered gender specific and sexual jokes to male associates who come into the office, loud enough for surrounding women workers to hear. This has occurred 99% of the days I have worked. Usually a woman will ask him to not render such material, but such a request only escalates his efforts to the extent that he follows a person and finishes his comments. Then he asks the woman her response. Miguel's comments are offensive to me in that they refer to an aspect of my private life that induces derision among co-workers. His comments are disrespectful, outside the realm of the working environment, and make me angry to the point of affecting my ability to concentrate on my work. I no longer feel capable of managing this situation.

And what do I want? I want Miguel to stop his inappropriate comments to and about me. Period. Since the moment I told him I was filing a formal complaint and he watched me go across the hallway, his remarks have ceased. He is doing his work and carrying himself as a professional—all business. The entire office is relieved; however, the investigation into his conduct continues. I am going to take it all the way. Whichever way this all turns out officially, I have won this.

Thanks, Anita Hill. We deserve full and total respect everywhere. And we are not the enemy after all.

Terri L. Jewell is a Black woman writer who works as a clerk for the Michigan state corrections system.

THESE TEACHERS

Elizabeth Kadetsky

Waiting for orientation to begin that day, I got what I thought was an invitation to belong. It came in the form of the dean walking through the pack of gray-eyed students as if on a mission, like a racehorse exiting a stable. He stopped a foot in front of me and offered a massive hand. He had a self-effacing grin, pleasant if saggy features and a corpulence that made him not threatening, but not blundering either; his bulk simply lent him an imposing presence. I felt the heated stares of the female students, the mocking scorn of the males.

"Who are you?" he asked, with an emphasis on the "you." I detected a sexual hint at once, but then I thought of every male professor who had slighted my female colleagues and me, and in a short second I rationalized this bit of undue attention. More perceptibly, I felt bolstered by the subtle expectation that I would succeed. It was as if he had blessed me.

I avoided the dean after that, until I needed help wrangling with the university bureaucracy. To him, my craftiness and perseverance proved my ability to make it in this profession, where wile and will are perhaps the two greatest assets. Or so he said. He was quickly a fan—for whatever reason—soliciting advice in matters of deanship and offering to look at my work.

In fact, we were friends. Throughout those weeks I mistrusted his motives, but I also came to like him. I believe I even developed a crush on him. I grew to expect his undivided attention each time we passed in the hallway or when he would introduce me to professors and visiting dignitaries, people I had fantasized about meeting but had been too shy to call, people who could help me in my career.

The questions naturally arise, as they did for Anita Hill's persecutors. How did I encourage him? Did I have an overt crush or a repressed crush? Did I manipulate him for my benefit, advance my career, use him, tease him?

There are no categorial no's in answer to these questions. He inhabited my dreams relentlessly. He would often metamorphose to my father, his contemporary, and then to the man I lived with, a lover significantly older than I. In one dream I planned to lunch with the dean, until another professor—handsome, young and accomplished—asked if I'd have lunch with him. I guiltily broke the date with the dean, lying so he wouldn't feel jealous. Other times I confused him with an appealing former college advisor, the man I secretly wanted to marry. Or he was the young professor who offered me a job only after he interrogated me about my love life and discovered I was single. In other dreams he became the portly high school math teacher who pulled me from my adolescent alienation with warm hugs—too warm—and a note in my yearbook: "You are one of the most special people I ever met here."

They are one person, these teachers. They were notorious among my girlfriends: the flirty, lonely, charming men who offered us enigmatic encouragement and praise, the men who seduced us into complicity by finding us "special." As much as I've felt disgusted by the inappropriateness of their advances, violated by their lust, part of me craved their attention, polluted with sexuality as it may have been. For a mentor to have deemed you exceptional in any way was better than getting an A; it meant earning your welcome into another generation's ranks. In competitive environments, it gave you an edge, suggesting you were deft enough to gain the respect of the erudite. Meanwhile, to sleep with a professor—a master, an intellectual—has often been a mark of distinction among my peers. The older man has a certain mystique.

It was with an awareness of this duality that I approached the dean's office one winter afternoon. From the windows overlooking the campus the trees looked so frigid they might crack. With my coat and sweaters in my arms, I filed papers with his secretary, ministered to bureaucratic business with the staff in his hallway, and glanced expectantly to see if he was in. He waved me inside, dismissing the student in front of his desk and motioning for me to sit. He looked especially bulky as he moved around the desk and took the chair next to mine; he leaned forward to rest his elbows on his knees in a gesture that accentuated his loose cheeks and darkened eyes.

"What will you do next year?" he asked.

I told him of a few job prospects, including one for which I'd unsuccessfully interviewed that week.

"Who interviewed you?" he asked, incredulous that I wasn't hired, leaning further forward on his knees. "A man or a woman?"

"A woman," I responded. I pushed my coat and sweaters forward on my legs as he edged closer in his seat. His pantleg touched my coat. I shifted my chair so I was almost in the corner.

"How do women respond to you?" he continued. In his imperious and condescending voice there was a familiar inflection, the same tone I heard when the professor asked if I was single, or when another advisor demanded to know if I lived in keeping with my political philosophies. It was paternal, too personal, authoritative in a disturbing way.

Faced with the choice between answering his question and telling him he was out of line, I merely giggled. I worried about alienating him. I wondered if I'd encouraged him.

He moved closer. "If it had been a man," he said somberly, "he would have hired you."

I giggled more, confronting what I feared might be a fact. His observation rang truer than I wanted to admit. The dean appreciated me not for my work, but for my femininity. My success thus far hinged on my beauty; my skills were secondary, my talent questionable, my only genius my charm.

Leaning even closer, he grazed my coat as he looked in my eyes. "Don't you agree?"

"No."

"You can get anything you want," he continued with a mixture of hostility and flirtation. "How long," he added, shoveling words like heaps of books on top of me, "have you been manipulating men?"

Elizabeth Kadetsky is a writer living in New York City, whose work has appeared in The Nation, San Jose Mercury News Sunday Magazine, New York Newsday, *and elsewhere.*

This is not just a woman's issue. This goes far beyond that...this is humanity's issue. I want a world where women do not have to carry the burden of others' sexual distress and power trips.

—Jennifer Werner

When I look back on my sexual harassment experiences, the commonality those men shared was the absolute sense of entitlement to dominance.

—Karen Carlisle

Every woman in the country has been given a chance to look at the sexual harassment she's had to deal with at work, at school, on the street, etc....Let's dump those dirty secrets in the public arena and, yes, on the floor of congress if that's what it takes to erode the foundations of the father's house.

—Diana Rivers

Men *know* what a bully is and bullies know they make people miserable.

—Carol Atkins

At 66, I still have to distance myself from my own body.

—Betty Summa

It was suggested that Professor Hill could not possibly remember what had happened ten years ago. I remember incidents that happened almost sixty years ago.

—Ninette de Vries

A CONTINUUM

Sheryl Karas

I think: going for an hour walk every day would be the perfect way to get some exercise and quiet time to be with myself. I live on a relatively busy street but in five minutes I can walk to a quieter neighborhood and in fifteen minutes I can be at the ocean. I decide to give it a try.

On the first day of my new routine the weather is cool and foggy. I'm dressed in jeans and a baggy sweater. I can tell this is going to work beautifully before I've even left my street. The stress of the day starts to drip off as soon as I walk out the door. By the time I return, I feel refreshed and calm.

The next day the fog has lifted. It's sunny and hot, maybe 90 degrees. I'm dressed in a skirt that falls to my knees but is full enough to swing slightly as I walk. My shirt is sleeveless as is appropriate for the weather. I feel good.

I haven't gone more than a couple of blocks when a car horn blares loudly right behind me. I jump and my heart pounds. I haven't been paying attention to the road. But when I turn to look, prepared to dodge flying metal, I don't see anything—only the car that has just passed me.

A few feet later another horn blows. This time I look up to see a man driving slowly beside me. He's looking in my direction and grinning. He gives the thumbs-up signal as he goes by. A compliment? A minute later another horn blares. This time the car is filled with young adult men. One of them hangs out the window. "Fuck me, mama!" Then he wiggles his tongue at me. His friend screams "Cunt!" The look on his face is anything but complimentary.

I'm honked and gestured at twice more before I get to a less traveled road. I'm flustered and angry. I catch myself wondering if I'm dressed too provocatively. I try to tell myself to lighten up—don't take it so seriously. But after an hour I still can't set aside my fury. I can't help but notice how many women my age are wearing baggy unattractive clothing despite the heat.

I used to live in Boston and ride the subway to work everyday. The return

144

trip was usually unbearably crowded. The cars were packed as tightly as possible, bodies crammed against bodies. Sometimes a man would get a hard-on. Annoying, but to be expected. But even the most understanding woman should not have to tolerate that hard-on being rubbed against her thigh or a stranger's fingers groping at her crotch. More than once I have loudly confronted a subway molester. "Whose fingers are these?" "EXCUSE ME! Is there something you wanted?" "Get your hands off me!"

The response was always the same. The man would take two steps back. (There was always room to take two steps back.) The look on his face would register disbelief, shock, sometimes outrage. He'd mutter something about me being crazy. Must have a dirty mind. Everything in his persona would say, "Don't believe this lunatic. How dare she accuse me of something like that?"

The last time I saw that expression it was on Clarence Thomas' face.

My first job out of college was as a paste-up artist in the advertising department at a large department store in Boston equivalent to Macy's. I worked with three other women in the paste-up department. We were all young, just starting out in the world of business. We each worked very hard to do a good job and make a good impression as we hoped these entry level jobs would lead to better things.

The assistant production manager was a man in his early thirties but he acted like a college sophomore with a bunch of his drinking buddies on their way to the beach. He'd gesture obscenely with a sick grin on his face whenever we passed his desk. "Ooohh, baby," "Hubba-hubba," wolf whistles, Mick Jagger tongue action—he knew *all* the moves.

We didn't know how to act. This man was the BOSS. Most of us tried to pretend we didn't notice him but Didi didn't have that option. She was cursed with a cute face and curvaceous figure so Bossman concentrated his attention on her. He'd drape his arm around her shoulders while he checked her work, and occasionally his fingers would "accidentally" brush her breast.

Sometimes he'd tell her that he saw a hot peep show at the Zone and thought of her. He always announced what X-rated movie was playing and, in a mocking tone of voice, would invite Didi to accompany him to it. Didi always cracked a mocking sort of joke back. Growing up mostly with brothers, she learned early on to roll with the punches.

Sometimes, though, she would try a different approach. Trying to strike a balance between standing up for herself and being nice she'd attempt to tell the Boss to stop. The response was always surprise, denial, ridicule. "What's the matter, Didi? On the rag? I thought you could take a joke!"

One day at lunch Didi confided how much she hated working late when the Boss was on duty. He never went further than talk and shoulder-hugging but she could never be sure that wouldn't change. Despite her easy-going appearance she was not at all at ease with this situation.

"Why don't you tell him off?" Helena asked. "I'd never let him talk that way to me."

"I NEED this job! I can't afford to be fired." We understood. We all worked too many hours to have much time for job-hunting, and we got paid too little to leave without having another job lined up.

The next time Bossman came into the production office and put his arm around Didi, she batted her eyes at him and told him how glad she was to see him in her most seductive voice. Then we all reached for our squirt guns and aimed for his crotch. His eyes widened and his mouth dropped open. Didi said, "What's the matter, darlin? I thought you could take a joke!"

Early one Sunday morning I left a friend's artist's loftspace in Fort Point Channel, Boston. At that time Fort Point was a warehouse district—completely deserted and a little frightening. I remember struggling with myself over whether to call a cab. A cab would be safer but it would cost $15—more than I budgeted for a week's groceries in those days. The subway was just a ten minute walk away, if I hurried, and cost fifty cents.

I decided to walk quickly and carry my kubotan. A kubotan is a black plastic martial arts stick with a pivoting piece of hardware at one end to which one attaches a full set of keys. The idea is to hold the stick and swing the keys at an attacker with a loud karate yell. In experienced hands it can be a vicious weapon. Unfortunately, I only had an afternoon workshop and never practiced after that. I'm five feet nothing and weighed 100 pounds on a fat day. Still, I thought it would be safe enough.

Halfway to the subway station I noticed a man following me. He looked suspicious. Of course, any man at that time and place would have looked suspicious to me. And besides, maybe he was walking to the subway station, too. I decided to test him.

I crossed the street. He crossed the street. I crossed again. He crossed again and sped up. He *was* following me and in just a few moments we'd be at an alley where he'd be upon me. I knew I couldn't outrun him.

I started to cross the street again and halfway across I spun around, planted my feet in a fighting stance, and swung my keys into my hand once with a decisive SWOP.

"Have YOU got a problem?" I yelled and angrily stared into his eyes.

"No!" he yelped. Then he turned and ran away.

I ran, too. When I got to the subway station my heart was beating wildly, and I was shaking all over and couldn't stop. "I could have been raped and murdered." But soon the terror was replaced with exhilaration. "I frightened away a rapist.

I intimidated HIM!" I was sure I would never be intimidated by a man again.

I have been intimidated since then. Nice girls don't use kubotan sticks in social situations, at work, or at home. But my perception of what I was capable of changed that morning. That victory laid the foundation for many more victories and told me that, with a little help in working through my fears, I didn't have to accept abuse as a condition of my womanhood anymore.

Most men would take offense at me lumping a complimentary car honk with attempted rape. What they don't understand is that rape, verbal and physical battering, and economic discrimination all create a climate where a "compliment" can be perceived as a threat. Because of sexism women receive ten times as much attention for their looks as they do for their brains or skill. Most of the time men and women don't notice this. It's hard to see oppression for what it is unless you have an opportunity to step outside of it. When looks are used as an excuse for rape or abuse ("she was dressed like a whore—she was asking for it"), compliments that focus on a woman as a sexual object become a form of intimidation, a way of maintaining domination.

I'm a heterosexual woman. I'm married. I don't hate men. But I *am* angry and I'm tired of seeing women treated in this way. Even "feminist" men unconsciously act out their sexist conditioning at times. It's time to put an end to it.

Sheryl Karas is an artist and nonfiction writer currently working as a graphic designer. She lives in Santa Cruz, California, not far from the beach.

Up for Grabs

Chris Karras

Thirteen years ago when I re-entered the workforce at age forty-four after a long absence, I didn't quite know what to expect from my new, male-dominated environment. I was soon to find out.

Within weeks of being on the job, a piece of paper with a dozen drawings of women's breasts in various shapes and sizes landed on my office desk. Each pair of breasts was named: Droopy, Floppy, Barely...

Given that I worked for a thirty-year-old employer, John, and his sixty-year-old relative and business associate, James (the one with the financial capital that had gotten John to where he was), I took a wild guess and identified James as the one with the breast fixation, especially since his wife had already confided in me that James was, well, impotent!

Handing the sheet with the artwork to him, I said: "I believe this belongs to you?"

I obviously had the right man because he wanted to know: "Are your boobs on that sheet?" I replied: "No, they're under my sweater."

John and James laughed uproariously and entirely missed the point. Unfortunately, they mistook me now for a good sport because I had neither blushed nor reacted indignantly. After that initiation into the heavily charged sexual atmosphere of my workplace, it was open season.

James kept a special file, an inch thick, filled with dirty jokes, most of them grossly demeaning to women, in his desk drawer and felt compelled to share the material with me, even though I had repeatedly refused to handle his papers and mentioned that my sense of humor lay elsewhere and that he had the wrong audience.

That did not stop the flow of papers from his desk to mine; nor did John, who had hired me, put an end to it. In the game of politics and business of this particular family, James seemed to be on top. The advice given to women to go to the top could be scratched from my list of options.

Next, I was treated by James to a baby photo of himself in the nude. The picture featured a giant, erect penis, super-imposed on little Jimmy's wee-wee. I wasn't surprised: I had figured James for a guy whose ego was permanently located in his crotch, and when he asked: "Waddayo think of that?" I said: "Not much!"

Once I asked the woman who had the job before me and who had retired at sixty-five if James was known to behave like this in the office when she was still there. She assured me he had and added she had all of his joke material at home, and the guys at the Legion, where she and her husband took to drinking on weekends, were crazy about it.

I struck out! On occasion I mentioned the annoying behavior of my boss's partner to my husband, but he kept advising me not to react and to ignore the Neanderthal. My husband had been around offices longer than I had and commented that, regrettably, the workplace was like that and probably always would be. He felt I was handling the situation well enough by not taking the jerk too seriously.

James now took to body-checking me full front whenever I had to squeeze through the narrow passage between our two desks. He pretended it was accidental; later, he accused me, jokingly, of purposely bumping into him every chance I got! John thought it was hilarious. The day James patted my backside when I had bent down to get a file from the bottom row of the cabinet, I said sweetly, but loudly enough for John to hear: "If you ever do that again, I'll have to take you to court!" When they laughed, their laughter had a nervous edge to it. I had finally pushed the right button and, for the first time, felt empowered.

For a while, the sexual innuendo, double-talk, and nonsense stopped—until it took a different twist; the men became interested in my menstrual cycle. As a result, I wrote this to a friend five years ago:

For the past eight years I have worked in a small office for a male employer and his silent partner, also a man. These two men are more than a generation apart, and one ought to have some hope for the younger man at least. But both of them view the menopausal female as a big joke and are anticipating my becoming one. I have been closely observed for telltale signs. The fact that the signs of my menopausal discomforts have eluded their scrutiny for three years now is more due to my efforts to hide my symptoms while at work than it is due to the men's lack of consistent inquiry which, lately, has become—"No hot flushes yet, Chrissy?"—"You still fertile?"—"You gonna get bitchy on us?"

One may or may not decide to be a good sport (and I consider all of this a nuisance, not to speak of the additional stress on the days when I'm not feeling well), but my quick response to these guys has been: "I'm surprised by your interest but, since you are so interested, I promise that you'll be the first to know."

This has been effective for the time being but it gives me an uneasy feeling about more serious consequences for other working women of menopausal age.

Men with such a mind-set tend to relate job performance to a woman's ability to menstruate. At menopause, she falls apart, can't do her job, becomes irrational (bitchy) and slow. Any legitimate reasons for assertiveness on the job (and there are many such reasons for women) are trivialized....I should really like to be able to feel more at ease in my working environment without inviting the obvious and traditionally known consequences.

Was the men's running commentary on the gender-specific issue of my menopause related to the more overt, sexual harassment of before? I think so, because James and John had merely shifted their focus from one area of personal intrusion to another, feeling entitled to consider everything about my sexuality up for grabs, including my fertility cycle and aging process. When John first hired me he joked that, in his client-centered office, he needed a sexy-looking chick and that I had gotten the job because I had shown up for the interview dressed in red and with long hair, then colored ash-blonde. Although far from young when I joined the company as its only employee, I was often called "Sexy" and "Chrissy" instead of "Chris," even in front of clients, and John had threatened, half-jokingly, to replace me with a younger woman when or if my looks went all to hell, something I once countered laughingly with: "No can-do, John! You know there's a law against that!" Both John and James seemed to have a healthy respect for the law; whenever I threw in "the law" or "the courts," I got a period of rest.

Because of my boss's sexist attitudes toward women in general and me in particular, I endured the usual indignities inherent in the workplace environment. For example: once, when in a particularly giddy mood and trying hard to impress another male, John introduced me to a salesman: "This here is our Chrissy! And she's housebroken too!" I expected him to follow up with a bark. The salesman, seeing I wasn't laughing, hesitated for a moment but then opted for solidarity with his fellow man, John, and giggled pathetically. I merely said: "My name is Chris Karras." It was just another one of those occasions when I showed my utter lack of humor.

Near the end of my menopause, five years ago, I decided to have my shoulder-length hair cut short and styled to prepare myself for going gray, naturally gray. With this personal decision, I provoked a major office crisis that lasted several months. John seemed personally offended by the change in my appearance and, I suspect, had there been a legal way to get rid of me then, he would have. His reaction told me that he had, after all, not been kidding about that sexy office chick. Hardly a day went by that he didn't try to chip away at my self-esteem with remarks about my aging and deterioration, all of which was more amusing to me than devastating. John played no important role in my private life, and his perception and opinion about my looks was no more than a nuisance factor on the job.

Menopause isn't called The Change of Life for nothing. I had definitely changed—even had written about it—and I was changing in ways that made my long blonde hair seem incongruent with my newly developed, inner state. I certainly felt no pressing obligation to explain the psychology behind my decision about as personal a matter as my hair to a man whose only concern should be how I do my job.

But John mentioned my gray hair once too often. That time I stared him down and said sharply: "I thought this is a business office and not a bordello!" To my deepest satisfaction, I saw him blush crimson.

Now that I'm fifty-seven years old, post-menopausal and aging, John no longer calls me "Sexy." Even "Chrissy" is slowly going out of style. James recently had a stroke and isn't the man he used to he. His file hasn't been updated for a long time, and he rarely visits the office now. The office is a drab and humorless place, because if the so-called humor on which men feed cannot be sexist and at the expense of women, it's not worth having from the male point of view. I get my laughs elsewhere, no problem.

In my final stretch, from fifty-seven to sixty-five, if the job lasts that long, my job will become what it should have been all along: a job, and not an arena for male power over a female employee, played out in countless offensive ways.

It always puzzles me when women are asked why we stay in a position when it is so unpleasant or even degrading. Should I leave a paying job and wander from place to place because men have a behavior problem around women in the workplace? Is it their problem or mine that men tend to go into a reflex action similar to Pavlov's dog at the ringing of the bell when a female enters their work domain?

In my case, there was no choice. My job supports me and my husband; I did not have the luxury of quitting, of looking elsewhere. And, if my husband is correct, elsewhere is no different, even if, as an aging woman, I could have landed another job. For many of us, those chances are almost non-existent.

As women, we aren't really supposed to share the male-dominated work-place, and sexual harassment is much more about power and male privilege than it is about sex. Men just have a hard time with the concept of the working woman. That, to me, is the subtext.

Chris Karras, 57, is employed in a client-centered office in Canada.

OPEN LETTER TO MY PERPETRATOR

Terry Kennedy

It was because of my father's regular and violent temper fits that I first began looking to you for guidance. I was 12 years old. I needed solutions to the family problems I was suffering. I needed spiritual and practical help. Instead, you helped yourself to my adolescence. You molested me in rectory bedrooms, in bathrooms, in cabins, in forests, in the back seats and front seats of your cars, in the church basement, and in the very sacristy itself.

You may have forgotten these places. I have not. They are vividly etched on my mind and branded on my heart. I do not always recall your physical acts beyond their repulsiveness. They made me want to throw up mostly, so I often disassociated myself from my body, separating myself from you while the abuse was occurring, not wanting to see it as real.

But I do remember the wallpaper, the furnishings, and the fibers of the rugs. I remember the dashboards, the car upholstery, and your Parliament cigarettes. I remember these details because I studied them keenly while you thrust your obese male body onto my girl being. Survivors of child abuse do this bodily separation-from-emotions act quite well. As children, we became hyper-vigilant, soaking up our surroundings like little sponges. We blocked our emotions because we could not cope with them. Some of us endured; others of us killed ourselves when we were 12, 13, 14. Those of us who did survive have paid a hefty price for our lives.

I believe that if even one victim goes to the grave without blowing the whistle on her perpetrator, it is one victim too many. So, I plan to avenge that child within me, the one that you damaged.

I am hurting, but I will not give up. I am hurting because you made me feel so ugly and so dirty. I am hurting because you intimidated me into believing I had no choice but to confess my "sins" to you. I felt shame and confusion, guilt and anxiety, grief and panic, headaches and stomachaches and nausea. I felt a hundred negative, swirling emotions sometimes, and I would employ every ounce of my energy to keep those emotions from coming out. These repressed emotions grew heavier and heavier, pressing on my heart like a marble tombstone as I prayed each night for God to deliver me from your hands, the tears pouring over me while I swallowed my sobs and my screams. I did not want to wake anyone up. But now the adult survivor is wide awake and it is she who shall avenge the child you damaged.

I am hurting because you convinced me I was evil because sometimes my body could not help but react to your probing. I would become aroused at times, and you told me this was my own lust, not yours. I never felt good in my heart about anything you did to me or anything you made me do to you. I never knew what an orgasm was until after my third child was born. I was like a puppet when you got hold of me. You pulled all the strings.

You took me to the movie "Lolita," starring James Mason and an actress that did not look anything like me or the girls in my school. After the movie you tried to tell me that it was normal for older men to have sex with girls. You suggested that I act more like this Hollywood Lolita. In the hotel room that you took me to that night, I got drunk on the brandy Alexanders you served me. I passed out before I could know what you were doing to me. My idealistic, small-town dream had turned into a shriveled up condom in the wastebasket of life. I was the next-best thing to dead.

Soon, I began to wonder whether you really did have the power to forgive other people's sins as you claimed you did. And when you told me some of the confessions of the other people in the church, I was shocked and scared. I did not know what to do. I hung my head in shame for the whole parish. I did not understand how a man who was doing what you were doing could absolve other people's sins. I was so mixed up. I felt sick kneeling in the confessional trying to explain myself to God—through you. It didn't make sense. It's a wonder I didn't kill myself or go mad.

I am hurting because you made me terrified of telling my own mother what was happening. I did not know how to stop your actions. I remember when you first drove me out of town to the lake. That was the first time that you sexually satisfied yourself using my body. I was certain that my mother would never listen to me if I tried to explain. My mother was so immersed in her own problems that she rarely had any time for me. And, you had become her hero. She cooked for you and my grandmother did your washing. What's more my father enjoyed your company in our home nearly every evening. His temper outbursts became less frequent. So I felt obligated to give in to you to keep the "peace." You knew this and taught me that what I did for you was a fair exchange.

My family looked to you for spiritual guidance. They were not learned people who read books in their spare time. They were working-class parishioners struggling to make ends meet. They took your words as dictums from on high.

At that point in time, you personified God in the flesh to them.

I do not know why you chose me as a victim. Perhaps all children are potential victims of people who commit sexual crimes. Or perhaps those of us who are selected appear to be more vulnerable. We may exhibit obvious signs of being easily entrapped. Like birds of prey who sweep down out of the sky, molesters grab up those of us who run a little slower, who move a bit more awkwardly, perhaps. I don't know for sure. I do know, though, that I was not your only victim.

It is possible that my parents suspected something was "not right." My therapists over the years have said that it is likely my family *did* suspect and that many people were aware of what was going on. After all, our town only had about 3,500 people in it. Maybe my family and the townspeople were truly blind, or maybe they were too afraid to see. Perhaps those that did step forward and report you to the bishop were simply ignored. You have always demonstrated a keen talent for worming your way out of accusations and parading before honest citizens as an exemplary person. But too many people know too many things about your dark side, "Father." And they will come forward.

People today know that it is illegal for young girls to go off to New York City for vacations with priests unaccompanied. No matter, you found a way to accomplish this and many other criminal acts—taking me over one state line after the other before I was 14 years old. I cannot help but wonder if the hard-working parishioners of our church were footing the bills for your extra-priestly "affairs."

I am hurting because I did not know how to get away from you. I was physically victimized by you for a period of six years. The psychological abuse continues. My mother, who I was only recently able to tell, refuses to believe that you could have hurt me. To keep her denial intact and to keep her world intact perhaps, she has chosen to disown me. Nearly a year has gone by and I have not heard my own mother's voice. Why? Because, for the moment, she believes what you told her—that you are innocent and that I've gone mad. I am far from mad, "Father," and even you must know that in eternity a moment isn't much. I know that my mother's love for me will eventually surface and then you will have her wrath to answer to—mark my words.

I am hurting because after years and years of therapy I am just beginning to understand healthy love between men and women, and I am only now learning about the joys of God-centered commitment to a marital partner. I am hurting because, in spite of the fact that my profession as a writer allows me freedom of expression, the little girl within me must continue to go to therapy in order to keep from repressing her nightmares, anxieties, and compulsions.

I am hurting because you paid for my abortion in 1962—a priest paying to destroy two people! I am hurting because I nearly bled to death on a dingy mattress. For three days I lay in a pool of my own blood with no one to take care of me, and you had the nerve to call me a whore.

Excommunicated from my church for getting a divorce from a man I loved, the father of my three children, a man with whom I could not function as a wife, my heart grew heavier still. While I was denied the sacraments, you were allowed live-in female companions half your age, late-model cars, and the most expensive booze. While I was supposed to hang my head in shame, you were allowed to go boldly on consecrating water and wine into the sacred body and blood of Christ. But the real Father, the Father of us all, was watching. He never excommunicated me from his omnipresence. He never stopped loving me.

I do not have the power to judge your immortal soul. God is the judge of that. But the man you are is still morally obligated to make recompense for what you robbed from me. There is, of course, no price that one can put on innocence. Originally, I had only wanted you removed from your priestly duties. But since my first letter to you and my two letters and one phone call to the bishop have produced no results, it appears that I have no further recourse than to file a civil suit against you. I have a grave responsibility to myself, to others you have hurt, and to those you are continuing to hurt. Therefore, I must see to it that not a single tear that any one of us has shed, because of what you did to us, is a tear wasted.

I will not rest until I achieve my goal—to have you stripped of your priestly duties and privileges and removed to a place where you cannot ever violate another trusting soul. I want any victim, past and present, who is still able to prosecute you, to come forward and do so.

I want financial recompense for all my therapy sessions over the years which document and record the suffering I underwent. I want financial reimbursement for the cervical cancer operation I had to have at age 26 because of the "early-age sex" you forced upon me. Gynecologists will testify that if a girl has repeated sex before she is old enough, the result is often cervical cancer.

I fully intend to continue my efforts to remove you from your position. With the support of loving family members, friends, and professional colleagues, I should be able to do this soon.

Terry Kennedy is a Hispanic poet and journalist who also teaches in the California Poets-in-the-Schools Program.

SUMMER LONG

Laura K. Koch

The memories ignite like fuel rods in a nuclear reactor. At eighteen I was so proud of my sophisticated first job. I was a small town girl who felt glamorous working at Howard Johnson's motel along the freeway which would sweep me off to college and the start of my real life in the fall.

When the manager gave me the two too-small turquoise and orange dresses, he said that since I was only there for the summer I need not buy new uniforms, these would do. Too tight, too short—I'm sure they did fine.

I bent my knees like a cocktail waitress to plug in the constant calls coming in on the old-fashioned switchboard. It was built in low and designed to be used sitting down but the chair had long since gone. I had been trained all my life to accept what was given to me and not to trouble anyone. "Thank you for calling Howard Johnson's. How can I help you?" from three to eleven with bended knee. By the end of the night sometimes I didn't care about modesty any more and I'd straighten my trembling legs and bend over the board giving the weary business traveler a glimpse of my underwear at no extra charge. I blushed when they told me I was sexy and pretended not to understand their comments and their jokes. Nothing in my past led me to expect to be given respect; I was grateful to be given the job. It seemed only right that I would wear what was provided and not sit unless I was told to.

The assistant manager looked like a cherub. Chubby, blond and curly, Ron waited and watched me each night as I struggled to balance my cash drawer. It grew into a nightly ritual; it always came out wrong. "I'll find your mistake if you give me a hug," Ron would offer at last. I'd hold my breath, tense myself and give the hug so I could go home. He was soft and squashy and a little bit damp. He'd hold me long and spank my bottom and laughingly warn me to try harder to get it right. I never spoke about this, never let myself know that it was more than just a part of my job. I accepted that I had been careless and could be excused from work only by paying the forfeit to the man in charge.

Russ, the bellhop, asked me out. Every day. Teasing me and pressing me for a date, his attention felt dirty and sticky and I dreaded seeing him. I fended him off with a joke, with a smile, with a reason, with a plea, with a threat, with a promise. I knew that if my jealous boyfriend found out there would be a terrible fight. I didn't understand why I was not flattered. I did not know how I was supposed to make him stop and still be nice. I did not have words for what was happening and there was no one to tell.

It must have started as a game with the other desk clerk but he hurt me. I do not remember his name. I was paid to be friendly and make people feel welcome and I did a very good job. In the back room this angry Asian permanent employee practiced karate in my face and I wasn't supposed to blink. His seniority required that I ask him each night if I could take my dinner break. Another ritual; I don't remember how it began. He'd twist my wrist until it burned and if I cried out I lost and he took my dinnertime and his own. If by my silence I won the game I gained his permission to eat.

I counted the days until September and clung to the fact that these people would be stuck here while I was bound for the glory of college. I held my tongue and kept the peace and was a silent partner in my own abuse. It felt familiar, I knew my role and I smiled and I smiled all summer long.

Laura K. Koch is a teacher and poet who lives in the Santa Cruz Mountains in California.

EVER-PRESENT

Debra Kuperberg

I attended Pomona College in Claremont, California, from 1973 to 1977. Pomona is a small, private, liberal arts college east of Los Angeles. During my junior year, I was taking a sociology class, and we were expected to do field work at one of the various institutions in the area. My professor assigned me to the California Youth Authority Youth Training School in nearby Chino.

I had no idea what kind of facility, or population, was in Chino. I had visions of a classroom full of Oliver Twists and Artful Dodgers saying "Good morning Ms. K.," as I entered the classroom. (My professor had told me it was a school for boys.) I found out very quickly that YTS was the only maximum-security prison for youth offenders in the state. The wards, as they were called, had been incarcerated for murder, rape, arson, child abuse, robbery—these were young men with two-year terms, and young men with life sentences. My Disney-esque fantasies floated out over the double barbed-wire-topped-walls.

The volunteer coordinator, Mr. David, was extremely helpful to me. He treated my questions and observations with honesty, candor, and humor. He introduced me to the teacher under whom I would be working as a tutor, and thus I became an unpaid teaching assistant in a remedial math class.

My first few days were interesting, to say the least. I was tested by the wards to see how I would handle myself, and was also tested by the line securing staff. The wards, it turned out, I could handle—they were roughly my age, and although I was relatively unsophisticated in terms of the "streets," I was able to hold my own by virtue of being on the right side of the bars, and being able to wield some power over them. The adult staff, on the other hand, was another story. These were men, not youths. And because of THAT dynamic, I was definitely at a disadvantage. Earlier that year, a woman staff member at another facility had been assaulted by a ward, and as a result, new security measures were instituted for all employees. Everyone was given a beeper to wear which would sound a silent alarm when activated from within a monitored building. As a volunteer, however, I was not assigned a permanent beeper; I had to go to the guard shack each time I entered the compound so that I could have a beeper checked out to me.

I learned to steel myself in preparation for the ever-present, never-ending onslaught of jokes, comments, and innuendoes that would commence the moment I entered the shack. I found it was easier to smile, pretend to be amused, and laughingly turn down their offers of dinners, dates, and sex, than to try to maintain my dignity by coldly rebuffing them. Also, I was scared. There was intimidation in their wolf-pack actions that frightened me. I did not know how to handle this type of "fooling around." One day, however, there was a man I had not seen before sitting behind the desk. When I asked for my beeper, he began to grin. "Beep her? Who wants to beep her? Or maybe you'd like a buzzer? Who wants to buzz her?" All of the men were laughing, and I remember feeling trapped. I tried to keep my voice from shaking as I repeated my request, but the man continued to play with a beeper that was on the desk in front of him, and did not answer me for a moment or two. Then he started to toss the beeper in the air and catch it. "Maybe I won't give you a beeper. Maybe you'll have to go into the classroom without it. And if you get into trouble, scream real loud, and if we hear you, maybe we'll come running out there to help you...maybe." I could feel tears of anger and rage welling up, and I turned to leave, not wanting to give him the satisfaction of seeing me cry. As I pushed by one of the guards, the man at the desk called my name. When I turned, he tossed me the beeper from the desk and smiled at me. I stormed out, slamming the door behind me, and started off towards my classroom. A moment later, a guard named Tony, who had always been pleasant with me, caught up to me. He handed me his beeper. "That one's defective," he said, as he took the other one out of my hand.

I was shaking by the time I got to Mr. David's office, and then the tears fell. That man was playing with my life! Mr. David agreed that there needed to be disciplinary action taken against the man, and as I did not know his name, we would talk to the head of line security regarding a grievance. Mr. David then escorted me through the halls of the administration building, and we went out onto the grounds. He gestured towards the tower. "That's the man we want, standing at the tower door." As I looked, my heart sank. The head of line security was the man who had been behind the desk in the guard shack. Needless to say, Mr. David told me that there was not much point in filing a grievance against him.

After that, I avoided the security staff as much as possible, and Mr. David obtained a beeper for me to keep. When another incident occurred a year later, after I had been officially hired as a teaching assistant, I complained to the superintendent (the warden) about the Gestapo-like tactics of his security personnel. All he did was smile and shake his head. "You know," he said, "if you were 45 years old and male, this sort of thing wouldn't happen to you. But being young and female—well, you've got to expect it. And there's not much that anyone can do about it."

I left the prison system shortly thereafter, feeling that I would not—could not—have much of a future there. I also carried with me an unflagging fear and hatred of that head of line security who had so casually toyed with my safety and well-being. Several years later, while I was at a large party in Claremont, he walked into the room, I felt myself become 21 again, and I froze with the paralysis of the impotent. At some point that evening, someone introduced him to me, and I searched his face, his eyes, for some sort of recognition, remorse—anything. But there was nothing there. What had been an incredibly demeaning, dehumanizing, and totally unforgettable experience for me had been nothing but words and wit to him. He had absolutely no memory of my face or my name, and doubtless none of that incident.

The term "sexual harassment" was not in my vocabulary in 1976. All I knew was that I could be kept down, and potentially hurt, by men who were in positions of authority in the prisons. In fact, I felt that I was in greater danger from them than from the young men who were incarcerated. As the superintendent stated, my age and sex allowed the male staff to treat me any way that they wanted, and no one, including himself, was going to stop it. The only way that I could end that type of treatment was to walk away from a potential career, and so I did.

Debra Kuperberg is 36 years old and has been a teacher for twelve years.

SYLVIA
by Nicole Hollander

THE FOUNDRY

Martha Lunney

Yes, I got it. An apprenticeship in a private foundry, one summer of grad school. I transferred as fast as I could into moldmaking. The department head there, Italian, had been making molds with his dad since he was a boy. They said he could cast anything.

Lunch hours I stayed inside working on my sculpture—that was the trade-off for getting paid shit at this foundry owned by a multi-millionaire who had made for himself a bronze sculpture of a laborer eating a Big Mac by a water fountain and reading a book titled *There's No Such Thing As a Free Lunch*. The technology of the place was state of the art. You could read every word on the page.

One lunch hour I sat, tool forgotten in my hand, stunned by a drama just beginning. The focal point: a larger than life-size woman in clay on a foot-high dolly. She was tall, you must grasp this. Hundreds of pounds of clay. A mold had already been pulled from her. Now the naked clay woman was useless.

The men lined up. It was hot and sunny outdoors; other lunch hours they'd be out playing volleyball, but this day they lined up with, I felt, a discomforting familiarity for their game. One by one they raced the few steps to this more than six-foot woman raised on her pedestal and kicked, trying for the most momentum they could—to kick away her genitals: first her vulva, then her breasts. Finally they tried for her face as well. Several times men almost fell over. They could have cracked their heads, as one might slipping on a banana peel with legs flying. It was not easy to get their booted feet so high. When many runs of this line of men could not produce the desired mutilation, and perhaps because lunch was nearly over, they armed themselves with tools—the various rifflers, knives and spatulas of the department—and took turns from their rowdy line and running start, hacking at the genitals of the woman in clay.

I needed to talk about this to someone and got little chance. The friend I told was revolted—but thought *I* was an accomplice for not quitting on the spot. It was a shock, but she actually severed our friendship that very day. This was a blow and, in the moment, all I could distill was a sense of a moral dilemma and a question of my courage to choose. Quitting could mean I would lose my apartment in this overpriced town. I would have to move.

I did quit the job. It cost me something and I don't pretend I thought I was "right" to quit; I only know I did, giving notice on my next work day. The director was upset. She drank beer with these "boys." In fact so had I after the sweat of pouring metal, the heat burning everything out of us. They were nice guys really, she said, and the department head—who I so much wanted to work with, who gave up his lunch hour and volleyball to perform in this grotesque ritual—why the department head had no idea...

She told me, after talking with him, that he wanted to apologize. She was upset because I was a student from a nearby Ivy League school, a school I was attending on a loan, scholarship, and multiple jobs, and their foundry wanted a link to our fine arts department. It wouldn't look good to have one of their first apprentices quit.

Before leaving I did run into the department head who did apologize profusely, insisting he had no idea I was a "radical militant feminist."

I caught a train back to Boston, homeless for the remainder of summer, sleeping in my studio with runaway mice and strange dreams at night in the part of the basement known as the pit.

Martha Lunney, 38, is a working-class Irish-American and a graduate student in clinical psychology in San Francisco.

Almost Always

Katharyn Howd Machan

Almost always it's the men
in cars—"Hey baby! Nice
ass!"—the ones who can escape

quickly, laughing, tires a squeal
of conquerors' delight as we
keep standing or walking, trying

not to listen or care or shout back
motherfucking bastards (those words
we've learned to make feel so good

in our throats even though they
are also about hating women),
the men who drink deer, hang

out in afternoon and evening
clusters, slapping shoulders, passing jokes,
comparing wheels and engines, riding

along thin streets like lords
looking for us, passing judgment, running
away in a snort of oily dust

before they have to speak with us,
before we are people, before we become
the women who will easily say no.

Katharyn Howd Machan teaches writing at Ithaca College and formerly directed the Feminist Women's Writing Workshops in New York.

2%

Geneviève Marault

So he says to me—
"But honey,
I'm so great to you
98% of the time.
Can't you overlook
that 2%
when I'm such an asshole?"
Well, let's see...

2% of the time
your one voice is raised against me,
calling me
a cold bitch—a selfish cunt.

2% of the time
your one hand
is cutting off the blood supply
to my lower arm,
your 5 fingers
leaving 5 marks
there for weeks to come.

2% of the time
you're one who could be called
a rapist,
if I didn't know you so well
and want you
some of the time.

2% of the time
you're one flaming,
drunken
lunatic,
your 2 hands at my throat,
and I'm so scared
I actually scream
before you set me free.

2% of the time
you're one faithless husband,
and I wonder
how many diseases
you're bringing home to me.

2% of the time
you haven't a clue
how much I'd like to hurt you.

So to answer your question—
no.

Geneviève Marault lives in Minneapolis.

It always puzzles me when women are asked why we stay in a position when it is so unpleasant or even degrading. Should I leave a paying job because men have a behavior problem around women in the workplace?

—Chris Karras

For a housewife the home *is* the workplace.

—Doreen Stock

Why didn't anyone notice that women were filing through the department like there was a revolving door?

—Jennifer Werner

There are men out there (they know who they are) who have not had to pay for their behavior.

—Barbara Unger

Then I seen his balls, and I bit his balls off.

—20-year-old victim of forced oral copulation

It is very difficult for a woman to go up against a man's denial.

—Catherine A. MacKinnon

How many more women would he intimidate in the years to come if I did nothing?

—Alice Irving

REPIECING

Joan McMillan

You must do the thing you think you cannot do.
—Eleanor Roosevelt

In 1981, I was a twenty-one-year-old senior English major at a Catholic university in Southern California. My ambition was to be a writer, first of all, and to teach at the university—a role I had formulated in no small measure by the example of my professors (mostly male) in the English department. By the first semester of my senior year, I had achieved some fine goals. I'd been on the Dean's list every semester since my sophomore year. Dr. Marley, the supervisor of the university tutoring center where I was employed, had appointed another woman and myself as student administrators of the tutoring program. I had friends and an on-campus apartment, which my roommate, Teresa, and I decorated on a K-Mart budget. In that highly Catholic and highly conservative atmosphere, I was also known as "the feminist" (as if I were the only one).

There were many secrets to my life back then. Only a few people knew that I had come to the university straight from eighteen years of a life replete with every form of abuse. My father had been a brutal alcoholic whose violence seared my life with deep emotional scars. My mother, an equally violent alcoholic, maintained a veneer of home life after she and my father got divorced. She also disappeared for days at a time, spent most of the household money in pursuing her various addictions, and fell into relationships with men as brutal as my father. One of these men molested me when I was fifteen; my mother discovered this, and blamed me for it so harshly that I was afraid to tell anyone else. I had never told her of childhood sexual abuse by male relatives, either, or of an incident in broad daylight on a suburban street where a young man grabbed my breast while he passed me on the sidewalk.

By the time I was seventeen, I vowed that I would leave home for good by going away to college. A counselor at my high school—one of the first positive male role models I ever had—helped me formulate my getaway, and I left for college with scholarships and a lot of hope. I still had to return to my mother's house for most of my college breaks, but the knowledge that I could escape back to my university kept life bearable for me. By 1981, I felt I could create a future for myself that had nothing to do with violence, shame, and cruelty. The problem remained that I stayed very naive about authority figures; I felt that nobody on earth could be as mentally ill as my parents, and I strove hard (however unconsciously) to idealize the people whom I admired.

One of these people was Dr. Winston, an English professor who seemed popular with many students. He was in his fifties, tall and thin, with long gray hair, a gray goatee, and small, almost colorless eyes. His face was full of wrinkles, and his nose was beet-purple and filled with broken veins. Most of the time, Dr. Winston wore Levi shirts, denims, and cowboy boots to class; he hung out between lectures in the hallways and quads, talking to students. He rarely taught in any conventional sense; his lectures were rambling and difficult to follow, but he was funny at times and didn't seem to care much if papers were late or classes were missed, as long as you explained why. Dr. Winston was married to a woman named Darlene, and his two children, Sam and Joy, were in grade school. Dr. Winston had been in the religious life for fifteen years, then left the monastery shortly before his marriage. He had been involved since my sophomore year with a "counseling group" which he said had changed his life after only three months. In fact, Dr. Winston liked to counsel people himself; if he noticed anyone looked a little depressed, tired, etc., he would swoop down on them for a counseling session in his office. I remember that he talked to many students, especially young women.

One of these women was a close friend of mine who told Dr. Winston that I had been sexually abused as a child. He immediately arranged for a counseling session with me, though I only knew him slightly at the time; I remember little from this session except for the fact that he stared at me intently. My friend remembers more about him: that he rubbed her arm during the counseling sessions or hugged her in a way that made her feel very uncomfortable. He seemed to especially befriend women who were on scholarships, from single-parent homes, or who were viewed by the campus community as being a bit different .

Dr. Winston remained a peripheral character in my life until my senior year, but I viewed him as someone who was genuinely interested in my welfare. I received As in his classes and praise for my coursework, and I remember only one "counseling session" in my Junior year, when I briefly split up with my boyfriend, Jay, a law student. Dr. Winston seemed happy for me when Jay and I reconciled after a couple of weeks. The first day of my senior year, I went to Dr. Winston's office to say hello, and found him hunched over his desk, smoking a

169

cigarette, his face very drawn. He only said, "You don't know what's happened to me, Joanie," and I retreated, not really able to formulate a reply. Soon after, I learned that Darlene had taken Sam and Joy to Northern California and moved back in with her mother, leaving Dr. Winston alone in his elegant, spacious home in an isolated area about a half-hour from campus.

My first semester that year was hectic; due to budget cuts, my financial aid was severely reduced for 1981 and I took on a part-time teacher's aide job at a local high school, in addition to my tutoring work and my full-time school schedule. Jay took a planned, temporary visit home to New York for a few weeks; the separation was deeply painful, and I tried to arrange a trip to New York to be with him over the Christmas break, which I could not take when yet another one of my grants was discontinued for the rest of the year. Instead, Jay returned to Southern California, took an apartment close to the university, and found a job as a law clerk while he studied for the Bar exam. I was often rushed, tired, and felt as if I had no time for myself; yet, as I stated earlier, I also felt that my life truly belonged to me and that my aspirations were within reach. At this time, Dr. Winston began to counsel me frequently in his office; aware of my financial situation, he gave me a job correcting student papers for him at a dollar per paper. He praised my work in this area, and I asked him for a letter of recommendation to graduate school, which he said he would write.

Dr. Winston's behavior towards me began to change somewhat as the fall semester drew to a close. Once, he wolf-whistled at me in the hallway, and I ignored him. Several times at student-faculty parties on campus, he showed up very drunk, and proceeded to leer at me and at other students, rubbing backs and hugging, then making loud, lewd comments about our physical attributes. The women students, in general, ignored this behavior or just accepted it; nearly everyone knew that the majority of our male professors made off-color remarks or jokes around us, whistled at us, talked about the breast size of the women students, pinched, and leered. In 1981, this was the atmosphere in which we were educated. My feeling towards Dr. Winston was that he was drunk a lot, missed his family, and that he would get back to his old, benign self again soon. I still trusted this man enough to housesit for him while he visited his family in Northern California over the six-week winter break; I felt like Jane Eyre at Thornfield Hall when I first saw Dr. Winston's house with its huge fireplace and its study full of books. Jay lived with me there for a few weeks before finding his own apartment, and we spent a simple, contented time together preparing meals, studying, and watching T.V.

One afternoon, when Jay was out, I was sitting in Dr. Winston's living room, looking at a few photo albums which had been left on the coffee table. Most were garden-variety pictures of weddings, trips with his family, baby pictures, backyard barbecues, etc., and so I was utterly shocked to find a huge change in

170

one of the smaller albums. The first few pages were of the same type of family photographs; the last few were devoted to pictures of nude children and adults, including one of Dr. Winston and his son as a toddler, seated on a bench in a child's room. Both were naked, and Dr. Winston, unsmiling, had his legs wide open and his hand positioned near his genitals. A glass of wine, blood-red, stood on the bench between his son and himself. I slammed the album closed and told myself that the pictures were just jokes, and that I had been prying into someone else's business. I shrugged off the disturbed feelings I had as "just my own prudishness"—but it was hard to entirely forget that incident.

Dr. Winston returned to campus that semester in a state of deep depression; most people, faculty and students alike, began to feel that he and his wife would soon divorce. I tried to keep my focus on my relationship with Jay, my studies, and my difficult struggle to make ends meet. Increasingly, Dr. Winston began to frequent the tutoring center where I worked in the evenings and on Friday afternoons. Few students came in and I could use the time for study. Dr. Winston began to tell me his many personal problems, including his violent upbringing in foster homes and the breakup of his marriage. This behavior became very intrusive and extremely difficult for me to deal with; once, I slammed down my pen on the desk and told Dr. Winston to leave me alone. The behavior continued, and finally, a day or so later, I went to my supervisor, Dr. Marley, and told him that Dr. Winston was "bothering" me. Dr. Marley spoke to him, and the behavior stopped except for a particularly humiliating incident when Dr. Winston came into the tutoring center one Friday before midterms, when the place was filled with students. I was tutoring someone, but Dr. Winston ignored that fact. Standing next to me, he said in a VERY loud voice, "Dr. Marley's noticed that you've been late to his class recently. I told him that it was no wonder, since you're always sleeping at your boyfriend's apartment." Everyone in the tutoring center laughed except for me; I felt mortified, but kept trying to work as if nothing at all had been said.

I was unwilling to burden Jay with most of this; by the end of February, he was preparing to take the Bar exam and was also working two part-time jobs, as his student loans were about to come due. Our times together, in retrospect, seemed like a small oasis for me; when I was with him, I did not have to think about what was happening at the university. We began to make plans for our life after my graduation, including the possibility of moving together to New York if he couldn't pass the Bar exam. Jay, who knew a bit about my troubles with Dr. Winston, told me diplomatically that Dr. Winston was obviously going through a rough time. I wanted to believe that, too, so I continued to work for Dr. Winston and accept any privileges which came my way, hoping that the troubling behavior was just temporary.

In early March, I was talking up the idea that I was going to become a college professor to everyone, including Dr. Winston. He mentioned that his friends had thrown a huge party for him when he received his doctorate, complete with presents. I asked him what kind of presents he had received, and he said that his friends had given him a book which couldn't be shown to everyone, a book of photographs showing a little girl and a man "together." I stared at him for a minute until it dawned on me what he was talking about. All I could manage to say was, "Isn't that stuff illegal?" and he retorted, "Not if the child consents to it!" I shook my head, made some feeble excuse to get going, and walked away feeling very shaken and disturbed.

In retrospect, these seem like not-very-frequent incidents, but they are significant in light of what happened to me near the end of March, 1981, when Dr. Winston's wife filed for divorce. Just before that, Dr. Winston wrote me a letter of recommendation to graduate school, one of three I relied on for eventual admission. When he told everyone that Darlene had asked him for a divorce, people tried to treat him rather kindly, including me. One afternoon—a Friday— Dr. Winston asked me if I could come to his house that evening and drop off the papers I had corrected, and also asked if I would just check up on him, confessing to me that he felt suicidal and needed help to "get through his problems." I decided to do so because I genuinely felt bad for him and because I felt I owed it to him somehow, in light of all that he seemed to have done for me. That night, this man—a friend, a mentor, someone who knew I had been sexually abused all of my life, someone whose troubling behavior I tried to ignore in a childish way, believing he would get back to his "old self" soon—raped me.

To say I went crazy after the rape is to not even approach the degree of disturbance afterwards. I fell into a cocoon of numb, silent shock; I blamed myself completely, feeling I had committed some terrible sin. For all the jokes on campus about my feminism, I did not know anything about acquaintance rape; I did not know there was a term for what had happened to me; certainly, there was nowhere on campus I knew to get help. About a week after the rape, my genitals broke out in white, painful blisters. I did not go to a doctor; I did not want to deal with it at all. Dr. Winston had assured me that students got thrown out of school for "fucking teachers," and I did not want to get thrown out of school just weeks before graduation. I knew that it would be my word against his, and I thought I knew whose words were stronger.

So, I kept going to class (I had no classes with Dr. Winston). I tried to work at my tutoring job and my teacher's aide job; obviously, I corrected no more papers for Dr. Winston. He went around campus as if nothing had happened; in my shock, I wondered if perhaps it had really happened at all. Yet it was as if someone had broken into my life and stolen it. A day or two after the rape, I ended my relationship with Jay, giving no real reason except that I could no longer be with him. Then I began to binge-drink on the grand scale of my parents, something I had never done before. I remember sitting in my supervisor's office in tears day after day, wanting to tell him about Dr. Winston but fearing the consequences. Dr. Marley was gentle and sympathetic, though he did not know what was going on, and gave me tasks other than tutoring. Finally, Dr. Marley arranged counseling sessions for me with the one harried priest who served the therapeutic needs of the entire university population. Father Joe rarely spoke during the counseling sessions, even when I alluded to the abuse, and I stopped making appointments to see him. Once or twice, I also tried to speak to another priest who was sometimes available for counseling during the evenings at the student center near my campus apartment. To his credit, he told me that I was not to blame for what had happened and that I had been "horribly duped" by Dr. Winston. Yet, in another session, when he asked me what I planned to do about it all, I stated that I wanted to just graduate and go on with my life. He agreed that it was best to "put the shame of it behind me." In addition, he said that if I had any kind of a "sexual history," it would count against me in "any type of action." "Do you have such a history, Joanie," he asked me kindly. I shook my head, and left the office. I never spoke to him again.

In May, I attempted suicide in my apartment when my roommate was gone for a few days. I took all the aspirins in the medicine cabinet, then lay down on my bed, covered myself with a thick blanket, and fell asleep, to dream that I was in a walled, concrete courtyard filled with folding chairs. One end of the courtyard had a partially open door; a siren was blaring out of nowhere and I was running towards the door, which was closing slowly. I never reached that door; instead, I woke and vomited. My ears were ringing and I felt too sick to move or to clean myself. Finally, sometime in the morning I felt I could get up, take a slow shower and pull the dirty linens off the bed. My roommate came home two days later to a clean apartment and my silence; I would sit mute for hours curled up on the couch or in a chair.

I graduated from my university at the end of May, barely finishing my classes. I did not receive my diploma at the ceremonies because I owed the university about a hundred dollars. I had left my job as a teacher's aide shortly before the suicide attempt, as my emotional state made me increasingly unable to teach and so I had no money to pay my tuition balance. Instead, I received a blank folder at graduation. While the graduating class was lined up, Dr. Winston walked by me and dove his hand down the back of my graduation gown. I yelled at him, but he had already moved on into the crowd.

A day later I left the university, my car loaded with my possessions, and returned to my mother's house. The sense of defeat I felt was total, and I was certain I had never really escaped my legacy of abuse at all. Yet, a few weeks later, a bright opportunity opened in my life: I travelled to Santa Cruz, California. Charmed by the redwoods, the ocean, the bookstores, and the man who would later become my husband, I decided to stay.

Eventually, I married and began a family, but my life after graduation slowly became an edging towards complete emotional breakdown. I became a published writer and a teacher in a nationally recognized arts-in-education program, but never tried to attend graduate school. I forbade myself to think of anything that happened to me before life in Santa Cruz. The amount of energy it took to try and put the rape out of my mind was staggering. Pictures of me from the years 1981 to around 1987 show a too-thin woman, pale with dark circles under my eyes. I remember the draining depressions of those years, the terror of being alone, the jumpiness, the inexplicable crying and hyper-vigilance, the night wakings when I thought I was hearing someone break into the house. I overscheduled my life for years with work, motherhood and many activities; it was as if I would not allow myself one minute of leisure. I went into therapy a few times, but left each counselor before any truly deep subjects were broached.

In 1987, my husband, two children and I moved for a year to a lovely but remote home in the Santa Cruz mountains. I was pregnant with my daughter Emily, who would be born exactly a year after the stillbirth of my son, James. It would be facile for me to say that his death tore the lid off my suppressed emotions and memories surrounding my rape, but I believe strongly that the deep mourning I allowed myself when my son died was a catalyst for older, buried griefs. In the last month of my pregnancy with Emily, nightmares began which centered around my university and the people I had known there. The first one involved Jay; one night, I dreamed that he was searching for me, that his spirit had entered my house after traveling a long way to find me; finally, in my dream, I could see him enter my bedroom and stand next to me. I woke with a shock, and ran upstairs. I sat in the living room until morning, totally unable to make sense of the emotions which the dream had brought up. After Emily was born, I began to slowly sink into truly unyielding depression; by January, when I was teaching again, I found I had become deeply dysfunctional and had to summon every internal resource I had in order to work effectively. Finally, I sought counseling, determining to myself that I would stick with it no matter how painful it got.

My husband and I bought our first home—again in the Santa Cruz Mountains—in October of 1988. In November, I told my therapist about the rape I survived at my university, after weeks of terribly disturbing nightmares, always with the central theme of losing something at my university—something I could not name—and searching for, but never finding, that nameless thing. I told my therapist about the rape as swiftly as I could, with a complete sense of numbness. Her reaction was of clear anger on my behalf—not blame, not judgments concerning the choices I had made at 21 to try and survive the rape. I misinterpreted numbness for perhaps having resolved it somehow and felt I could just tell her once and be done; I was not ready to speak of it again for months, though she tried to gently mention the subject often. By early summer of 1989, when I felt ready to speak, my therapy began to focus mostly on the rape.

I began to feel that my healing process was leading me to confront Dr. Winston via letter, using my post office box as a return address rather than my street address. I began to call different women's organizations in the area, trying to garner information on the confrontation process. Finally, I drafted a letter to Dr. Winston which I mailed to his department at the university (a few months later I sent a copy to his home address). I do not think I can ever express both the terror and the relief I felt when I put that letter in the mailbox—I wanted to grab it back out, fearing his rage after all these years, but I walked away and let it be sent.

And nothing happened. No one came after me, no one broke into my house, no one sued me. What began around the time I sent the second letter were sporadic hang-up calls early in the morning and late at night; I logged the times and the dates on my calendar and they ended after a few months. Around the time I sent the letter, it seemed as if a floodtide opened in me and I began to cry about the rape for the first time in eight years—in fact, it seems that I cried almost all the time that summer. When I wasn't crying, I was reading, mostly books on sexual assault, then turned to *The Courage to Heal* (by Ellen Bass and Laura Davis) and *The Courage to Heal Workbook* (by Laura Davis).

In addition to the letter of confrontation, I made contact after eight years with three people whom I felt I wanted to tell about my rape: Dr. Marley, who had seen my depression, shock, and crying jags first-hand; my former roommate, Teresa; and—most difficult of all—Jay. I had not been in touch with Jay since shortly after graduation, though I heard through the grapevine that he was living on the East Coast. A small amount of research showed that his parents were still living at the same address back East. I sent Jay a letter there, explaining to him what had happened to me and apologizing for the hurt I had caused him those many years ago. I made it clear that he did not have to reply to the letter, but enclosed my address and phone number in case he ever wanted to discuss what I had told him. A few weeks later, Jay called me from New York and we had the first of a few long, constructive talks which helped to heal many deep emotional wounds on both sides.

In addition, I made contact with Dr. Marley, who clearly remembered my emotional state that semester, and Teresa; both gave me a tremendous amount of feedback regarding their memories of me at the time and also gave me their support when I told them I had been raped and was considering telling the university about it. I realized that Dr. Winston had continuous access to young women and that the possibility that he had raped again was very high. The time period between August of 1989 and July of 1990 was thus taken up with my preparation for disclosure to the university (with a 7.1 earthquake in October and the Christmas birth of my last child thrown in for good measure).

The upsurge in emotions which I had experienced at the beginning of the confrontation process seemed to increase over time; I truly clung to my therapy sessions and kept a long journal. Nearly every night, just before I went to sleep, I thought I could hear someone breaking into the house and had to get up to make sure both entry doors were deadbolted. My nightmares reached an all-time high in frequency and I felt as if all my energy were being funnelled into just riding the emotional waves. Despite this, I began to prepare seriously for disclosure of Dr. Winston's abuse, trying to weigh every possible negative and positive outcome in therapy.

Finally, I woke up one morning and simply called the dean's office of my university. I asked the secretary if she knew who was in charge of receiving complaints of sexual harassment and other abuse. She said she needed to talk to the dean for a moment; when she got back to me she said, "The dean would really like to know right now who the faculty member is." I felt I would completely fall apart if I disclosed his name on the phone and I told her so. I promised her that I would send a letter to the dean. The letter detailed the circumstances surrounding the rape and the destruction it had caused in my life. I told the dean of my shock and severe depression, my drinking binges and the suicide attempt, and that I lost my job as a teacher's aide because I was dysfunctional after the rape. I told him of the blank folder at graduation and the fact that my student loans and tuition had been paid off for years; still, I had never asked the university for my diploma. Ten days later I received a letter from the dean, stating that he had begun a formal inquiry regarding Dr. Winston, that he would take appropriate action upon its completion and that he had arranged for my diploma to be sent to me.

One month later, in August, 1990, I called the dean to find out the status of the inquiry, which he said was proceeding and hopefully would be concluded no later than October. The dean—who at all times was highly gracious and very sensitive to the issue of sexual harassment, told me that he could not share the specifics of any personnel actions which might be taken against Dr. Winston. I was REALLY shocked; he then said he would ask the president of the university if there could be a special exception made in my case. After August, what I call "the quagmire of waiting" began in earnest. I felt at all times under a constant and stultifying pressure; I feared that Dr. Winston would find a way to my home and harm me; I watched my children in the front yard with a stronger vigilance. Then, one night, I dreamed that Dr. Winston had decided to send me a huge package containing objects I'd forgotten from my childhood. For some reason, that dream helped to keep my hopes up.

From September onwards, the sporadic phone calls which I mentioned before happened again, with the disturbing twist that whoever was on the other phone did not hang up for a while. Twice I listened long enough to hear faint office noises far in the background; once, I heard a chair on casters roll across the floor as the caller hung up. Again I logged as many of the dates and times of these calls as I could.

The inquiry which was supposed to end in October took much longer to complete; in December the dean finally called me, apologizing profusely for the delay and explaining that he realized how horrible the waiting period had been for me. He then informed me that "Dr. Winston had a long process of coming to terms with what he did" to me and had refused to answer to any of my allegations or even meet with the dean, reacted with rage and hostility when they did attempt a meeting, and, according to the dean, "did himself further harm in the eyes of this university." Dr. Winston had finally—perhaps the day before—sent a letter to the Dean in which he admitted to my allegations, said he had not answered to them for fear of losing his job and the regard of his colleagues, and said that he now had remorse and regret over his actions towards me. The dean paraphrased that part of the letter, saying that much of it was terribly confusing and meandering. He then told me that he was preparing to make his recommendation for personnel action, and gave me the scope of what those actions might include, from a letter of censure in Dr. Winston's file to termination, but that he could not tell me the specific action he would recommend, nor the final action which the inquiry board would take. He added, "I would like them to take steps which will insure that something like this never happens again to a student."

During this phone conversation, I also told the dean of the stay-on-the-phone calls, and he said he had a way to discreetly check past long-distance calls to find out if Dr. Winston was calling me from the university. (I never again received that type of phone call after I told the dean.) He then thanked me on behalf of the board of inquiry, which had included the university president, provost, and vice president, saying that they deeply appreciated my candor and willingness to come forward after so many years, and that they all wished me the very best in life.

For a time afterwards, I felt cloaked by a small triumphant glow, as if I had fought a very long battle and now the siege had reached a turning point. In April of 1991, a letter arrived from the university alumni office, informing me that a ten-year reunion was coming up for my class in November. At first, I felt I didn't want to go, particularly after I called Dr. Winston's department and found that he was still teaching at the university. ("But if you want to make an appointment to see him," said the department secretary, "you'll have to do that through me." "Why so?" I asked. "I can't really tell you," she said. I told her I didn't want an appointment, just information on who was teaching and who wasn't.)

I sent another letter to the dean, informing him of my desire to attend my reunion without crossing paths with Dr. Winston, that I had found out he was still teaching, and that I had truly hoped for a more just conclusion to the inquiry process. I also asked for a copy of the university's sexual harassment policy and expressed my fears for other women as long as Dr. Winston remained on campus. The dean replied with a letter stating that he had "taken actions which guarantee" that Dr. Winston would not be at the reunion, expressed good wishes for my return to campus and stated regretfully that personnel actions associated with implementing the university's policy on sexual harassment could not be shared except with a supervisor. He also enclosed a copy of the university's updated and comprehensive policy on sexual harassment, which included a clause prohibiting "...sexual harassment of...students, employees, and those who seek to join the university community in any capacity." I wrote to thank the dean for his efforts on my behalf and began to make arrangements to attend my reunion; I had not been on campus for the ten years following graduation.

I flew to Southern California with my husband on the day after Halloween. It was emotional beyond all words for me to return to campus; a few old friends attended the reunion party, but there was another highlight for me. All day, I was able to walk around the campus without fear, to look at students who were in the same age group as I once was and to know fully that I was not at fault for what had happened to me. I felt now that I took back that part of my life and that the healing I gained from the process of disclosing my rape was mine forever. In a letter to the dean after the reunion, I told him of my renewed sense of pride as an alumna of the university—something I had never once dreamed of having.

The fact remains that Dr. Winston to this day remains in his teaching capacity at my university. The dean had assured me at the end of the inquiry that, should Dr. Winston remain on the faculty, he would be under constant surveillance, and yet I wondered how long it would be before such surveillance was relaxed around him. In preparing to attend my reunion, I went to a rape survivor's support group and discussed, among other subjects, the minimal things I had been able to glean about the personnel action against Dr. Winston. The group facilitator told me that he might have been offered some options such as therapy as an alternative to termination, perhaps because Dr. Winston is close to retirement age; she added that perhaps the choice to keep him on such a small campus, where the dean and his supervisors knew what he had done, rather than let him go somewhere else where his background was unknown, was possibly not an unwise decision.

During my process of disclosure, I was not cross-examined by the board of inquiry. Dr. Winston did not ride the posse into town to get me; he did not take me to court. I still battle my emotional demons, but they've diminished considerably, and my life feels safer, richer and more full of possibilities than ever before. However, the news throughout that latter part of 1991 has reminded me yet again that the labor to protect women's rights is going to be a very long one indeed. Somehow, no matter how much I felt that the pain would never end, it finally became manageable. The only way out was to hold my ground and keep going; when I truly did what I thought I could not do, I received a healed sense of self, pieced from many fragments.

This knowledge has helped me to endure.

Joan McMillan *is an Italian-American mother of four children who teaches poetry in the Santa Cruz County schools.*

Viv Quillin

WHAT DINAH THOUGHT

Deena Metzger

This is the dream. Even as I was dreaming, I knew it was disappearing. I didn't have the guts to hold on to it. It faded, not as the Cheshire cat faded away but as colors on celluloid are bleached out by direct sunlight though they also depend upon projected light to be visible. The tormenter is clever: He can do his work and disappear before we awaken to the deed.

I am working during the summer for a temporary agency, the kind that sends young girls out to business firms to file, type, answer the phone. The girls work for a day or a week and then they're sent somewhere else, wherever this kind of laborer—simple, willing, accommodating, eager—is needed. I am glad to be working, have lied, as is traditional, about my age, grateful for the money. I have a Social Security number for the first time, a pair of stockings in case I cannot stop the run in the ones I'm wearing with the colorless nail polish I also learn to carry. In short, I have outfitted myself carefully to resemble the "older" women I admire in the subway, those who seem so self-possessed when they fold their left hands over the right in their laps, displaying the single-stone diamond engagement rings. In the dream I am quite young, too young to have working papers, am prettier than I am now and also more ungainly, awkward, not quite certain how a lady sits in a chair, how to smile; I am accommodating to everyone and everything. The man in the frock coat stands over me, to check on my typing, he says. I do make mistakes, out of distraction—I cannot concentrate on this work for forty working hours—but also out of nervousness and lack of practice. But then I stay after hours without charging the company, to correct my mistakes. I am conscientious. I am working for a charitable organization, they raise money for a yeshiva in Mea Shearim and my job is to type personal letters asking for donations. I am careful not to cross my legs, to wear long skirts, and to cover my elbows. My clothes are modest, even prim. When he stands over me, he makes me uncomfortable and my hands tremble a little so that my fingers miss the keys and I have to erase the mistakes and begin again and my fingers get dirty as I

180

correct the mistakes on the carbon copies and then the paper smudges or I forget to blow away the eraser filings and the second copy or third isn't quite legible. The typewriter is cumbersome and I must press the keys hard. My polished nails, transparent so as not to offend the rabbi, click on the keys. I have listened to this sound in other offices and understand that the long nails are required—they assure the employer through the constant tick—but, also, there is something about the impossibility of typing this way, the conflict between the limitation and the task.

As soon as he opens the door from his inner office and enters the room where I am working, I smell the sweat which is saturating his clothes. Then I feel his breath on my neck, a little moist and heavy with tea and sandwiches. Mayonnaise, soggy lettuce, kosher breast of chicken. Swee-touch-nee tea, two cubes of sugar, one rectangular, one square, two carrot sticks, a piece of honey cake. His breath is just a little fetid, just a little unwashed, as are his clothes; it's summer, noon and hot, the windows are closed against the noise, and there is no air circulating in the room. He twirls the buttons of his robe. It's a nervous habit so some are popped and the threads stand up alarmed, a bit of white undershirt peeking through the empty hole of his vest, the white of an eye. He bends closer; he says he can't see. "Shall I take it out of the typewriter for you, Rabbi?"

"No, don't bother. I don't want you to lose your place, then it won't line up correctly and you'll have to start again."

He is quite certain there is a spelling error or something he'd like to alter, or he is not sure that my phrasing is correct in the section he asked that I add. That sentence is awkward. Am I certain I didn't alter the text he gave me? He leans over my shoulder, pointing at the error. I can't see it. My vision blurs. I think it is his sweat dripping into my eyes. He drops the pencil just as I lean forward to examine the letter better, but his hand is already in my lap, looking for the pencil. He can't find it. It has dropped to the floor but he pulls me back not wanting to disturb me, to soothe me. It doesn't matter. It's only a spelling error, it won't ruin the letter, he isn't worried because he knows I'll find it later and correct it, it doesn't matter about the carbons, they don't need the spelling corrected, and it doesn't matter that he's lost the pencil, but maybe it is still in my lap not on the floor, he didn't hear it drop, his hand is on my shoulder pressing me back into the typing chair so he can look in my lap, among the folds of cloth, my skirt is very pretty, he is glad I am earning a lot of money, he thinks the minimum wage is very generous to young people and I can buy myself nice work clothes but did I think over his proposal that I donate some of my salary to the yeshiva because those boys are doing God's work for all of us, he always liked pleats, but they hide so many things. Did the pencil fall down my blouse, it was his favorite pencil, the blouse is very loose, did I know, sometimes he thinks women do not dress carefully enough, it's one of the banes of the orthodox tradition to try to instruct girls so that they will not violate God's laws. So often the mothers are lax or have forgotten all the injunctions, and what is a man to do, it is his duty, but still it is awkward, the pencil was a mechanical pencil, that is why he's making such a fuss though he's sure it isn't lost and maybe he left it on his desk, after all, but I did hear it drop on my skirt, didn't I, it has one of those retractable points that is protected within the metal casing when it is not in use, and it slides in and out very easily, but he thinks he ought to show me how to tie my blouse better, he'll look for the pen later when I get up, the blouse needs to be tighter or higher, though he agrees the style is very pretty, his mother always wore peasant blouses and now it is the fashion, imagine that. He is glad it has drawstrings, not elastic, so that they can be opened and tied tighter, no not up to the neck, but still a little tighter, there, let's see, he pats the blouse to see how it looks and lets the strings go so that it falls open and he sees that I'm upset, silly, he wants to calm me, please, it's only a spelling mistake and your blouse was not that open, not as open as it is now, but he'll fix it, no, don't touch it, he'll do it, he has to measure it, to see that it is exactly perfect, and he doesn't have a mirror for me to look in, better for girls to be without mirrors, but he can see exactly everything that he is doing, please don't cry, it's only a spelling mistake and a blouse, here, he'll soothe me, he'll pet me a little like he does his daughters to soothe me, calm me, he pushes my head back against his fat belly, relax, close your eyes, get calm or you won't be able to type and I'll just rub these little breasts, first one and then the other, you'll be surprised how very soothing this will be, just lean back in the chair, let it hold you as it is designed to do, it will catch me in the small of the back and if I raise my legs, I'll see, it will bend backwards, and he'll support me, it will be as if I'm taking a little nap and forgetting everything, I can just lie down and let him rub my little breasts, as long as I want, until I'm calm and not crying, just breathing deeply with my eyes closed, or until the nipples stand up very hard and tall and then get very soft again, it will take a little while but not too long, he's breathing hard, and rocking the chair back and forth against his thighs, and then, then, just another moment, oh what sweet breasts, we must keep them hidden but he won't tell anyone how sweet they are, as his hands rub my breasts and nipples inside my blouse and brassiere, it's too tight, it must be uncomfortable in this heat, here he'll take my brassiere off, pull my arms out of the sleeves of my blouse, no the blouse doesn't have to come off altogether, just a minute, he knows I'm so hot, I'll faint, he doesn't want me to faint, and he's unable to open the window or unlock the door into the corridor to let in air, there, the brassiere is off and the blouse is down to my waist but he pulls it up and puts my hands back into the sleeves so he can put his hands back into the blouse, the brassiere is in the wastepaper basket, he'll throw it away somewhere else later, no, he doesn't think I ought to wear it, an undershirt perhaps or a little white camisole, it's not good for the lungs, the body needs to be free, and he thinks it is OK because my little nipples don't show through the cloth because I'm just a little girl so it doesn't matter, and it is also proper for a little girl like I am always to wear white, no, don't cry, just rest and lean back against me and I'll rock you, while I put my hands in your lap, I'm sure the pencil is here, there, spread your feet just a little and we'll see, there, that's the girl, and rest against me and soon everything will be soft and then you'll be easy.

Deena Metzger *is 55, Jewish, a writer and counselor.*

Viv Quillin

AND IF I SPEAK...WHAT THEN?

Jane L. Mickelson

There is a story told of scientific research, perhaps apocryphal but no less applicable to the subject of sexual harassment for that. It seems a scientist places a frog in a beaker of boiling water. The frog immediately scrambles to escape. The second time, the scientist places the frog in a beaker of cold water which is then gradually heated to the boiling point. The frog boils to death, at no time making any attempt to escape its fate. It never senses that time at which the water in which it sits becomes deadly. The line differentiating the acceptable from the unacceptable is so gradually drawn that it is nearly invisible.

I hear people say, in cases of sexual harassment, "Why didn't she tell? Why didn't she report it, if it was upsetting to her?" I will tell you why.

I am twelve years old. It is 1957. I am in the seventh grade. My breasts are beginning to develop and they are sore and tender much of the time. The moment there was anything to jiggle, I had been popped into a bra and girdle. Nice girls don't jiggle. I go to a square dance at the old Congregational Church with Bruce, a boy from my dancing class who is in the same homeroom as I. During the punch and cookies break, my school bus driver comes up to me. I had not known that he worked as janitor at the church. He takes me out into the hallway beside the recreation room and starts to make conversation. I haven't much to say to him. When he is done, he hugs me. He hugs very hard and tightly. It hurts to be pressed against him and I try to pull away, but I do not want to hurt his feelings. I am confused. I want to be back with the other kids. After that event, any time I am the last one off the school bus, he hugs me again, always jolly and friendly. I start getting off a stop or two ahead of mine, and walk home from there rather than be alone on the bus with him. It never occurs to me to report something I cannot even understand. And to whom would I report it? My parents, uncomfortable them-selves with my growing young woman's body, have placed as many physical restraints upon it as they know how. If nice girls don't attract un-nice overtures, then the fact that I am attracting them makes me somehow not nice. I feel as if

I have done something wrong, something which has not yet even been clearly defined for me. The water is getting warmer.

I am in the eighth grade. It is 1959. I feel less and less comfortable walking alone in the streets. Guys drive by in cars and shout rude comments. Men in trucks make "appreciative noises." I tell my mother. She says to remember that I am a lady. I am above such things. Pretend you don't even hear them, she says. I learn to walk slightly slumped over to hide my breasts; to duck my head a bit so no one can look directly into my face; to keep my hips still and make sure that my bottom doesn't sway from side to side. I have learned how to walk like a victim.

I am in the ninth grade. The boys at school, the ones who we would, in a later era, call "greasers," are starting to become bolder. They come up behind girls in the halls and unhook their bras, then laugh and leave. This has not happened to me, but I have heard other girls telling of the humiliation. They make vulgar remarks from their desks in the back of the classrooms, in loud whispers, then smirk and snort with amusement if the girls blush or act offended. Some of the girls preen and return sly smiles or slightly hinting retorts. They seem to find it flattering. I do not. I find it embarrassing and I wish they would stop, but to whom could I report it? It never occurs to me to tell the teacher. What good would that do? If the teacher disciplined the foul-talking boys, what would they do to me in return? At the very least, I would suffer social stigma for being a goody-goody, a tattletale. At the worst...well, I was not about to risk it. And after all, it was just words. But the water was definitely getting even warmer.

It is the Fourth of July, 1961. I am 16 years old. My friend Nancy and I have packed a picnic lunch and taken it down to the local swimming hole to celebrate the middle of summer and the fact that we still have weeks to go before school starts again. After we have been swimming a while, two boys, young men, really, show up. They start to ask about our schools, what grades we're in. At first we are a little flattered. They are, after all, high school graduates and we aren't even juniors yet. Then, things start to turn ugly. Innuendoes, off-color comments, are introduced into the conversation. At first Nancy and I try to laugh them off, but gradually we begin to feel more and more vulnerable. We are alone with these two men. No one else is anywhere nearby. The swimming hole is isolated, at the end of a long road and far from the nearest house. Suddenly, as I swim in water well over my head, one of the young men swims up beneath me and grabs my nipple in his fingers. He twists it, hard. I gulp water and flounder as he laughs. Then, as quickly as I can, I swim to shore. I am terrified. What if he had pulled me under? I whisper to my friend that we must leave. We pack up our lunch and head up the hill. At the top of the hill, we see a neighbor family arrive with their three children. We sit down and watch for a while, loath to give up our swimming on such a beautiful hot day. The two young men eventually leave and we feel safe to go back to the water, but the day has been tainted. We swim, eat our picnic, talk, then, as afternoon becomes early evening, we start to walk home.

We have not gone far when I hear a noise. I turn and see the two young men, standing in the middle of the dirt road behind us. My mind goes numb. I cannot think. I can only remember my mother's words. I say to my friend Nancy, just keep walking. Pretend they aren't even there. The next thing I know, I am face down in the dirt. A hand is tearing at the straps of my bathing suit. Another hand is grabbing my crotch. I force myself around and see eyes, crazy, hard, determined eyes. His arm is now over my shoulder, the hand now scrabbling at my breast. I can think of nothing to do. Instinct steps in and I bite him, on the upper arm, as hard as I can. He yells. I bite harder. Blood is running into my mouth. He tears his arm away and I scream for the father of the family swimming down in the swimming hole. The two young men disappear into the woods. I send my friend to get the father of the swimming family. He drives us both to my house. My parents are out. When they return home, they listen to my story. "Did he hurt you?" they keep asking. What they mean is, did he rape you, but they cannot bring themselves to use that word. They call the police. A man in plainclothes shows up. He listens to my story. We are all very polite. He asks me where the young man touched me. I gesture to my breasts and my crotch, too embarrassed to say the words. He stays a long time, asking for any detail which might help to identify and find the two young men. He also asks me to show him, several more times, just where I was touched. I am in shock. I cannot imagine why he needs to be shown, over and over, where I was touched, but I do as I am told. I tell him that they ought to call the hospital, that I hurt the man and that he might have gone to the hospital for help. Instead, over the next week, I am shown year books from all the junior and senior highs in our city, shown group photos in which each head is a quarter of an inch high. Was this the one? What about this one? I am terrified of what will happen when they find them. I don't want them to ever, ever know who I am, where I live. The police promise me, over and over, that I will be able to identify the suspects through a one-way mirror at the station house, that I will be able to remain anonymous. My parents are now acting as though nothing has ever happened. They want to forget, to pretend that it never occurred. When, after two weeks, the police finally check the local hospitals, they find the name and address of a young man from our neighborhood who came into the emergency room on the 4th of July for treatment of a severe laceration on the upper right arm.

I am at my friend Nancy's house. My father telephones. He says I want you to come home, right away. I walk home. I walk into the driveway where there is a police car. Sitting in the back seat of the police car are the two young men who attacked me. In my own driveway. Glaring at me out of the car. I run into the house. I fling the front door open so hard that it crashes against the wall behind me and bounces back. I run into the living room and shake my fist in the face of the plainclothes officer who had interviewed me over the past two weeks, the one who had wanted to be shown, over and over again, where I had been touched. "You promised me," I shout. "You said he'd never know who I was or where I lived and then you brought him to my house!" He says nothing. A small, nervous man sits on the couch next to my parents. I am introduced to him, as though this were a tea party. He is the father of the man who had attempted to rape me. He keeps saying that his son is a good boy, really. The implication is there, unspoken, but there. What had I done to tempt this good boy, this good boy with the weeping, confused old father, to do such a dreadful thing? My parents say nothing.

Where in all this was there anyone to defend me? Where were my parents? Where were the police? Why was everyone pretending that this was something that would just blow over, a slight social faux pas that was best forgotten? No, no, of course there was no question of filing charges. After all, I am now 16, the age at which my name, and the circumstances of the unfortunate event, would be published in the paper, in the police blotter. Think of the shame, they tell me. Think of what people would say. And so he is not charged. And one month later he rapes and murders a young woman in our city. And I had learned my lesson. I had told. I had reported the crime because that fine line had been crossed, from the humiliation of words to the obscenity of physical attack. I had turned him in and look what had happened.

It is the summer of 1964. I am 19 years old and walking along Lexington Avenue in New York City. It is broad daylight, the streets are filled with shoppers and workers on lunch hour. It is not an ominous or seemingly dangerous hour for a young woman to walk alone. Along the sidewalks are buckets of flowers for sale, piles of brilliant fruits and vegetables, fascinating store windows to examine. I am breathing in the diversity and color of an exciting city, delighting in my solitary adventure. A nondescript-looking man walks straight up to me and grabs both of my breasts in his hands, then immediately continues walking down the sidewalk, blending quickly into the crowds. I freeze to the spot, all pleasure in the day extinguished. A greengrocer standing outside his shop snickers and turns away, part of that great fraternity of men whose world does not seem to include compassion for the other sex.

I go through college and graduate school with acquired selective deafness, as do most young women. We laugh off or walk away from the mildly or openly obscene comments of young men at fraternity parties, dances, blind dates, even, occasionally, from professors. We shrug and accept the fact that guys will be guys. We try to forget the date rape that took place because we went off with someone we hardly knew, just to go to a college weekend. Whom would we tell of these events? There are no date police, and I already knew how police handled such incidents.

It is the summer of 1968. I am 23 years old. I am working as a waitress after my first year in graduate school. I am the only unmarried woman working at the

Chimney Corners, a self-consciously old New England-style, upscale restaurant. I am fair game for the waiters, the barkeep, the chefs. In order to get the drinks I need for my customers, I have to go back into the storeroom with the bartender. Luckily, he is an older man who merely wants to put his arm around me and pinch my cheek, but if I do not do that, I do not get the drinks and my customers grow angry and do not leave me a tip. The waiters are gross in language, but do not try physical contact. The chefs, however, have no such compunctions. They make comments when I come back to pick up meals. They make lewd hand gestures. I tolerate it, telling myself it is only words, I am a lady, I do not hear, I do not respond. Then comes the night when I am standing at the freezer, bending over slightly to scoop up a dish of ice cream. Suddenly one of the chefs is standing behind me, wrapping his arms around my waist, thrusting his hips into my buttocks. It is a classic edition of the dry hump. I break away, dropping the ice cream dish which shatters and spills. He and the other chefs laugh uproariously. I am shaken and stunned. I will not tolerate this. Filling another dish with chocolate ice cream for my customer, I go to the manager's office on my way back to the dining room. I report what has happened. He laughs and asks me if the other one gives vanilla. I realize that in my anxiety I have been holding the dish of chocolate ice cream up against my heart.

Somehow, word gets to the chef that I have reported his behavior. When I go on duty the next evening, I must go to the cook station and get popovers, the restaurant's famous offering, from the chefs. I am scared. The chef who I had reported signals to me to go with him back to the ovens. I shake my head. He shrugs. The message is clear: if I don't go, I don't get the food I need to serve my tables. I follow him, leaving a safe distance between us. After all, I think, I can always yell if he touches me. We aren't going out of the restaurant, just to the back ovens. In the passage is a huge scullery sink, where the restaurant pans and pots are set to soak before being washed. It is as large as a small bathtub to accommodate the institutional-sized cookpots. A two-inch layer of orange grease floats on the filthy water. A stack of used pots towers at the edge of the sink. As the chef walks by, he deliberately cocks his elbow against the pots. They cascade into the sink. I am covered from head to toe with a backwash of greasy, dirty water. I have to go home, shower, wash my hair, change my uniform and return to work having lost several precious hours out of my salary. Report this event? To whom? Not long after, I quit and return to school early.

What is sexual harassment? Is it the incidents I have lived through? Is it the adored uncle who turned funny after I hit puberty, who told me off-color stories which made me uncomfortable, who took me aside to show me how to do a breast self-examination when I was fifteen, who tried to French kiss me, and held my face, forcing it back to his mouth, when I attempted to turn away? Is it the head of the department who, when I went for an interview to go back into graduate school for my doctorate, told me that I would need to get a rich husband to put me through? Is it the man who regularly came into the library where I worked later, and routinely brought the topic of tampons and sanitary napkins into his conversations, while pretending to need reference help?

When a person grows up in a culture which tolerates or even applauds the overt sexual behavior of one gender at the expense of another, it is often impossible for the individual to draw the line between the tolerable and the intolerable. When is the water so hot that it will kill? I only know this: the day it got too hot for me.

It is 1975. I am 30 years old. I am coming out of a grocery store. It is a magnificent afternoon. I am in love and engaged to be married. I am buying the ingredients for a meal for my fiance. A man walks past. He mutters something. At first I am so bemused that I actually say, "I beg your pardon?" He repeats his comment. It is crude and has to do with the size of my breasts. For a brief instant I find myself retreating into past conditioning: remember that you are a lady, pretend you do not hear, walk away as if nothing has happened. Then, something snaps in my head. I find myself shouting at the top of my lungs: "How dare you speak to women like that! You filthy creep! What right do you have to say things like that!" Everyone in the parking lot turns around to see what is happening. The man disappears so fast that he must have rolled under a car. I feel strong and good about myself.

I tell you this: I will never, ever allow things to be said to me without a response. I will never again participate in the silent condoning of verbal abuse. And I will never, ever allow someone to physically assault me again. I will go for the throat this time; for the eyes or the genitals. I will play for keeps. I will neither expect quarter nor will I give it.

Jane L. Mickelson is a freelance author and voiceover narrator living in Northern California with her husband and son; her interests include women's spirituality, environmental protection, travel and music.

WHAT'S CHANGED?

Lisa Morekis

The television's blue presence cuts through the smoke of the bar. Hours of hearings pump heated accusations and flat denials into this meeting place for Savannah's Old Guard, and conversation tonight turns to controversial subjects.

"I bet Charlie Joe is feeling like a long-tailed cat in a room fulla rocking chairs right about now," says Jimmy, a coat-and-tied regular. From behind the bar I hear the name and a picture of a greying, beer-bellied man enters my mind: Charlie Joe, the owner of a small tavern I'd worked in four years ago.

"Yep, I bet he's about ready to leave town in the middle of the night and move up north where they don't give a damn, what do you think?" comments another from the polished oak bar.

"Is it true what they say about the girls who work for him, about those bonuses and fringe benefits?"

I cut the limes in front of me, juice squirting onto the wooden board. Jimmy leans over to his friends and murmurs something, and they all silently regard me. I look up from my limes and want to laugh at their curious faces.

"Lisa, didn't you used to work over at Flanagan's?" says Jimmy, the spokesperson for the group.

"Of course I did, Jimmy. Don't you remember? I had to kick you out at closing plenty of times."

The others laugh and pat Jimmy on the back as I automatically empty their ashtrays.

"So, uh, how was Charlie Joe to work for? I mean, was he an easy person to work for, or was he picky, or what?"

I set down a fresh Dewars and water on the clean napkin in front of Jimmy and mark a little "one" on his tab. "Jimmy, if you're asking me did he ever try to get in my pants"—I hear an intake of breath at this— "well then the answer is yes."

The bar is filling up and the boys talk among themselves while I serve cold beers and cocktails to people who've drunk the same thing for years.

190

The television shows a close up of the witnesses, sincere in their testimony. I can't tell which person they are defending.

Jimmy is not through with me yet. "Well, aren't you gonna tell us the rest?" I look from face to face knowing what they want: dirt. I don't want to say anything, make them wonder, but silence is the admission of guilt in this bar.

"Guys, look, would you screw Charlie Joe for an extra fifty bucks a week?" I ask. "Or for that matter, a hundred?"

"Yeah, but we're not a woman."

"Why Jimmy, I would certainly hope not, after all these years of watching you chase skirt. Then I'd have to say you were a lesbian." The laughter is long and cuts out the pleading voices from the television. I make sure I am busy for the rest of the night.

At closing time, the hearings still drone one. I think of the implication Jimmy had made, that if a woman is offered financial reward or status for sex, that she would take it. And I think about Karen. Karen had started at Flanagan's a week after I did. She was cute and friendly but not organized or efficient. She couldn't cope with a packed bar and soon no one wanted to work with her. Before long she was drinking shift drinks with Charlie Joe and his friends, and the two of them would leave together in his van. The affair (he was married at the time) was blatant, and although I was repulsed, I was also envious of her special treatment. I had to wait on her.

"Charlie Joe's got some property I'm interested in," she'd say to me, drunk on expensive liquor. "We'll be back in a few minutes." But they'd not come back. I'd see her car still parked near the bar when I'd leave at three a.m.

One day Karen showed me an engagement ring—she and her former boyfriend had gotten back together, and he had asked her to marry him. She was ecstatic. The boyfriend came in that night while Karen happily worked, and she asked to leave early. Charlie Joe and his cronies glowered in the corner. Within the next few days, Karen no longer worked at Flanagan's.

"So I hear you work for Charlie Joe. Just watch your ass," people warned me from the day I started. What's all the fuss, I thought, thinking about Charlie Joe's conversations with me, which all went something like:

ME: It was a good night in here last night.

HIM: I heard. We did $900.

ME: Damn.

HIM: You're doing a great job.

ME: Thanks.

The most personal thing Charlie Joe said to me was "Don't wear jeans to work." That is, until Karen quit.

One day I'd come to work in a slim skirt and matching blouse. "Mmm-mmm...I really like that outfit on you, Lisa." I accepted the compliment but felt as though I were being tested somehow.

I really like that outfit, Lisa," he emphasized, looking up and down my body as I came to the table he sat at every night.

"Thank you, Charlie Joe. Can I get you another drink?" I was unsure of this new behavior.

Charlie Joe's alcohol intake seemed to increase, and the flattering remarks gave way to a more insistent tone. "What are you going to do about this?" he seemed to say.

Then we entered a strange stage. Charlie Joe was cordial and distant in the daytime, and rudely provocative at night.

After I served him his usual soup and sandwich for lunch, he read the paper and barely noticed me. At night he would sit in the corner like a spider, waiting for women, including me, to come into his web.

I agonized over what to wear to work. Thinking that drab, loose-fitting clothes might deter him, I opted for outfits of beige. Gone were the dangling earrings I loved so much. I sighed as I put on pearls.

But Charlie Joe was out of town for most of this, and I got used to the freedom of his being gone. I wore a saucy red dress to work one night, and there sat Charlie Joe, back early from out of town and drunk already at five o'clock.

In this stage, the cat-and-mouse days of my fleeing from his advances, I wondered why I couldn't tell him I wasn't interested. I just couldn't say the words. He'll probably fire me, I thought one night, dangerously close to saying something. Or, worse, make me regret I was born.

"Lisa, come here," he said one night, and I knew I was in trouble. "I've been thinking," he said, putting his arm around me and guiding me to the hall next to the front door. Customers were watching us and my cheeks hurt with a blush.

"What is it?" I said. He was so close I could smell his cologne.

"I've been thinking. You need a vacation."

"A vacation? I don't need a vacation."

"Yes you do. You need to come down to Florida with me. We'll sit by the pool and go to nice restaurants and just relax." He had pinned me against the wall by the men's room. "You need to get away from this joint," he said.

This man is physically detaining me, I thought as I tried to move against his bulk. He was stronger than he looked. The thought of going anywhere with him disgusted me. But I smiled and said, "I couldn't possibly leave. We're short as it is. I have to work six days a week!" A customer watched us as he went to the men's room. I saw the look on his face.

He leaned even closer to me and said, "You'll still get a paycheck." I wrenched myself out of his grasp, but he still held on to my hand. "Think about it," he said. Later that night I waited until the crowd had died down and spoke with Kelly, another bartender.

"Has Charlie Joe ever said anything to you?"

She knew exactly what I meant. "Oh, sure. He's talked his trash to all of us," she said, ringing up a drink.

"Well, he's doing it to me and it's getting worse by the day," I said.

"Just tell him you're not interested," she said. "He'll keep on until you do. Just tell him to go to hell! We all have, Lisa. That's why he doesn't bother us."

But I couldn't find the words. The distaste and confusion at being pursued by someone I had no interest in did not outweigh my fear of retaliation by a spurned man.

The situation ended when I fell in love with my husband-to-be. I soon left without giving notice.

"Have you ever been sexually harassed?" asks Mrs. Bazemore, the night auditor, bringing me back to the present day. She is watching the television and does not let me answer. "You girls have it made in this day and age," she says. "In my day a boss could ask you anything he wanted to, and if you were asked to make him a cup of coffee, all you could say is, 'What do you want in it?' "

I watch the people on the screen, think of Charlie Joe and of my never once thinking of taking him to court, and wonder if anything has really changed.

Lisa Morekis is 28, married, the mother of a two-year-old, an avid beginning writer, and works in food and beverage.

CHEMICAL FALL-OUT

Marjory Nelson

Walking across the bridge that spans the Raritan River and the canal next to it, I get to feeling that something terrible is about to happen; perhaps the bridge will shake and break and I'll go tumbling into the muddy waters below. I'm eight years old, thrilled with the independence of being able to walk to school, but something is wrong and I'm not sure what it is. I keep walking as fast as I can.

Now I've left the bridge and must pass an old factory and three blocks of run-down hotels and buildings. Wounded veterans from World War I gather here with other homeless men to sell pencils and beg for money. It is 1936, and I have grown so accustomed to this symptom of the Great Depression that I've hardly thought about it as my mother has driven us back and forth to our school. But now, I'm not in a car, nor do I have the protection of my father with whom I usually walk.

"Hey girlie, come over here, I wanna show you something." The voice is gruff, insinuating. The men around him laugh. I look at him briefly, notice that he is missing one hand, and that the man next to him has no legs. I turn away in shock. "I'm talking to you, girlie, you with your head in the air. Don't be afraid," he coaxes. "I'm not gonna hurt you. I got something real nice to show you." Again the men laugh. I hug the curb and walk as fast as I can, for I'm in a quandary. I don't want him to think I'm repulsed by his injury, and yet, I'm frightened. I hear the words my mother etched in stone across my still shoulders: Good girls don't draw attention to themselves. If the boys are bothering you, it's only because they want your attention. Ignore them and they'll leave you alone.

It's like trying to ignore a wild dog charging at you. Do I dare run? Pretend you don't hear them, mother's voice commands.

Another man speaks up, "Hey blondie, where'd you get that cute little ass, I bet you're soft all over, ain't you? Come here and let me have a feel."

I could choose to walk on the other side of the street, but then I'd have to cross two dangerous intersections. Most days, I opt for the traffic; sometimes I take the bus.

Six years later, our country has entered World War II. The old veterans have disappeared, there are no more homeless men asking for handouts, but now our town is filled with floods of desperate young GIs on their last leave before being sent overseas. All the streets are dangerous, and we girls are encouraged to walk with a buddy, or if alone on a dark empty street, stay in the middle of the road and be ready to run up onto anybody's porch. But nobody calls their assaults on the women and girls of our community sexual harassment. Men will be men and everything is for the good of the troops, for the morale of the boys in uniform.

My mother, who was raised in a household of Victorian ladies, knew about men. She knew enough to teach me that I must never try to defend myself, but to find the strongest man around to fight for me, to walk beside me, to protect me. My mother knew. She beat me and scolded me and locked me in my room when she saw me raise my fists against my brothers who were all older than I. Good girls don't fight, she'd hiss.

Growing up in the nineteen-thirties and forties, learning to be a girl meant learning to take sexual harassment; to turn my head away, lower my eyes, cross my legs, silence the roaring voices in my ears; stay out of trees when the boys were around because they could see your underwear so then of course they'd be driven to pull at your legs, make nasty comments about you, haul you down out of the sweet sanctity of green bowers. If the boys were upset, mother would say, you shouldn't have been there.

And so I learned to be a woman. The line between sexual harassment and sexual terrorizing is blurred in my memory. A neighbor boy ties me to a tree and throws a hard ball at my undeveloped breasts and my soft belly while he taunts me for being a girl. My brothers threaten me with knives and ropes, dangling me out of my second-story window or down the clothes chute, my dress down over my face, and the threats they hurl at me have to do with my being a girl.

An ugly voice inside my head tells me that a fat girl like me is only indulging in wishful fantasy. The voice is real: the voice of my brothers, of my best friend's older brother John, of the comedians on the radio, everyone saying that only an attractive woman gets harassed, how dare the "dogs" complain? They're either envious or must be man-haters. If you're going to complain, you'd better prove that you're not one of them: starve yourself, dress femmy, look vapid so you can make a legitimate complaint.

On my nineteenth birthday, I married an ex-marine, then had three children. Now it's 1964, and I have just returned to college at the University of Akron, Ohio, to finish my Bachelor's degree and start the Master's program. I'm a serious student and want to make up for all the years of being home alone with my babies. Several of the professors take an interest in me. One invites me to his home and as I read him the paper I've written, he tells me over and over that I am beautiful. I want him to tell me I'm smart, and once when I ask him, he says in a very off-hand way, "Of course you are, you're working with me." Other professors sit in the graduate student office making snide comments about women's legs and breasts. I start dieting more strenuously than ever before in my life, for now it seems clear that my professional advancement depends on how thin I am. None of the male graduate students are subjected to this.

It's 1970, and I'm living in Washington, D.C., working on my dissertation about the militant suffragists. At the women's bookstore, I find a stack of cards that read:

> *You have just insulted a woman.*
> *This card has been chemically treated.*
> *In three days, your prick will fall off.*

With my new feminist friends, I roam the streets. We stop a car whose driver has made catcalls at us and scream back at him; I hand a card to a well-dressed man who looked me up and down and then said angrily, "You could be so pretty if you dressed like a woman. And why don't you smile?"

I feel angry all the time. I feel alive.

It's 1991 and I'm enjoying my morning walk in the San Francisco neighborhood where I now live. Behind me, a bus has just unloaded a group of students bound for the junior high school across from my house. I hear boys giggling behind me, and as they draw closer, one of them calls out, "woh, man, look at that motion." The others join in laughing. As old as I am, I can't believe they are paying attention to me, so after they have passed, I turn around to look behind me. There is no one else on the block. What shocks me is that they can still bother me. They rob the peace that somehow I'd come to believe I was entitled to at sixty-three.

At the warm pool in the Recreation Center for the Handicapped where I swim, there are old men, some without legs, who hang out making comments about the women's bodies, telling jokes about women in voices loud enough to be heard around the entire pool. I think of the World War I veterans of my childhood, and wonder who all the fighting has been for and what we have won. No longer repelled by missing limbs, I feel great rage, and also sadness, for it seems that something so much more important is missing from these men.

Marjory Nelson is a 63-year-old writer and hypnotherapist.

Sexual harassment was never a major issue as long as it only threatened the careers of millions of women. It only became a major issue when it threatened the career of *one* man. Click!
—Susan Pepperdine

My life is one big sexual harassment experience, from the time I leave my house to the time I come back home.
—Cheyenne Goodman

Somehow, these remarks seemed so out of context that I refused to believe I was hearing them.
—Abby Lynn Bogomolny

For those women who can effectively engage in denial, the problem simply doesn't exist.
—Mark E. Smith

For two decades now I've encouraged women to break any law that discriminates against women, and to ignore any social custom that keeps women in the place of second-class citizens.
—Nikki Craft

The reality is that sexual harassment—like rape, like abuse, like pornography—unites women.
—Ellen Goodman

Such Great Knockers

Carol Potter

Hey what knockers, what tits just for fun, just for
fun they were yelling from the boat the two women
crouched in the surf, the man's hand on his cock

love oh love oh careless love he was
singing in the boat load of men come in close
to shore to see two women swimming naked in

the surf as close as they could come without
running up on shore his hand on his cock by the side of
the road he slowed down his car he called out

to the girl, hey you want to fuck he called
hey you want to fuck the boys are in the bushes
and they're playing a game with sister they

invited her to play with them they want her
to be the wife, slut,
hussy, whore they will call her later for going

along with them whore you fat bitch you slut and
some friend of her brother's has invited her
into the room to see through the microscope so he

lifts her up slipping his hands into her pants so she
can look into the microscope & brother
is behind the door with his penis in his hand

and he is calling to little sister come in
please he says I have
to show you something I have to show you something

I have to show you something said the man
in the barn this time he wants to
show her something he wants her to see something his

pink penis standing up in his hand don't tell
anyone don't tell he tells her in the bible it says
he who goes about as a talebearer reveals secrets

but he who is trustworthy in spirit keeps a thing
hidden a thing hidden he says slowing the car down such
great tits such knockers hey you wanna fuck?

Carol Potter is 41, a teacher, and a lesbian single mother.

FROM BREEZE INTO BLIZZARD

Amy Diane Purcell

With my first period came a new smell from between my legs. My new shape found a mirror all around me. Sometimes it was in the eyes of men who looked; their nods and the fire in their eyes was a confirmation of my beauty. I began to understand it was one of the most important things for a woman to possess and cultivate. But other times, they touched. I remember one man, a "family" man, who had two children. One evening at a gathering he greeted me by grabbing my chin and capturing my head in his large hands. He puckered his lips and kissed me long on the mouth. His lips were warm, wet and fat. I was disgusted and very upset that this was my first kiss by a man: an old man with a large belly and hair creeping from his nostrils that hissed with each breath. I hadn't chosen him for this first, special kiss. He chose me. This became a ritual each time I saw him. I was only thirteen and he towered over my body. A "friend" of the family. And when I told my father that I didn't like what this man was doing, he didn't tell him to stop but shrugged off the man's behavior as simply a greeting.

My social world grew as did my curiosity about my body and the boys I liked. We petted and kissed in cars on dark streets with the eagerness of adventurers discovering a new and untrodden place.

My freedom and instinct to explore was exciting and terrifying. My circle of friends grew and I began to find myself alone with older boy/men. Without my consent, hands seemed to be grabbing and prodding. Lips forced their way onto my mouth when my own were closed. I was never asked; I did not matter. Only the sum of my parts gave meaning to what was happening.

Turning here or there, I heard whispers of what this man wanted to do with me or what that married man had done with a prostitute. I began to learn to be clever, to strategize and endure when I could not escape. What was I doing wrong? Or what wasn't I doing that could stop these men whose only focus seemed to be sex? My father didn't teach me how to stop the "friend" of the family. No one taught me to say, "No, I don't like this." And everywhere I looked, women were being subjugated, dominated, over-powered, harassed or raped by men. So, if this was "normal," why did I have such a problem? Why did I feel powerless and violated? And worst of all, it didn't stop there.

When I was sixteen, I spent the summer at my grandparents' home on the coast of Florida. The days were a lazy blur of sunshine and sea but the evenings were long as I dodged my grandfather's pinches to my buttocks and arms. One day, as I ran around in my swimming suit getting ready for the beach, I found myself in the kitchen with my grandparents. Suddenly, my grandfather reached out and clamped his hand on my breast. It felt like a claw as it dug into my body. I stood in shock as my grandmother said, "You had better not do that or Amy will think you are a dirty old man." He never apologized or showed shame. I attempted to tell my mother who brushed off his actions as those of a sorrowful, old man who was incapable of showing his feelings. With my eye on the bedroom doorknob, terrified that at midnight I would see it move, I waited out the end of summer.

Time passed and my body continued to grow but in a different way. The outlines had been formed and now each curve and angle filled up. The longing, vitality and desire began to focus on something for which I suspected all these changes were preparing me. This was somehow aligned to the wolf yells following on the wind of a passing car full of boys. It was connected to the strange hands fondling me on a bus, to the knowing glimmer in my teacher's eyes. I wanted to make love—not to these men, but to a male who would be gentle, loving and respectful. One who would go with me to this secret world alluded to in every book, movie or song I encountered. I worked for months attracting and getting to know the boy of my choice.

One day the world I worked hard to create shattered in the walk home from school. "Whack!" I thought that it must be my step-brother surprising me. Maybe he got off a different train car and I didn't see him leave the station. With my rear-end stinging from the slap and a hopeful/angry feeling inside, I turned expecting to see my brother, grinning at his joke. Instead, I found myself staring into the wandering, unseeing eyes of a man—a man with a grin on his face, his hands reaching out for me. I am running, the distance home seeming miles longer. I feel him behind me and turn to see his pants undone. I don't take the time to look but I know that his penis is out of his pants and I reach to hit him away. He grabs my hand but somehow I yank it free and run. My one-inch heels are painful, slowing me down, and my toes smash against the front of the shoes. I feel a cry and scream choking my throat but I contain it as I run faster than I ever thought possible. I burst into my home where screams and cries tear from my throat. I am hysterical and my mother's terrified eyes make me scream louder. Once I am able to get the story out, she calls the police but is told that before they can send someone, she must come and fill out a report. An hour to and from the station and by then the man would be far from the neighborhood.

The following day I tell my boyfriend and he laughs at my story. Later, he tells me that he did not know how to react so he laughed. But I cannot touch him, his hands are those of the dark-haired man. His body, the one I couldn't ever seem to leave alone for long, terrified me. Whose penis was whose? Why did I begin to shrink inside? Why wasn't anything done? And why couldn't that man have been punished?

Time healed or time forgot and I felt the exciting urges coming back as well as the power and control over my own body. Graduation and the bitter-sweetness of leaving my first lover concluded the summer. A year later, I looked around and spotted a blue-eyed, curly, blond-haired boy. A connection is made and we begin the game, the dance of courtship, where roles are vague and experience is young.

My second date or third? Francesco invites me for dinner but I arrive at his house to find an empty table and a "I don't know how to cook" grin on his face. He grabs my hand and drags me to his bedroom. A single bed, barely a bed and more like a cot, and a dirty window at the end of the narrow space is his bedroom. I blink and suddenly, we are on the bed. This must be, I tell myself, one of those passionate scenes I see over and over in the movies. But wait! Why and how did I get undressed? No!!! He's naked and my eyes barely blinked for the second time. He tells me to shut up and covers my mouth with his hand and I cannot tell what I heard. A giggle? A cry? He is gone and I am left with my legs spread apart, my knees looking scrawny and skinny and ugly. Something fell under the bed and I know it was a huge piece of me caught under the rickety, bare metal frame of the bed. What had happened? Where did I go? I convince myself that I had wanted to have sex in order to pick myself up from under the bed, shake off the dust balls and put myself back together.

In the months to come I realize that there really isn't a difference between the wolf cries and this boy/man. I excelled in college but inside he wore me away piece by piece. My buttocks and breasts were ugly beacons to tempt a man, he told me over and over. He asked why I had spread my legs so easily. He told me that I shouldn't do that for boys. (Was he not naked as well? Was he not the other half of that night?) I tried to leave the relationship and to get away but couldn't when I found my hands crushed in his own as he used them to beat his face. I was afraid for my life. The school year ended. I left and never saw him again.

By now the holes had multiplied all over my body. I tried to fill them with drugs, alcohol, caffeine and nicotine, blurring the edges between my life and reality until I forgot what I once cared about, who I was and how I deserved to be treated. My dreams faded and a numbness filled its place. Whom could I confide in?

And so I learned to look away from the gleam in men's eyes, to ignore the calls on the street and to remain still until everything was absorbed like an old sponge. I struggle to re-learn what is right, wrong and inappropriate without the fantasies and stuff of Hollywood, novels and insensitive people telling me that there is no other way for men and women to treat each other. If ever someone comes to me in pain and confusion about being violated and harassed, I will believe and I will not shut my ears to them.

Men such as those who wronged me will not cease existing as long as our children are not taught differently and unless we create new myths, images and ideas about how to love and respect our sexuality within ourselves and each other. In the meantime, I try to become aware and rub awake this numbness. So that next time, just maybe, I will fight back before it's too late and experience grows into another mountain too big to contain.

Amy Diane Purcell is a 27-year-old artist who has participated in and organized several art exhibitions in her local area and internationally.

Marian Henley

MY LUCKY DAY

Clarinda Harriss Raymond

Sexual harassment, by definition, is a misuse of power. The very young are very powerless: anyone "bigger" in any sense of the word can dictate what uses are to be made of their bodies. Like most women, I suspect, I can look back at a great many early experiences. Which of them shall I choose to write about? Which of them made me feel most literally raped?

I reject the earliest incident, a memory so far back in my childhood I've lost all but the main outlines. A New York restaurant, a table full of old Herald Tribune cronies, my parents' friends from their Bohemian days. Me small enough to be lifted playfully onto the lap of one of those friends. And bounced on his knee—playing horsie! Whee!—holding onto a pommel that sprang out of his pants. Whee! Everybody thought my screams were screams of infant delight. And after a while he put me back in the high chair.... I reject several small incidents that occurred in what was briefly my workplace, a respected savings and loan association where I was hired as a vacation stand-in secretary every summer while I completed college. I recall but put aside the memory of the man whose eyes startled mine as I bent over the office watercooler: "My buddies and I have a bet going. MY money says they're real." His eyes examined my black, too-dense, carefully plucked eyebrows while his hand examined the contents of my shirt....I likewise put aside the memory of the elderly, drunk senior officer at the same company who pinched my bottom black and blue at the annual Labor Day party. Some years later, seeing a grainy videotape of that party, seeing myself dance the boogaloo in a fringed dress that jiggled like Shazell Shazaar's famous tassels down on Baltimore's infamous Block, I was so appalled I could almost concur, momentarily, with the wisdom of the day: "She asked for it."

I also reject the incident that took place many years ago at the sedately elegant University Club, site of a debutante party. As one of Baltimore's most unwilling and most ill-suited-for-the-role debutantes, I was grateful when an elderly, tuxedoed gentleman suggested I step outside the stuffy party for a breath of fresh air on the marble porch. And stunned to near-catatonia when he drew my hand into his open fly. He was the grandfather of one of the debs! A Maryland highway was named for his family! I stood there passive as one of his family's famous brood mares. Finally I got up the gumption to duck back inside—where, within the hour, I became known as the Slut in the Pink Dress.

I settle on the one incident that keeps resurfacing in my memory even when I'm not deliberately trying to recall incidents of sexual harassment. This one did not occur in a workplace. It occurred in a play-place, under a cloud of cherry blossoms.

Druid Hill Park is beautiful, even now, and back then (only a few decades after the idyllic "sleep-out" shown in the film "Avalon") it was almost safe. At least during the daytime. At least when you were there for an innocent stroll or picnic or visit to the zoo.

The picnic I was there for was not innocent. I was a seventeen-year-old college freshman. The man for whom I had fried chicken and brewed ice tea was a junior professor at another college—married, with children, whose photographs I had seen. I was afraid of my parents' outraged sense of decency and propriety, my friends' censure, my own scared aspirations toward being the Other Woman. He, a devout Irish Catholic, was afraid of hell-fire. But he was a poet, and I was an aspiring poet. We had explained to ourselves that this picnic was about sharing poetry.

Though I belonged to a jeans generation, I had dressed for the occasion in a ruffly pink silk blouse, white skirt and flowered sash. Lying on my back in the petal-strewn grass, I took the two big brass hairpins out of my huge mop of hair and let the tangles trail on the ground, the better to feel like a Gainsborough painting. I held his slender manuscript (O what cliches we were!) outstretched above my face, almost at arm's length, reading along while he murmured the words. When his arm fell across my body, and one chino-panted knee nuzzled my legs, the gestures seemed as accidental as a boy's arm across my shoulders in a movie theatre. It was easy for me to pretend not to notice. Being a teenager during the late 1950s, I'd already had a lot of practice at not noticing that sort of thing.

I lay there pretending to read. Until four heavy black shoes planted themselves against my ribs and my hip.

"Let's see some identification," demanded the two policemen looming above my poet and me.

My poet jumped to his feet, but one black cop-shoe held my thigh to the ground. Under the black shoe, I sat on the grass rummaging through my purse till I found my almost-new driver's license.

"Goddam, seventeen, can you believe it?" The two policemen looked at me and shook their heads solemnly. "Bringing her tricks to do it right here in the park," said one, "and no older than my baby sister."

205

My poet, pocketing his own ID, demanded to know what they were talking about. "Keep your mouth shut and get lost," one of the cops responded, "unless you want to get cuffed to that fence." My poet glanced at the chain-link fence guarding the duck pond at the foot of a hill about twenty yards away; then, at a peremptory jerk of one of the policeman's heads, he walked downhill to huddle against the forbidding metal posts.

"Had a lot of complaints about you," the older cop told me. "Red-headed hooker brings her johns to the park and does it right here in broad daylight. Makes a decent citizen want to puke."

"Stand up," ordered the younger cop. "I bet you're one of those broads that doesn't wear a bra." I stood. He stuck one hand into my blouse, yanking my pink ruffles aside. "Well, well," he greeted one modest handful of white Maidenform. "Now let's see about what's under here." He lifted my skirt with his billy-club and ran his free hand over my white cotton Lollipop panties. He stuck a finger inside the crotch. "Wet," he informed the older cop. The older cop shrugged and sauntered down to the fence where my poet stood rubbing his tweed-jacketed shoulders against the steel mesh like a flybitten horse. The older cop's passing joke about "whether she's a real redhead or not" hung thinly in the flowered air.

"I'm going to have to take you in," the young cop announced.

"You can't! It'll ruin everybody's life!" I wailed, and then, ridiculously, though I meant it at the time, "I'll kill myself if you arrest me!" My two brass hairpins winked in the grass. I stooped, grabbed one, and started sawing at the blue veins in my wrist.

"Hey, Reds, take it easy." The young cop's big hand closed over my arm. The other hand pried the hairpin out of my grip, and that same hand twisted me down onto the grass. He ran the tip of his billy slowly up and down the stretch of white skirt where my squeezed-together legs met. "What's it worth to you if I let you go?"

"Everything," I whispered. "Everything?" he grinned.

"Only I don't have any money."

He laughed aloud. He held his billy upright between his squatting thighs and waggled it toward me. Light dawned.

"And I can't...make love to you."

I actually said "make love."

Maybe that was what did it. I'll never know, but looking back on the incident I feel certain that if I'd said "I can't fuck you" or even the briefly-popular "ball you," he'd have hauled me over to Northern Police Station right away.

He stared at me and at my driver's license and at my not-very-red hair. He glanced downhill to where the other cop stood, legs akimbo, broad back turned toward us solid as an oak door. There my poet was saying something inaudible, miserably gesticulating. Then the young cop sat down on the grass beside me, thumped the ground with his billy like a gavel, and said: "If I let you get away, will you promise me to be a good girl and never see that man again?"

I nodded. I had already made up my mind to be a good girl and never see that man again. A few minutes later, when that man and I—not looking at each other—climbed into his poetic old Renault to search for my own parked car and then leave Druid Hill Park forever, the young cop didn't seem at all put out that I'd already reneged on my vow. In fact, both policemen tipped their caps with their billies, and then burst into guffaws we could hear through both sets of car windows. I guess the guffaws are what I really remember. That laughter, and the old question: was I sexually harassed, was I as raped as I felt, or did I just get lucky?

Clarinda Harriss Raymond teaches at Towson State University in Maryland and co-directs the National Campus Violence Prevention Center.

Just Trying to have Some Fun

Mardi Richmond

Jack sometimes worked in the shop. He was big and tough and strong and rumored to be about the best carpenter in this county. One thing for sure, he always seemed to know what he was doing. He was about as confident as they come, cocky in a way.

Jack reminded me of two boys that I lived next door to when I was a kid. They were big and tough and strong, like Jack, and they wore their hair in a short, almost crew-cut style, like Jack.

When I was eight years old, the two boys next door paid me a nickel to come into their house when nobody was home. I didn't want to go in because their house was dark and always smelled like their dad's cigars. But they said, Come on in, we just want to have some fun. So I went inside. They shut and locked the door behind me and one of them grabbed my arms and the other pulled my pants down. They took turns holding me and touching me in ways I did not want to be touched. Then the oldest boy, he must have been fifteen or sixteen, tried to stick a broom handle up inside of me. I started crying so hard that they let me go, but not before they made me promise that I would never, never tell anyone what they did. Then they gave me another nickel and said, Stop crying, we were just trying to have a little fun. I ran straight home to my room and made myself sit in the corner. When my mom came in and asked me what was wrong I told her nothing. I never, never told, but I knew that what they had done was not fun.

Fourteen years later, at work, Jack took a stick—it could have been the handle of a broom—and stuck it between my legs when I was bent over nailing off a toe board on a cabinet. I turned around furious and told him to cut it out. He said, Hey, I'm just having a little fun, and walked off laughing.

The next day, Jack did it again. This time he grabbed my breasts and started making remarks about how I liked it and wanted it, in front of all the men I worked with. They all started laughing. I pushed Jack's hands off of my breasts and walked away, mad and scared. That time, I could not even find the words to tell him to stop. A feeling of terror filled my heart and the words would not come out.

Later the same afternoon, when I was carrying one end of a one-foot by one-foot by eighteen-foot fir beam, he grabbed my ass as I walked by. I jumped, startled, started to drop the huge beam, and felt a twinge of pain in the small of my back as I caught it. Three of the other men I worked with laughed, one frowned. Later the man who had frowned, carefully out of ear shot of the other men, told me he did not think it was right for Jack to treat me that way.

I went home from work that day scared, not knowing what to do. I was afraid to tell anybody. I heard the voices of those boys in my childhood memory saying never never tell. And I felt, much as I had when I was eight, that it was my fault. When I was eight, it was my fault because I went into their house for a nickel; now it was my fault because I had lost my voice. I was not able to tell him to stop.

I tried to tell my husband about it. He was furious and threatened to find Jack and punch him in the face. My husband could make him stop temporarily, but could I feel like I was strong enough to take care of myself if he did? And how could I keep working with men who thought this was funny, who were likely to do it again, if I couldn't take care of myself? I knew I had to find my own power to make him stop, and I knew that that had to start with finding a voice with which to say no.

I found that power and that voice through the anger of another woman. I visited a friend, and told her about the harassment. I told her about Jack grabbing me and touching me. I told her about his constant words, threatening and loud. I told her about the laughter of the other men. We were walking down the street when I told her and she began yelling at the top of her lungs. She yelled how fucked what he did had been and she yelled how fucked the other men were for laughing. When she stopped yelling and when the people driving down the street stopped staring, I felt my own surge of anger, and of energy. I realized how his words had stolen my energy and when I felt it coming back, I felt my voice coming back. My friend and I talked for hours that night about how to make him stop. I knew that shrugging it off would not work, and I knew that in a non-union shop I had very little political recourse; there was no one to complain to. What I realized I had to do was to confront him directly and loudly, the very next time it happened, before he had a chance to steal my dignity and energy again.

The next day, Jack took the nozzle from the pneumatic hose and blew air down my shirt. I grabbed the hose out of his hand, stood as tall and firm as I knew how, and told him loudly but calmly that it was not OK with me for him to do this and he had to stop right now. And he was never to touch me again. This time when he said he was just trying to have a little fun, I told him it was not funny and he was never to do it again. And he never did.

About a year later, another man I had worked with for several years approached me outside the building, saying he wanted to talk to me about something. I went over to the doorway where he was standing, and he grabbed me, pushing me into the doorway. He stood with his arms on either side of me, blocking my way out, and leaned his tall frame over me, to kiss me, trying to force his tongue in my mouth. I did not even hesitate, I pushed him away with all of my strength yelling NO. My yell startled him enough that he staggered backwards, just as several faces looked out of a nearby shop. Hey, I wasn't going to rape you or anything, he said. I was just trying to have some fun.

Mardi Richmond spent the first twelve years of her adult life working as a cabinetmaker and finish carpenter; today she is a freelance writer.

Jan Graveline Eliot

THE MAN

Victoria Alegria Rosales

The year? 1979. 1981. I really don't remember. Or don't want to remember. I'm 34 years old. The memory of the man is with me. I'm terribly afraid of him. I work at the Seventh and Mission Post Office in San Francisco. When I least expect it, he emerges from the crowds and bumps into me.

I work as an armed security guard. I have a B.A. in Spanish from U.C. Riverside. Big deal. I have not been able to get any other kind of job. I feel ashamed. Angry. My family mocks me for the many years I went to school. I know I deserve better. Shit! I see his eyes. He stares at me. His hands motion to his penis. I pretend I don't see him. I find protection in helping a woman use the zip code directory.

Security guards are subcontracted by the Post Office, earning $3.48 per hour. We work under the supervision of highly paid Federal Protective Officers. I have talked to my bosses about this man. The Security Guard Chief knows I want a transfer. Weeks go by. I stand at my post, watching. He bumps into me again. Boy, I'm pissed. I talked to Willie, one of the Federal Officers, about the harassment from this tall, dark man with a crew cut. He must be 6'2" tall, weighing over 170 pounds. I am 5'3", 145 pounds.

The majority of the Federal Protective Officers are retired. Most of them are very mean, especially Captain Lopez, who doesn't allow us to sit down.

Willie is one of the few nice guys. He promises me that he will speak to the man who is harassing me. Later he tells me he has spoken to him.

I feel a bit better after Willie tells me this. I stand at my post, trying not to tense up. If I get caught sitting, I'll be reprimanded by Captain Lopez. I hate that man. No wonder people call policemen "pigs." I lean back on the table to rest. The thought of having to confront the man who is bumping into me drains my energy. I quickly stand up as the judges and other attorneys pass by on their way to the courts. They never say hello. The only people who talk to me are the employees or the custodians.

I don't care if I have to work as a security guard. Things will change. I'll be able to get a job as soon as we have a new government and new president. Women like myself will get jobs and be paid a living wage. Hell, the man is there. He slides his hand as if unzipping his pants. I'll go on my rounds. Speak to Willie again. I hate to bother him. Why haven't I been transferred? I stand by the window, pretending I am writing. Perhaps the man with that ugly-looking cut will go away.

My paycheck is just enough to pay rent and buy food. I live in a studio on Divisadero and Haight. Friends don't want to visit. Isn't this a dangerous area, they ask? This was the least expensive place. When I get off work it is a relief to lie down on my bed and look at the trees. I live at the back of the building. Shit, the man followed me today. I lost him in the crowd on Market Street. What if I were to open the door and he was there? I begin to panic. To forget him as I begin my house chores, I eat a slice of cold stale pizza. I don't dare go out to the store.

Willie tells me that he spoke to the man again. Can't do much, he apologizes. He is just a patron of the post office, he says. I argue that there must be something I can do. Willie looks at me with sad eyes. Sorry, he tells me. It is about eleven o'clock.

Would you like to buy some handcuffs, someone asks at the post office. How much? Two bucks. You can always do a citizen's arrest, Willie laughs. What a great idea. Why not? I'd accuse the man of sexual harassment. I'd tell the police how this man interrupted my work by bumping into me, sometimes hurting me. Other times he'd just stand making sexual gestures at me. On two or three occasions, he tried to follow me home.

My friend Chessa stops by to see me at work. She's working on a play at the Mission Cultural Center. Would you like to be in it, she asks. I get excited. The part will be a distraction from my life. Sure, I say.

The part I want you to play is that of a victim. In the play the woman gets beat up, Chessa says.

Stop it, I shout. People stare. I feel my anger rising. Chessa's jaw hangs. I walk fast, doing my rounds. The man bumps into me, this time grabbing me by the shoulders. His hard swollen penis is on my back. I want to yell for help but can't talk. Creep, I finally manage to say, freeing myself. I run to the bathroom and cry.

I'm going to kill him, I say to Willie. Why didn't you make a citizen's arrest, he asks. I didn't think about it. I was so frightened, I say.

He attacked me in a dark corner. Judges and lawyers were locked up in their chambers. The post office was open only for those coming to pick up their mail from p.o. boxes.

From then on, I walked fast to catch the bus home. Every man seemed to be him. Even a wino emerging from a doorstep frightened me. I arrived home not knowing what to do. I glanced at *Plexus*, a woman's paper, and saw the ad for a therapist. I called. Can't really afford it but I'll manage. I have never been to a therapist.

I'm going to kill him, I tell the therapist.

What about jail?

I don't care. I'm tired of his harassment. I explain my ordeal in great detail. Soon the hour is up. I'll come back, I promise. A week seems such a long time to wait. I call the security company and they inform me that they can't transfer me. Sorry, they say.

I'll quit, I tell the therapist the following week.

What will you do for money?

I don't know.

I go home and look at the newspaper. It's depressing to look at it. I don't have the experience most employers are looking for. Nor do I have the wardrobe to apply for an office position.

The man bumps into me again. I blame myself. I should have had my eyes open for him. This time I smelled his sperm and sweat. I will not submit. I will not become a victim like when I was married. I will fight back. I'll talk to Willie again. I look at myself in the mirror. My eyes have dark circles around them. I haven't been able to sleep. I don't have the money for the therapist this week. What am I going to do?

The man is waiting for me. Willie isn't anywhere. I tell another officer that I don't feel well and that I'm going home. I walk through a path known only to the post office workers. I want to change my uniform. Besides, I have to lock up the gun. Just as I walk through the hall, the man is there. He comes toward me. I know he is going to bump into me again. His penis is the first thing I'm going to feel on my belly. I freeze. I won't become a victim, I say to myself, unfreezing. I take the gun from its holster and shoot. There's a loud boom throughout the corridor. The burning smell of gunpowder fills the post office. A few employees come out to stare. The man is crouched, in a fetus-like position on the floor. His hands are wrapped around his head. He is shaking. "Take this crazy woman away from me," he screams. I now realize that I missed. My gun still points at the man, this time he is an easy target. Willie rushes to my side. Very gently he gets hold of my hands, the way men did when they were teaching me how to shoot a gun. Willie looks at me. His eyes tell me: shoot the bastard. Go ahead, this is your chance. I look at the man, still shaking on the floor sobbing. I think of his mother. Am I not a mother also, I ask myself as I allow Willie to take the gun away from me. Someone handcuffs the man and takes him away in a police car. My bosses rush to the scene. I leave Willie to explain.

The man comes in wearing a suit, with a lawyer. I am called to testify. I recount my story just as I do here. Why do I have to do the talking? I am angry.

213

I am being psychologically raped by this court. The perpetrator sits there, staring at me.

"Miss Rosales," the judge finally says, pointing his finger at me. "If you are going to continue in this profession (profession? I laugh to myself. A better word would be oppression) you must use better judgment in the future." Turning toward the perpetrator, the judge says as if addressing a kid who has misbehaved, "Mr. Kichens, please learn to recognize when a woman isn't responding to your flirtations. Is that clear?"

"Yes, your honor," the lawyer answers for his client. The client stares at me with hateful eyes.

"Case dismissed," the judge roars, and walks out of the room.

The new job requires an unarmed guard. The pay is less than the post office. I asked for my last check to be mailed.

"You could have sued," someone says.

"How could you have done such a thing?" a woman at Kelly's bar asks. I decided then to keep my mouth shut. Until now.

Victoria Alegria Rosales is a San Francisco poet born in Mexico; she is presently working on her M.F.A. at San Diego State University.

214

THIS IS MY SIDE OF THE STORY

Samantha

It has happened before, but never seemed this bad. This time it's the boss and very direct. He reserved a hotel room, tried to get me in it; he followed me home and managed to force himself on me for a "kiss" before I could shove him off and run. Not to mention all of the touches to my thighs, my neck and attempts to kiss my face. NO meant nothing to him.

I couldn't afford to quit the job and I rationalized that since I didn't have to work with him that I'd be able to handle it. But he would drive up to us in his fancy air-conditioned car as we worked away in the hot sun, asking my foreman about me. Watching. He often called me at home on the pretense of business and then asked me out.

> *he said "you're beautiful, i love you"*
> *so many times*
> *that i couldn't stand to hear those words*
> *even from my lover*
> *for months afterwards*
> *he'd known me from a ten-minute interview*
> *and my resume.*

I bought an answering machine to screen out his calls. After a month, I got transferred to a department where there were other women and I told everything to the union steward. She told the other women and said she'd warn any of the new women who came. I asked her what I should do and she advised against going to the union or Human Rights. It would be my word against his and the all-male union, except for her, would support the boss. She thought I would be harassed by other workers and wouldn't put further violence past this man if I were to challenge him. I needed other women to go against him with me, but could find none.

> *some friends said i was too naive*
> *mom was ashamed of me because he had a wife and son*

dad wanted to nail him
my sister said i should be flattered
my partner offered support.

A couple of months later, the boss approached me while I was working and said he was doing a survey and report on sexual harassment for the organization. He'd volunteered. He wanted to know if I'd ever experienced sexual harassment. I could not speak. I leaned on my shovel and stared at the ground. Then he asked my supervisor the same question. After he left I asked my forewoman if I could go tell him off. I went up to his office, waited for ten minutes beside the secretary and then I was let in.

He asked me why I was there.

He said that he never sexually harassed me, that he was just being a man and acting on *normal* feelings toward a woman.

He told me that he really was a good boss. Hadn't he hired a black man without even an interview, a seventy-five-year old man and a female foreman? He said all he needed now was someone disabled and someone gay. Then he laughed.

He whispered, "Stop yelling! Do you want everyone in my office to know?"

YES! I WANT EVERYONE IN YOUR GODDAMNED OFFICE TO KNOW. He finally admitted to the sexual harassment and apologized, which was an accomplishment. He promised me he'd never do it again.

I know he probably said that to shut me up, but it gave me strength to yell at him as he sat behind his big desk.

Some feminists have tried to put me down for not quitting or taking my boss to court. This was upsetting for me because I felt like such a failure, a coward. At a workshop on sexual harassment, the women convinced me to go to court. I went home with my information and my feelings of support. Then I was faced with the nights alone and relentless fears. Where were the women from the workshop who wanted me to do this for "all women" when I needed them most? I had to think of myself, of my own safety. I also worried about my lover, who worked nights and what would happen if our lesbian relationship became known to co-workers. I would have lost what little support I'd acquired and put both of us in danger.

A woman must go by her own feelings on this. Of course I'd like to see the boss fired and help stop assault and harassment, but at that time in my life confrontation and self-preservation were all that I could handle.

Samantha lives in Ontario and works as a laborer in the trades; she has a degree in Women's Studies/English and is trying to find her way back to the country and to a job she enjoys.

THE REVEREND

Janet Sassi

When I was 19 and in college, I took a weekly job cleaning house for Reverend Gruman and his family. I adored Reverend Gruman's wife; she was beautiful, active and politically aware. The year was 1973, when being free with your love and sexually liberated was considered progressive. It was a time when I was trying to figure out what I believed.

I worked for the Grumans every Friday morning for a whole semester. I would vacuum, wash the kitchen floor, dust, make the beds and tidy the rooms. Once in a while, I would be left in the house alone with Reverend Gruman; he had an office off the dining room and he usually sat there, doing his work, and left me alone.

Occasionally, he would pass me on the stairway when I was dusting the banister, or vacuuming, and say, "Janet, hello. How are you?" and give me a hug. I had seen him with others, and I knew he was an outgoing, affectionate person by nature. I remember always feeling flattered that he hugged me, yet somehow uncomfortable. The hug was too tight, too phony, and it lasted way too long. He never did this in front of his wife, although she was often in the house in another room. Yet I accepted it as his way, because there was the whole thing of him being a minister, which I respected. I also felt a certain camaraderie with him inasmuch as I did volunteer work at my church. In my college town, ministers were not just ministers; they were often social activists, as well. They were working for a better world; a world where all people, including women and minorities, were treated fairly and justly.

Boy, was I naive.

One day, Reverend Gruman passed me on the stairs, and gave me a hug. His hand slid over my breast at one point. It seemed somewhat deliberate yet I couldn't accept that. I determined that it must have been accidental. I told myself that he was "open" and that I was "closed" and that I should be more "open" to affection, yes I should. I told myself, well, so what if his hand slipped on my breast; we are all human, this is my body and I am supposed to be proud of my body. I remember telling myself that. I remember telling myself that because I felt, at this time, socially awkward, inept, and afraid of involvement with men. I had been raised in a rather stiff home and I felt (now that I was at college and living away from home) that I should loosen up a little bit.

Something was happening to me, but I didn't know what. I was trying to be something I wasn't, to accept behavior I didn't like or respect. Trying to feign comfort with a situation I wasn't comfortable in. I think it was probably very obvious to the Reverend that I was young, impressionable, and somewhat intimidated by his outgoing presence. I think my faith in his goodness was being abused by him. One day Mrs. G went out to shop. I was left in the house alone with him. He was working in his office. He came out and saw me on the stairs, vacuuming. He came up behind me, and put his hands on my shoulders. Then he hugged me and slid one of his hands right up my shirt and fondled my breasts. "Oh," he commented. "They're not as big as I thought they were."

"They're big enough for me," I replied miraculously from a state of shock, standing there, letting him do it, terrified and confused inside, asking myself what it was I was supposed to be doing right then.

I wasn't pushing him away because I was taught to respect elders—especially clergy. I was never taught to stand up for myself against authority, even abusive authority. In fact, at that very moment, I couldn't accept that I was being abused, even though I was.

Afterwards, he went on about his business, eventually going back into his office. I finished my work in a fog, terrified he'd come up behind me again and put his hands down my pants this time, or grab my buttocks, or something unsavory. It was a horrible hour and a half. I was single-minded, fearful of being touched again, horrified at what had happened and wondering if I'd let it happen. I remember, at one point, even questioning if it wasn't my fault because I hadn't worn a bra underneath my sweatshirt.

The next week, I didn't go. I called Mrs. G and told her I couldn't make it because of tests. Truth was, I was ashamed. I didn't know how to face her, or face him. I felt humiliated, like I'd humiliated myself, too, because I didn't ask him to stop.

I told some of my close girlfriends, and only then did I begin to recognize it as abuse. One good thing about the women's movement of the seventies was that women became much closer to each other, and began to talk about their feelings. The support and comfort I got from one of my friends in particular was helpful. Although we have each moved on with our lives since then, we still keep in touch and, occasionally, see each other. With friends' help, I was able to clarify my feelings about what Rev. Gruman had done.

The week after, I went back. By that time, I'd resolved in my mind that I was going to clean once more and then quit. I had also decided that I wouldn't say a word to Mrs. G. She was too nice, I told myself.

I went to clean, and the whole time I was cleaning I was thinking only about quitting. I had decided I was going to tell both of them I was quitting but give them each different reasons.

While I was cleaning that day, I recall a young lady coming in to speak with the Reverend in his study. She was kind of on the buxom side, and I kept thinking, I'll bet he's feeling her up too. I'll bet he feels up all the women who come to speak with him about their problems. I remember feeling outrage at that, because it occurred to me just how terrible an abuse of his position this was. The young woman did not stay in there long, and then she left. The whole thing disgusted me even though nothing may have happened. Just knowing the kind of man he was made it hard to take. After I finished cleaning, I looked for an opportunity to see Rev. Gruman. I knocked on his office door and went in. I told him I was quitting. I told him it was because of what he'd done two weeks earlier. He looked at me, and said nothing.

I remember his response angering me, and I recall speaking with fire in my voice. "You had no right to do that!" I said to him. "And I am surprised at your behavior because of your profession. You have a lovely wife, too. How can you do that to her!" At that point he got somewhat upset. He said he was sorry, but that he had a problem. That he just couldn't help it. I remember being angry at that, and I told him that he should get help if he had a problem.

Then, I told him that I wasn't going to tell his wife the truth of why I was leaving because I respected her too much. And then I left. I never did tell his wife.

The incident happened 17 years ago, yet I feel as if it was yesterday and my emotions still get stirred up. Yes, I talked to my women friends about it at the time, but I guess I need to say more or I wouldn't be writing this. I guess I need to tell everybody.

I believe that this incident left me slightly fearful of men. I love having sex with men, and have a daughter from one of my previous relationships. But I have never married, and seem to have difficulty when a man genuinely cares for me and not just my body. Somewhere along the line, I became convinced that it is my body that men want, and that I am a "fallen woman." (At one point about seven years ago I even became a go-go dancer, where I performed in a bar half-naked for tips.) I can't believe some of the put-downs I've dished out to myself over the years.

When Anita Hill spoke, I felt a rush of emotional release I'd never felt before. I was struck by her intelligence, her calm, her candidness. I felt as if she were speaking for me, speaking about something that I never felt I had a right to speak about except in the company of women. Even then, I could tell others what happened but I couldn't discuss the effect that it had on me, or the negative impact it may have caused in my relationships with men, and with my own body, over the years. There has been enough shame, suppression and self-denial.

Janet Sassi *is 37, a fiction and free-lance writer, and the author of a novel,* Chance Discovery.

Cath Jackson

Throughout My Career
Judith H. Semas

Union Bank (1966-1974)

In 1971 the small independent bank of which I was an officer was merged into Union Bank, a much larger statewide organization. I worked in personnel. After a few months I was offered an opportunity in the Northern California Corporate Personnel Division in San Francisco. I accepted; however, at that time, my burning desire was to get into Union Bank's loan officer training program, as I knew that was a faster track for promotions. I was twenty-eight years old and married at the time.

During those early months I met an executive officer of the bank; in subsequent years, this man became president of the bank. At the time I met him he was one of three executive vice presidents. He demonstrated what I thought was sincere interest in my career goals, and so I told him of my wish to enter the Bank's loan training program.

Soon after that he called me from Los Angeles and said he'd be coming up to San Francisco. He said he wanted to take me to dinner to discuss how he could help me get into the training program. He said dinner was the only time he'd have to talk with me about this, as the rest of his schedule was packed. I suggested we meet at the restaurant, but he insisted on picking me up from the bank and driving me to the restaurant. He said that would give us more time to talk about my career.

My husband had serious reservations about this man's intentions; however, I naively felt that he really wanted to mentor me and would simply be advising me about—perhaps even recommending me for—that training program.

While driving to the restaurant, he reached over and tried to pull me toward him. I resisted and moved back to the passenger side of the car, next to the door. Once seated at the restaurant, he began groping me under the table and trying to get me to sit on his lap. He'd had a bit to drink, and it was clear that I needed to get out of there. I excused myself on the pretext of a trip to the ladies' room, called my husband to come get me, and waited out front for my husband to arrive. I never went back to the restaurant, nor did I ever speak to that man again.

A month or so later while in Los Angeles meeting with other female bank officers, I mentioned the incident. The women I spoke with said that this man was notorious for such behavior, but that no one would speak out for fear of losing her job. Besides, everyone knew this man was slated to become president of the bank and we all feared criticizing someone of such power in our organization.

The following year I was being given my performance evaluation by my vice president. He stated that my performance was outstanding, by far the best of anyone in his unit. He said he'd like to give me a substantial raise; however, if he did, that would put my salary ahead of the men in his unit, and they would never stand for it, even though my performance was exceptional and theirs only mediocre. So, instead, he raised my salary the minimum amount, and gave them the bigger increases.

One evening on the long ride down the elevator, my arms were filled with files to work on at home. The man next to me glanced over and, seeking to compliment me, said, "Boy, I sure wish my secretary would take home work like that," to which I replied, "I sure wish mine would, too."

City of Santa Clara (1974-1980)

A peer department head would frequently slip up behind me as I stood talking with someone else in the hall and quickly unzip, then rezip, my dress, as he strolled by. This same individual would also attempt to discuss pornographic movies, give explicit details of his sexual activities, ask about my sex life, etc.— all despite my attempts to change the subject and my protests that I did not wish to discuss such things, feeling that they were inappropriate subjects for office conversation. He would also occasionally run his finger quickly down my spine, from top to bottom, as he walked by me from behind, on occasions when I'd be vulnerable to such an approach because I was facing away from him and talking with someone, or involved in doing something on which my attention was focused. Sometimes he would approach me from behind and, placing his hands on my shoulders, begin to massage them. Even though I'd pull away, he'd just laugh and say I was being silly.

The city manager would frequently complain that I should be home raising children instead of working. He felt that way about all women and was quite vocal about it. Despite those comments, however, he did promote me and increase my responsibilities.

Hope Rehabilitation Services (1981-1990)

Although I subsequently became president of this organization, my initial position was director of development. My male supervisor, the executive director, would routinely tell dirty jokes to me and other women, despite our statements that we found them offensive and wanted him to stop.

A peer department head routinely called me "Honey," despite my attempts to get him to treat me with professional respect. He also would attempt to touch me inappropriately. He behaved in similar ways with female office workers working two and three levels below him. Because I refused to submit to his advances, this department head conducted a vendetta against me, seeking to undermine my image and reputation whenever he could. He wrote abusive memos, criticized my performance in group meetings, tried to characterize as irrelevant any comments or suggestions I would make, and sought to present as unimportant my accomplishments and those of my unit. When the executive director was told of these behaviors, he just laughed them off and refused to take action. He told me that it was my problem. According to him, I just didn't know how to get along with this man.

As it happened, though, one year later I became the man's boss. The morning he learned of my promotion to president, his secretary smiled and said to him, "See, it pays to be *nice* to people." Unfortunately, he made no changes in his behavior. It wasn't long before new complaints came to my attention. They were acted upon immediately and resulted in his dismissal.

There are many, many more such instances, but these give examples of the type of discrimination and harassment I've experienced in my career.

Judith H. Semas is 49, a bank vice president, a business consultant, a free-lance writer and motivational speaker.

HAIR

Eva Shaderowfsky

I was sixteen and hairy. I had a sparse, but dark mustache and some light fuzz on my cheeks and chin.

"We have to do something about this," my mother said.

She had very little body hair. I probably took after my father, I thought, with a feeling of shame. I even had a few hairs around each nipple and a line of hair from my belly button to my pubic bush.

She bought me a kind of sandpaper glove, the kind she used for her legs.

"Use this, in a gentle circular motion. I use it on my legs."

I knew that. I had seen her sitting for hours, the swishing sound of the fine sandpaper set my teeth on edge.

"Why don't you use a razor?" I asked.

"Because the hair grows back stronger and coarser."

I certainly wasn't going to shave my face. So, I tried the sandpaper glove and got a slight, pink rash.

"Well, you can bleach it. Then it won't show." She bought me a bottle of hydrogen peroxide. But it seemed to bleach the skin, too, so that I had the circumoral pallor of heart disease.

"How about that depilatory cream?" I asked as we stood in front of my bedroom window, my chin in her hand, as she angled my face to one side, then the other.

"No, people get bad reactions to that. It's a very harsh chemical. I think we should let Dr. Morris take a look."

My father was a general practitioner and Dr. Morris was a dermatologist. All the doctors I knew were German-speaking, from Austria, Germany or Czechoslovakia—which is where we were from. We lived in Kew Gardens, New York. Some people called it Jew Gardens, because of the many, many refugees there. They had also settled in Forest Hills, not in the restricted part, and in Jackson Heights. A few of them had known each other in Europe, but most of them had met here, after escaping the Holocaust in the early 40s. They had developed a tight, closed referral system. So, naturally, if I had to see a dermatologist, I'd see Dr. Morris.

At least once a year, my parents gave a big party for their doctor friends. Year after year, as I was growing up, I met the same doctors and their wives. When I was younger, the men pinched my cheeks, pulled me up onto their rough, suit laps, squeezed me in the circle of their big arms, rubbed their sandpaper faces against mine and said how sweet, cute, pretty, clever, I was. They no longer did that once I was a teenager, of course. They confined themselves to a wet kiss on the cheek and a heavy arm around my shoulders with which they would often crush me to their vested chests. Or, more delicately, they would proffer a tobacco-smelling cheek for me to kiss. I knew Dr. Morris from these parties.

Dr. Morris was squat and hefty, with thinning red hair, a bristly, dun-colored mustache and loud adenoidal breathing. A rather distant, unsmiling man, his greetings to me were rather formal, a nod which suggested a military click of the heels and a small bow from the waist, accompanied by a pat on the upper arm. He even addressed me with the formal *Sie*, not the familiar *Du* that most of the others used with children.

My father, I must add, thought my mother's concern with my facial hair was exaggerated. He rarely contradicted her, but I do remember one night at the dinner table he said, "Women who have hair on their faces are very sensuous, very sexy," and then he smiled at me sweetly, lovingly, as he always did. That did it. My mother called Dr. Morris the very next day.

A couple of days later, I took the subway directly from school to Roosevelt Avenue in Jackson Heights and walked four blocks to his office. He lived in a brick house, one of many in a row of identical ones, on a tree-lined street. His office was downstairs in the front. Almost all the doctors worked where they lived. My family had two large, adjoining apartments, one of which was largely devoted to my father's practice. It had a treatment room, an office and even an x-ray room. The foyer and living room were used as a waiting area during his office hours. I hated office hours, because I had to keep quiet during them and couldn't use the wonderful, huge radio in the living room.

When I arrived at Dr. Morris' house, I fully expected to catch a glimpse of Mrs. Morris or their ugly, redheaded, toad-like son who was still in grade school.

Dr. Morris let me in without a word or a smile. He showed me to a very small waiting area in a hall just outside the living room, which was long and narrow and seemed to have doilies on every flat surface. The waiting area was dark, though there was a lamp on the little table next to the straight-backed chair on which I sat. There was a pile of worn *Time* magazines on the table. With a magazine in my lap, I waited nervously, listening to the sound of his footsteps in the next room. I heard a long roll of paper being pulled and torn. I knew he was covering his treatment table with fresh paper just as my father's nurse did between patients. He didn't seem to have a nurse. No other sounds in the house, not from the kitchen or from upstairs. Mrs. Morris and son didn't seem to be home.

His sudden appearance at a door just to one side of my chair startled me. With a grunt, he motioned me into his treatment room. A large room, facing the street, it had an examining table right in the middle of it. I stood there, just inside the door, now knowing what I was expected to do.

"Your mother said that you want to get rid of the facial hair," he said with a heavy German accent, as he brushed his thick mustache up from his lip with two quick motions of his index finger. I had seen him do this before.

"Yes," I said. "I tried bleach and that sandpaper glove. They didn't work too well. Mommy won't let me use a depilatory."

"She's right," he said, "you could get a reaction to that. I've seen it many times." He walked towards me. "Let's take a look," he said as he switched on the huge, bright light over the table. "Sit down, please," he said, motioning to the table.

I sat on the edge as he pulled my chin up towards the light.

"Well, you have a choice of electrolysis which is somewhat painful or hot wax. I think we should try the wax," he said as he moved my face to one side and then the other.

"I have a friend whose mother does electrolysis," I said to him, wondering what *hot* wax was.

"Get undressed over here, down to your underpants."

Undressed? Had my mother told him about the hair around my nipples?

"You can put your clothes on this chair," he said and turned his back to me. "Cover yourself with the sheet on the table."

There was a neatly folded sheet at the foot of the table. But where was the screen where I could take off my clothes? There was none. His back was still turned and he seemed to be doing something at a large, glass-fronted wooden cabinet against the wall. As fast as I could, I took off my clothes, except for my underpants, and piled them in a heap on the chair, sure that he would think me a messy teenager. A few fast, barefoot steps to the table, and I climbed up on it and tried to cover myself with the sheet as quickly as I could. Suddenly, I felt very large. The sheet wouldn't cover me. It didn't fit.

I settled it over my breasts and under my armpits just as he turned around. His left hand was covered with a thick, green glove and in it he held the handle of a little, gray metal pot. I saw that he had a wooden tongue depressor in his right hand. The smell I had barely noticed before grew stronger. What's the tongue depressor for, I wondered. He tipped the pot towards me so that I could see some green, waxy stuff in it. Wax! Of course. The tongue depressor was to put it on my face. I understood.

"Now, he said, as he leaned over me from the top of my head, "hold still. This will feel a little warm. It won't burn you."

He put some of the warm stickiness on my upper lip and on my cheeks and chin. It wasn't too bad. It didn't hurt.

As he stepped back, he said, "Now, we wait for it to cool."

I could feel it tightening as it cooled.

"You have good skin," he said. "Very smooth. Good quality."

I looked down and could see an edge of the wax on my cheek.

"Don't move," he said. "Just lie there." Then I felt a prodding pressure from his fingers on my lip, under my nose. Before I knew what was happening, and without another word from him, he ripped the wax off my upper lip.

"Ow!" I said, more in surprise than pain.

"That didn't really hurt," he said, as he scratched at the edge of the hardened wax on one side of my face. "You're a big girl. Just be still." And he ripped the piece off my cheek. "See? Look!" he said and held the wax up in front of my face.

I could see that there was fuzz stuck into it. It looked something like mossy green velvet.

"Good. Now, one more," he said, scratching at my jaw on the other side. He ripped that piece away.

My face was tingling, slightly numb, and both hot and cold. I wanted to cover it, to touch it. I lay there without moving a muscle. Then a burning started, like the worst blush, like a sunburn.

"That didn't hurt," he said as he picked away at a few stray pieces of wax.

"I guess not really," I said, rigid to my toes.

His shoes made squishy, squeaking sounds as he walked back to the wall cabinet. I looked. He was standing over a hotplate with the little pot on it. I now understood that the wax had to be melted. That's how he did it, on that hotplate. That's what he was doing as I got undressed. That I understood the procedure finally gave me a feeling of relief. I sighed and tried to relax.

As I lay there, it dawned on me that we weren't done, that he was heating up more wax. The smell grew stronger, something like hot crayons. Before I could consider the thought, he came back to the table, this time standing by the side of it, looking down at me.

"Your mother said you had other hair to remove."

"She did?" I said, tensing.

"Yes. Around your breasts."

"Well, there's only a little..."

"The wax is getting cool. I have to do it now. Pull the sheet down to your waist."

I did. My face was burning up as I pushed the sheet away from my breasts.

He applied the hot wax around one nipple, slowly, carefully. The touch of the applicator was very gentle, around and around it went. Then the other nipple, slowly. The wax piled up as I watched the applicator moving from pot to my nipple. Like a dream. I felt I was running naked in the high school halls, everyone staring at me. I heard his breath through his nose, coarse and uneven.

He stepped away and put the pot on a little table next to me. I hadn't seen it before. He stood six feet away, arms folded, facing me, his glasses reflecting blank white from the examination light. The sound of his breathing continued, ragged and loud.

"You have very beautiful breasts."

"Thank you," I said, having been taught to answer politely, especially to my elders.

"So high and firm," he said, still standing in the same place, in exactly the same position.

"You're so young. You will be a beautiful woman."

I tried to smile. My face burned, tingling with little sharp points first in one place, then another.

He walked towards me, took the glove off his left hand and laid the right one on my breast, cupping it. His hand was hot. I felt I had armor over a part of my breast where the wax had completely cooled. Very gently, he picked at the edge of the hardened wax, his breathing the only sound in the room.

"Your skin is so smooth," he murmured and then ripped the wax away.

I gasped at the pull and the cold air hardened my nipple. Time seemed endless now. One more side to go, I thought.

Again, his breathing loud, he cupped my other breast in his meaty hand. Maybe, I thought, he's warming up the wax a little. His hand rested on my left breast. I couldn't look at his face. As he leaned over me, hand on my breast, I could feel his breath on the skin of my chest, on my neck. He removed his hand and picked with those large, sausage fingers at the edge of the hard wax. A ripping sound. I gasped again and bit my lip. He put the wax on the table nearby.

"There," he said very quietly, "all done." He stepped away. I sat up, pulling the sheet under my arms again. "No, lie down. I have to apply some ice." His shoes scrunched over the linoleum floor as he walked to the other side of the room. Next to the cabinet was a small, white refrigerator. He opened it and I heard ice cracking. His white-coated back was to me as he did something. When he turned around he had some sort of white bundle in his hand.

"Put this on your face," he said, handing it to me. It was an ice pack, about six inches square. I took it from him, trying not to touch his fingers. I put it on my upper lip.

"Put it on your cheeks, too," he said, his back turned to me again. I watched as he cleaned up, first over by the cabinet, then at the little table next to me. I heard him open a floor-pedalled garbage can and guessed he threw my wax-imbedded hair into it.

My face was numb and hot at the same time, as I moved the ice pack from cheek to cheek. My nipples were sore.

"Now on your breasts, too. Don't forget," he said, as he turned to me once more.

I took the ice pack and moved it under the sheet to one breast.

"You can do it that way, if you like. But you don't have to be embarrassed. I've known you since you were a little girl."

Once more, he stood near me, by the side of the table, arms folded.

I moved the pack to the other breast, under the sheet.

He sighed, then said, "Well, you can get dressed now. I'll give you some cream to put on later." He walked out of the room and closed the door.

I threw back the sheet and ran to the chair, putting my clothes on as fast as I could. Just as I pulled the sweater over my head, I heard him come back in.

"If you have any tingling, use this three times a day for the next couple of days."

With my long hair still inside the neck of the sweater, I took the little silver tube he handed me.

"I've made another appointment for six weeks from now," he said, handing me an appointment card. "You can show yourself out," he said and turned away.

"Thank you, Dr. Morris," I said as he closed the door to the examination room.

My mother was home from work already and cooking dinner.

"Let me look at you," she said and put on her glasses. "It's a little red, but you look better without that hair."

"Mommy, it was strange. Dr. Morris put his hand on my breasts."

She took off her glasses and turned back to the stove.

"He did that, too?" she said, stirring the soup. "That's good. It takes quite a while to grow back. Some of it doesn't grow back at all, you know. You won't have to go for another month or so."

"Six weeks, he said."

"Six weeks, then. Set the table, will you?"

I took off my jacket, hung it in the closet, and started to set the table. I tried to think whether I should say it again, maybe in more detail. But then, she called everyone for dinner and I didn't have a chance.

During dinner I said to my father, "Daddy, I went to see Dr. Morris today."

"Oh? And how is he?"

"He did that waxing."

My grandfather flared at me with disapproval. This was not dinner table talk.

"It looks much better," my mother said as she passed my father the salad.

"The redness will be gone by tomorrow."

My mother came to my room later that night, as she always did to spend a few minutes with me. I was in bed.

"Your face isn't as red now."

"Yes, I know. But...Dr. Morris put his hand on my breasts while he was doing that."

"What do you think? Of course, he put his hand on your breasts. He waxed them, too, didn't he?"

"Yes, but..."

"It's nothing." She frowned at me.

"He was breathing like a pig and he put his hand on my breasts, not just..."

"Nothing happened. *Nothing at all.*"

She gave me a goodnight kiss.

"Sleep well," she said and left the room.

Eva Shaderowfsky is 53, lives in Rockland County in New York, and works as a photographer and writer.

Some women have a story of rape, some a story of incest, but every woman has a story of sexual harassment.

—Janine Canan

Men who sexually harass women are, I suspect, the same men who clamor loudest for war.

—Amber Coverdale Sumrall

We collaborate in our own victimization by remaining silent during this war that men are waging against us....If we, women, are to survive, we must learn to fight back, and that means fighting back by any means necessary.

—Tara Baxter

If we took the level of violence against women seriously, the revolution would start tomorrow.

—Gillian Greensite

A woman's denial is the ultimate enemy.

—Susan Carol

We'd rather see a woman spend her money on a .357 magnum than contribute to her therapist's BMW payments for the next 30 years.

—Nikki Craft

I'd like to have an annual national holiday called Anita Hill Day. It would be a working holiday.

—Ursula K. Le Guin

BUT WAS HE SMILING?

Carole Sheffield

In the spring of 1973, I was interviewed and hired by the Department of Political Science at William Paterson College. The position was advertised at the assistant professor level but I was told that one had to have the doctorate in hand at the signing of the contract and because I didn't, I had to be hired as an instructor. Even though I received my doctorate in August of the same year the college refused to upgrade my contract.

When I arrived at WPC, I soon learned that a doctorate was not, in fact, required for appointment to rank as assistant professor. I accepted, unhappily, that I had been duped and applied for promotion to assistant professor through the regular promotion process. That year, five men and no women were recommended for promotion from instructor to assistant professor; three of the five men did not have Ph.D.'s. I filed a sex-discrimination grievance. Later, in spite of having won an arbitrator's decision upholding my claim of sex discrimination, no promotion was forthcoming. I had been advised by the Union to continue applying for promotion even though other litigation was continuing on the refusal of the college to honor the arbitrator's award. Being untenured, young (26 years old), and having won the first sex-discrimination case against the state of New Jersey under the AFT contract, I became somewhat of a cause celebre on our campus.

During the second attempt to apply for promotion, I was propositioned by the chair of the All-College Promotion Committee, identified here as Prof. Everyman. He asked me, in front of witnesses, to step into his office for sex. While he didn't directly state that a reward for doing so would result in a promotion, the conversation prior to his "invitation" was about my application for promotion. This incident took place two weeks prior to the promotion committee deliberations. In addition to his proposition, Prof. Everyman objected to my concern for promotion. He said that I should be grateful for the job and shouldn't worry about the rank. Before and after this particular encounter, this full professor, with whom I was barely acquainted, insisted on calling me "honey," "sweetie," and "dear."

Not surprisingly, I was again turned down for promotion. Prof. Everyman publicly referred to me as "a bridesmaid, never a bride." I also filed a grievance for this denial of promotion. The arbitration hearing is one I will never forget. I worked as hard as I could to describe my experience of what is now commonly referred to as "sexual harassment." It seemed straightforward enough to me: Prof. Everyman was chair of the promotion committee, he asked me for sex, I said no; two weeks later I was turned down for promotion. Prof. Everyman called me honey, sweetie, dear. How objective and professional could he be in reviewing my application for promotion? Moreover, he commented, in gender-specific language, that he considered me a loser.

When the hearing was over and everyone was packing their briefcases, the Union official and the President's representative began informally discussing another case. The President's rep—a black male—objected to the characterization of the case as "ugly." I suggested that if he thought about it from the perspective of the victim, he might understand. At that moment, after having spent the last hour listening to me explain the dynamics of sexist language, he leaned forward, looked directly at me and very deliberately said, "Sweetheart, I could write a book." At that moment, the feeling of erasure was nearly overwhelming and overshadowed Prof. Everyman's offense.

I lost the grievance. The key issue in the mind of the white, male arbitrator was whether Prof. Everyman was smiling when he asked me into his office for sex. Of course he was smiling! Why wouldn't he be? The fact that I was embarrassed and humiliated by his public proposition meant nothing to the arbitrator. He later wrote in his opinion that the fact that he was smiling was an indication that he meant no harm.

When I began my academic career, I didn't know very much about feminism. In my first year at the college, the department asked me to develop a course on "Women and Politics." The political activism around issues of women's liberation was just beginning to impact on the academy and while I had no graduate preparation for this, I was curious enough to agree to undertake such a course. Serendipity played a hand here as the request paralleled the experience of sexual harassment described above. As I read, voraciously, the early feminist writers of this "second wave of feminism"—Betty Friedan, Kate Millet, Shulamith Firestone, Germaine Greer, Juliet Mitchell, Mary Daly, Andrea Dworkin—I began the journey, unique but at the same time nearly identical to the journey of thousands of sisters before (and after) me. I realized, in a sudden and explosive way, that the personal is political. As I read and studied, my life played out before me, as if on a movie screen, and I watched it with a new and profound understanding. The things that had happened to me, the past encounters with male supremacy, experiences with sexual harassment, sexual terrorism, were *not* accidental, random, or individual; they were political, systemic. I was not alone.

The course, "Women and Politics," never materialized; instead, "Politics and Sex" was created. The course has been offered two and sometimes three times every semester since 1975. It has become the focal point of my emergence as a radical feminist and as an activist for women's rights on my campus. I even wrote the sexual harassment policy for the college and spent seven years getting it accepted by the administration. Through teaching the course, I have introduced feminism to hundreds of women and men and encouraged them to think differently and to ask new questions. Teaching about the oppression of women sustains and nourishes me. I am challenged every time I walk through the classroom door.

The irony *is* amusing. I am the one who smiles now.

Dr. Carole Sheffield, 43, is a professor of Political Science and Women's Studies at William Paterson College and is currently the Director of the Women's Studies Program.

A RESPECTED MEMBER OF FORCE

Deirdre Silverman

I grew up in a small town on Long Island, New York, not far from the ocean. One night in June, when I was 15, I went to the beach with a male friend. We parked at the beach club that was closed for the night, climbed over the fence and walked onto a completely deserted stretch of beach. We swam and built sand castles for a while, and when we began to get cold, walked back to the car. My friend climbed the fence first, but jumped back down on my side. There was a police car parked next to his.

We didn't know what to do. The clubs on this beach were all closed at night, so we had been trespassing and could have been arrested, but we couldn't think of how to get away. There probably wasn't another person within several miles, and we were beginning to shiver. Since everything on the road was closed, no cars were driving by, so hitchhiking wasn't an option. Reluctantly, we climbed the fence.

The policeman told me to get into my friend's car. He took him into the police car and talked to him for a few minutes. Then he asked me to come over "for a chat." As my friend passed me, he shrugged as if to say, it isn't that bad.

The cop started asking me questions about what we had done on the beach. He refused to believe that nothing sexual had happened. He repeatedly asked if I had taken off my bathing suit. His questions became more and more specific and, as they were very embarrassing to me, I sat looking out the window. Suddenly he said, "Oh Jesus, look at this!" I turned to look and saw that he had opened his pants, and pulled out his erect penis. I had never seen a penis before, and I was terrified. "How am I going to go home like this?" he asked. "You have to help me out. We can't leave till we take care of this." When I asked what he meant, he indicated with his hands that he wanted me to jerk him off.

I panicked. I started to cry and told him a totally untrue story about how my father had a heart condition and I was applying for college scholarships and if he found out anything about this it would kill him. I just kept crying and talking. I think he found my story so depressing that he lost his erection, because after a while he sighed, zipped up and let me go.

I didn't tell anyone about this for nine years. When my friend asked why I had been in the police car so long, and why I was crying, I said nothing, mostly out of embarrassment. I felt filthy. I never spoke to the boy again. The cop was a "respected member of the force," and I didn't think anyone would have believed me. I knew that my parents' main concern would have been why I was on the beach at night with a boy, and whether anyone would find out about it. In the two years before I left for college, I saw the cop several times, and he always gave me a big smile. I was always afraid of him. Once, when my family and I went to a diner in his town, he turned on his stool at the counter and winked at me. My parents didn't notice, but I was unable to eat. When I first started talking about this incident, I was teaching women's studies courses. I found that a number of my students had also been harassed by policemen, or had witnessed their mothers in such incidents. Using their power to intimidate and punish, police had demanded sexual favors in exchange for tearing up traffic tickets, not reporting violations, or lenient treatment. No one had filed a complaint. Who would have believed us?

Deirdre Silverman is 46 years old, mother of two, and works as Development Director of HOMES, Inc., a human services agency in Ithaca, New York.

236

ACCIDENTS
Sky

How often do I read "She asked for it," or "She was upset because he rejected her"? Many times these words are said in response to a woman claiming sexual harassment. Why is it so difficult to believe a woman's truth? Her words are simple; "He harassed me."

I work a part-time retail sales job in a large and busy building supply store. Most but not all of the managers are men, as is the sales personnel. The harassment I experienced came from my immediate supervisor, a married man in his early thirties.

The first incident left me feeling puzzled. Surely it was an accident, I thought. He really didn't mean to "bump" into me. Selling retail is stressful and physically demanding work, particularly at holiday time. When the rush is on, clerks and bosses alike work fast to throw freight, look for invisible prices on hard-to-reach boxes and lunge for the ever-ringing phone, all the while striving to keep the hoards of customers happy. When Alex approached me as he did many times during the day I did not move back. He reached past me for a tool on the counter and "accidentally" squashed his penis against me and rubbed. I was startled.

The second time this happened I sensed it was intentional. The third incident turned my job into two jobs, keeping track of my work duties, and keeping track of Alex.

Alex was a "good boss" in all other areas of work. He and I related only as the job required. We exchanged conversation about duties, rarely if at all did we talk of anything beyond store business. He never once indicated an interest in me personally. I remember being relieved when I first began working with him because he stuck strictly to business. I escaped the usual curious inquiries into my life and crude sexual jokes offered as "just kidding around" by many male bosses. This is why his first offense was confusing to me. His sexual gestures were prurient and self-gratifying. He never followed the incidents with a change in communication. Nothing was said or implied either verbally or non-verbally to indicate my job depended on my pretending his behavior was unintentional, but we both knew it was. Finding proof of these happenings would be difficult. It would be my word against his. And whom would I report this to? Another male boss, of course.

I began looking for a pattern of when or where he would choose to turn a benign movement into an offensive gesture. He often selected busy times at the front counter when many customers were present. The counter was elbow high; all that showed of the sales clerk was the top of an apron and a "May I help you?" smile. Alex's gestures happened so fast I wouldn't see them coming.

I began carrying a clipboard, and kept an eye on Alex as we worked the counter. One day he made a familiar reach for the credit printer but continued to push his body into my space. I flipped up the edge of the clipboard. "Ouch!" Now it was my turn. The days went by and he repeatedly found the sharp edge of the board instead of me.

Another man became involved, whether by accident or plan I don't know. I found myself at the counter flanked on one side by Chuck and on the other by Alex. Usually I would move to the side to avoid close contact with Alex. Chuck's near presence hindered my movement, giving Alex his chance. Alert to Alex's movements I stepped back just as he thrust his pelvis forward. Chuck also made a move toward me, or more precisely, to the place where a split second before I had stood. Ah yes, it was sweet. The two men met pelvis to pelvis. The ensuing scramble to assure each other and the world they were "regular" guys was a delight to watch.

Shortly after the Chuck and Alex incident, Alex transferred to an out-of-state store and I to another department. I am certain Alex took his practices to his next job. I never mentioned it to anyone. The clipboard and collision with Chuck seemed to do the trick.

Sky is a lesbian, a half-century old, and fills the open spaces in her life with writing.

SEXUAL HARASSMENT: NOW YOU SEE IT, NOW YOU DON'T

Mark E. Smith

Sexual Harassment is magical in its ability to appear to some while being totally invisible to others. When surveys show that some women claim to have been subjected to sexual harassment, while other women insist that they have never been sexually harassed, the tendency is to think that the women themselves must be in some way responsible for their experiences. Those who claim never to have been harassed are thought perhaps to dress more conservatively or comport themselves more carefully. Those who claim to have been harassed are suspected of dressing or behaving in a less reserved manner or of simply being supersensitive to innocuous or even flattering remarks.

As a woman who has been living as if I were a man for the past ten years, I have found myself in the privileged position of being backstage with the magicians, able to see exactly how the startling and otherwise inexplicable appearances and disappearances of sexual harassment are accomplished. But knowing for a fact that sexual harassment, even while hidden from the audience in the lining of a top hat, is as real as the wriggling rabbit that will eventually be produced with a flourish, I feel compelled to give away the secrets of a very profitable and powerful trade.

During the confirmation hearings on the nomination of Justice Clarence Thomas to the Supreme Court, a great deal of tension surfaced in this country. Feminists were deeply concerned that if Professor Anita Hill were not found to be credible and Thomas were confirmed, women with lesser credentials would never be believed. And if the charges were true and he successfully denied them, would it be possible for women with sexual harassment cases to gain a fair hearing before him in the future?

Men felt the strain of the hearings as they began to worry about their own past behavior and future careers. Could a simple flirtation deny them a promotion or cost them a job? Would they have to be even more careful than before in deciding which women in the workplace could be safely harassed and which ones could not?

The tension was almost palpable immediately after Thomas's confirmation, when I attended an evening meeting of a rather conservative community organization. Though this group has no declared political position, I think of it as conservative because I have often heard members say things such as, "This country has the best health-care system in the world" or "Anybody who really wants a job can get one." They seem to be living in the past, unaware of our high unemployment rate or the fact that we are one of the few developed countries in the world that lacks a national health plan. They don't seem to recognize that many Americans have no access to health care, while others, dependent upon Medicare, Medicaid, the military, or limited health plans, receive minimal, substandard care. But they are such nice people, one wouldn't want to hurt them by bringing them into contact with reality.

At the meeting following the hearings, several of the men made jokes about sexual harassment at every opportunity. Their jokes sounded like the sort people make in wartime when a bomb or a bullet comes close but misses, and the survivors need to relieve the tension and dissipate their fears.

The meeting proceeded in accordance with its agenda. The previous meeting's minutes were approved and one item after another thoughtfully dealt with. Discussions took place. And then a woman rose to make a routine announcement.

Dedicated to her home, her husband, and her children, this woman is also a hardworking volunteer, exhausting herself in efforts to promote the organization she belongs to. She has the air of a professional caregiver, which she was for most of her life. She is modest, self-effacing, and supportive of everyone she comes into contact with, young or old, male or female. Her enthusiasm is almost childlike, as is her high-pitched manner of speaking. Although one of the most capable members of the group in every activity, she is always careful to say things like, "Well, of course we women don't do all of the things that the men do," despite the fact that not only she but also most of the other women do them quite well indeed, sometimes better than the men. But most importantly, she is the type of woman who never does anything publicly that could be construed as either competing with men or as inviting or provoking sexual harassment. She is a sweet, humble, caring, and proper traditional woman.

But this evening, this evening after the Thomas confirmation, she had the misfortune to be the first woman in the group to rise to make an announcement. And no sooner had the first words passed her lips than one man rudely interrupted her with a loud and obviously sexist comment. It wasn't anything obscene or vulgar, and it wasn't a sexual invitation—not there in front of so many people. It was just a means by which he could demonstrate to the other men that he, and they, were okay now—the bomb, or bullet, of the Thomas confirmations had missed them. Everything could go on as it had before. He wasn't an impolite man or the sort who you would think of sexually harassing women. He simply needed to break the tension, so he said, "Aha! I see we have an attractive woman making an announcement!"

The other men knew what he was doing and were grateful. One quipped, "Isn't that a sexist remark?" The woman's husband, who was running the meeting, chimed in, "Would it be okay if I said it? After all, she's my wife." All the men laughed happily. Sexual harassment was alive and well—they could do it. They hadn't lost their privilege.

But what of the fact that they were being rude? What of the fact that they were out of order? And what of their victim, whose only sin was an attempt to make a routine announcement, such as she usually did at meetings?

Ah, here's where the magic comes in. The woman who was interrupted stopped speaking immediately. As the men made their comments, she tilted her head toward the ceiling, and her eyes focused off into the distance. She was determined to ignore what was going on, and she did so very well. This is something that can only be done with years of practice, and then only by the most proficient actresses. You could almost hear her saying to herself, "This is not happening. I am not here. This cannot happen to me. I do not hear anything, and as soon as they stop, I will continue my announcement as if nothing had ever happened." And she did! Furthermore, had you questioned her after the meeting, I'm quite sure she would have sworn that she hadn't heard anything, and that if anything at all had been said, she was sure that they really didn't mean it. This was a woman who could easily tell a pollster that she had never been subjected to sexual harassment in her life, nor had she ever witnessed any. Now you see it, now you don't.

And what about me, invisible to everyone but able to see what goes on from both the magicians' and the audiences' points of view? Am I a traitor to my sex because men no longer subject me to sexual harassment, since they do not realize I am female? I am well aware that merely acting and dressing like a female attracts sexual harassment, so I don't choose to do so. Nonetheless, I consider myself a feminist.

I don't wear female clothes, but I'm not a transvestite. A transvestite is one who wears clothing of the opposite sex for sexual or sensuous reasons, and the clothing I wear is neither sexual nor sensuous. I'm not a lesbian, because although I like women, I have no desire for them sexually. And I'm not a transsexual because, although I live as if I were a male, I have never had, nor would I want, a sex change. I'm just old and tired, and I find that my life is much easier now. Nobody talks down to me, men don't make comments when I walk down the street, and I don't have to be constantly afraid of assaults. Or be constantly subjected to sexual harassment. And now I'm free to see it, without having to pretend it isn't there. After all, it's only a power play, a ploy to reinforce and perpetuate the patriarchy. It isn't actually harassment in many cases; sometimes it is merely rude and insensitive behavior. And it often isn't sexual at all, just a way to differentiate patriarchal gender roles and act them out.

True, I felt guilty when I got home from the meeting. Why hadn't I pointed out that a woman was trying to speak and that the men were being rude? Perhaps because I could see that I would not have had any support. When a woman's survival depends upon denying that reality exists, to point it out is not a friendly or even a sisterly act.

In browsing through the library, I once came across a reference to a doctoral thesis entitled "Schizophrenia: An Essential to Survival in Our Society." I don't know if the thesis itself addressed the question of sexual harassment, as I never read it. But the title, I feel, is an accurate description of women's status in the battle of the sexes in the United States today. For those who cannot readily divorce themselves from reality, the fight against sexual harassment can be extremely frustrating and can often cost them their careers. For those women who can effectively engage in denial, the problem simply doesn't exist. They swear to it.

Mark E. Smith *is an older woman, working on his autobiography. A feminist, he continues to prefer inclusive pronouns.*

Marian Henley

HOSTING HARASSMENT

Ellen Snortland

I live in L.A. and have worked on and off in the entertainment industry for years in many capacities: actor, writer, producer, director, mostly in television.

I responded to a friend's urging that I entertain some couples in the "business" because of what it could possibly "do" for my career. It made sense to me although it felt odd to have an ulterior motive rather than just liking the people you eat and socialize with. My husband and I are not very good at the game.

We both enjoy the company of the women of the couples we entertained that evening. We noticed, however, that the men dominated the conversation with their "deals," their golf anecdotes, and gossip about other men in the Hollywood community. My husband commented to me privately, "Male dogs, relieving themselves on each other." They never appeared to be curious about anything or anyone else. My husband and I bustled around, trying to hear whatever the women might be able to slip in occasionally, without being impolite to the incredibly rude male guests.

I went into the kitchen to attend to the poultry and one of the husbands followed me there. He had had too much to drink and grunted, "I'd forgotten how attractive you are." He grunted again and went back to the dining room.

Dinner was delicious. Before I served dessert, Mr. "Grunt" needed to use the "little boys' room" so I showed him the way. I opened the bathroom door for him and he groped for me. I couldn't believe it. I pushed him away. I was so humiliated that no words would come to mind...the verbal freeze response.

I went back to the table and continued the evening. I couldn't look at Mr. or Mrs. Grunt. The evening was blessedly over and I told my husband what had happened. At the time, we agreed that Mr. Grunt was indeed a beast but it would be best not to do or say anything, primarily because of Mrs. Grunt and her four little ones. We're still in a quandary about what we should have done. Or what

I could have done in the moment.

It's been almost vogue since Anita Hill went through her ordeal to shake the head, click the tongue and say, "The men just don't 'get it.'" There are people who apologize for the behavior and misogynist, socially damaging product of film and television "guys," with basically, "They don't get it." Interestingly, the men I know and love who respect me "get" it.

I'm sorry, if our leaders in government, corporations and entertainment are that dense, is it a comfort to have our country run by the "thick ones," that can't "get" the effect they have on us via their lack of understanding of gender relations?

I dare say, the only "getting" that's really involved is in "getting away" with it. We all let these guys "get away" with everything from squeezes to murder. That's why they have more to gain by women not having any real power. We are caught in a vicious circle of being cowed by the power plays that these fellas know how to use.

They "get it," alright. Let's say that the gentleman had seen me as a powerful person, a person of consequence. Do you suppose he would have given me a squeeze? No way, in his cups or not. He would have perceived that it wouldn't have been good for his career. At some level, reptilian perhaps, he assessed that I would not scream, hit or tattle. He was right. He also was aware that he had any number of defenses that he could use. It would come down to his word against mine. He knew that I cared about his wife. He knew he could damage my career and I couldn't touch his. He also figured that I would never be in the position to buy a project from him or hurt his standing with his peers, which include no women.

Is this guy a genius? No, I'd say his IQ is a little higher than his body temperature but not much. But he understands power as it exists right now in Hollywood. It's not much different from Washington, D.C., either. Those in power will do whatever they can to stay in power. Those who are perceived as above or potentially more powerful are kowtowed to. The others are used, abused, or ignored.

I'm afraid many Hollywood guys want to cast women only in their "proper" roles of wives, secretaries and mistresses. I certainly didn't feel respected as a peer or even regarded as a human being.

Perhaps some would say I was making too much out of nothing. If he'd been the only guy to pay me unwanted attention or insult me in my life, perhaps. Did he touch me because of his great regard for me, my talents, my abilities? Did he even like me? No. The accumulation of slights, digs, teasing, uninvited touches, comments and condescension I have experienced just because I'm a woman has eroded my self-esteem far too long. I'm now resisting with all my might and doing whatever I can to encourage other women to do the same. My dignity used to be nothing. Now, it's everything.

We haven't seen the Grunts socially since the pawing because we can't bear to be around him. What would I do now, after Anita? (A.A.) I still don't know. It looks like I lose with any option I come up with. Or his wife, sons and daughters hurt. I don't want him in my home or to show him to the bathroom again, that's for sure. I fantasize about one solution. These occurrences boil down to my word against his, right? Well, if that's true and he could get away with denying he touched me, I could get away with denying I kneed him in the groin, couldn't I? I could say my knee slipped...why, he just doubled over from too much wine...He's just saying that...He's got some kind of paranoid fantasy going that hostesses like to connect between his legs....Perhaps a well-placed knee could deter him from mauling another woman. They say pain is a great teacher. It's a wonderful fantasy.

Ellen Snortland is a Norwegian-American who loves her husband and dogs and is working on a book from which her piece is an excerpt.

INTRO

Judith Sornberger

If I were to see the syllabus now for the Introduction to Poetry course I took as a nineteen-year-old in 1971, I would be instantly alerted to danger. Not a single woman poet. Not a one. And if a Dr. Michael McBride sauntered into the room now and assessed his students one by one from behind the lectern with an ironic half-smile and one eyebrow arched, I would recognize the type. But it was my first semester in college, and I had worked at a dull job as a hospital accounting clerk for a year to earn the money to be there. I was prepared to love everything about being in that classroom. Prepared to find Dr. McBride as brilliant and debonair as he found himself. Prepared to enter this new world on its terms, whatever those might be.

Although this wasn't a writing course, I shared with most of the other students an ambition to be a writer. I had always assumed I would be one, as I had always known I would one day be a mother. My great-aunt had been a war correspondent during World War II and had been married to a bestselling author. Although I never met the illustrious pair, I had grown up on stories of my aunt's heroic acts and glamorous life after the war. Winning a prize in a poetry contest sponsored by *Highlights* in third grade cinched it: I was destined to become a poet. I'm certain that most of us in the class entertained such romantic notions of our futures.

Dr. McBride seemed to believe his mission was to show us the error of our ways, to demonstrate our ignorance and poor taste in poetry. Most of us had a pretty limited background. In high school I had written under the spell of Emily Dickinson's poetry, trying to mimic her terse wit, her syntactical revelations, and especially her odd capitalizations. Among ourselves we had probably written hundreds of haiku in the tradition of Matsuo Basho. Before we knew better we revealed our tastes. Among Dickinson, Basho, Walt Whitman, William Carlos Williams, and of course, e.e. cummings, we admitted during the first week to liking Leonard Cohen and (yes, I'll admit it) Rod McKuen. Dr. McBride raised his bushy silver eyebrows, gave a few tugs to his salt-and-pepper beard, and shook his head as if he were about to give the bad news to a terminal patient. "You have entered this course not a day too soon," he said. We knew that Dr. McBride's strategy would be to trap us in our ignorance and shame us into seeing things his way.

Dr. McBride was handsome in the craggy, robust way of the middle-aged Sean Connery, and perhaps the two men could be said to share a similar view of women. I wonder if at nineteen I would have been less appalled than I was a few years ago to hear Connery tell Barbara Walters in a television interview that he thought that some circumstances made it entirely appropriate to knock a woman around. Dr. McBride's methods of educating women on their proper place were slightly more subtle.

He told us many times that women were "cows," that they had only one proper function: "the propagation of the species." Although we read no women poets, women were the subjects of many of the poems we read and offered numerous opportunities for such pronouncements. If the women were good, they were usually dead. Otherwise, they were objects of desire—temptresses or withholders of pleasure—to be either pursued and conquered or castigated. At first we women students timidly countered these charges. He answered us by pointing at the challenger and saying just wait, despite what we said now, in five years we would all be pregnant, fulfilling our "natural function." We tried various arguments from time to time, but always knew who held the control and that that control confirmed the validity of his remarks. He had established himself as master, and we were so afraid to reveal our ignorance that we found ourselves most often giggling nervously in response to his pronouncements, as though they were meant in fun, rather than to engage us in a rhetorical battle he had already proved we were not up to.

One day I couldn't stand it, though. I answered his "just wait" by saying I would "never, ever as long as I live bear a child." My cheeks burned and there were tears in my voice as I said it, maybe out of shame or regret for what I was relinquishing in that moment. Yet, I had no idea what I was agreeing to by saying this: that bearing children made women brutes, creatures incapable of thought or artistic creation. No idea I had agreed to accept or reject my role as a woman on his terms. "Well, we'll see now, won't we, Mrs. Cleasby?" I had married at eighteen—a fact that had shocked my counter-culture friends—hence, the "Mrs." and perhaps also my especial need to proclaim my independence from such expectations.

Once, noticing that our professor wore a wedding band, another young woman said, "What about your wife? Why would you marry her if you thought she was a cow?" None of us saw the problem in that question—that the idea of women as cows fit in very nicely with our culture's traditions surrounding a woman's role in marriage. He didn't point it out either. Instead he answered, "Mine is a marriage of convenience." We had read enough literature to have an idea what that meant. None of us asked "Whose convenience?" because that was a given.

So well had we been raised to admire mastery in a man that we women students accepted, for the most part, Dr. McBride's tyranny as his right. The first time I read Sylvia Plath's "Daddy" several years later, I would cringe at the line: "Every woman adores a Fascist." I would resent that generalization as I had resented Dr. McBride's. But the fact that we admired him, despite or because of his scorn, bore out that line. Something in our upbringing had trained us not only to bear that scorn, but also to believe it was our due, to welcome it even as we were incensed by it. With an instinct toward survival of the herd, we were careful (although we never discussed it among ourselves) not to leave one woman alone as the focus of his scorn. He had ways, however, to divide us.

The Socratic method was naturally fitted to Dr. McBride's proclivities. One day he asked a question requiring an analytical answer about one of the poems and called on one of the male students, as he was wont to do. "Uh, sorry, I don't quite get this poem," the student responded. "And what about you, Mr. Olson? Do you 'get' this poem?" Dr. McBride snarled. "I guess I'm not quite sure what you want to know," my friend Rex answered. "I see," said Dr. McBride, raising his eyebrows and looking from one of us to the next, choosing his next victim. "What about you, Mrs. Cleasby? Have you an answer to this very simple question?" I had, and I answered in what must have been a satisfactory manner because Dr. McBride turned back to Rex and asked, "Would you have thought of that, Mr. Olson?" Rex smiled sheepishly and said, "I guess not." Dr. McBride grinned back with contempt. "No, I guess not." He paused and looked at me, as though with a shifting sense of my worth. "That's because Mrs. Cleasby is a rare thing—a woman who thinks."

I want to say that I challenged him, that I claimed to be no different from any other woman in that class. That I at least squirmed in my chair or thought of saying something. I want to say that I did not walk out of that classroom as starry-eyed as a high school freshman who has just been invited by the captain of the football team to the Homecoming Dance. I think I felt some embarrassment after the initial flood of pleasure, but it was a secondary emotion. Maybe it was the way Miss America feels after the first wave of elation at having been chosen has subsided and part of her attention now picks up the stifled sobs of the other contestants, carefully disguised as tears of joy and congratulation.

In the next three years I would divorce my husband, marry a second husband, and give birth to twin sons. I had planned to return to college after the baby was born, but then there were two and they had been premature and were sick all the time, and I had no help. I was lonely and kept the t.v. on for the company of adult voices. One day as I fed the boys applesauce in their highchairs, I was watching "Good Morning, America." The collected poems of Yeats had just been published, and a representative of the publishing company was on the program reading aloud from the poems. I sat there dipping the spoon in the jar of food, and moving it from open mouth to open mouth, dipping and feeding, dipping and feeding, letting the tears drop into my lap as I listened. I don't remember which poems were read. What made me weep was my overwhelming sense of loss. In that moment I believed every word Dr. McBride had said about women. I had borne out his prediction. I had violated my sworn promise in his classroom never to bear a child. I had proved that my biological destiny was even stronger than his momentary belief in me as an exception. I certainly wasn't that, was I, I thought, washing the sticky fruit from the boys' faces and fingers.

From time to time when there was money for tuition and a sitter, I would take a course. Then, when the boys were six and I was a divorced mother, I quit my full-time job and went back to college. I received my B.A. the next May, the first person in my family to do so. I went on for a Master's degree and a Ph.D., one right after the other, as though if I ever retreated from that world again, it would vanish along with my dreams. I kept writing my poems, and eventually began publishing them.

Last year I started my first tenure-track position as an assistant professor of English and women's studies at a small state university in rural Pennsylvania. Since I had a teaching background in women's studies as well as creative writing, my institution hoped I would help start a Women's Studies program. It was a huge job, I knew, but I was charged up about it.

I had been looking forward not only to the job itself—the teaching, colleagues and better salary—but also to receiving the respect that I believed I would be entitled to thereby. I had worked many jobs to support my sons and put myself through school, and each one had been low-paid, low-status work. Graduate school and my subsequent temporary teaching jobs had offered their share of indignities as well, but now I would be a professional in my field.

A week before my first fall classes began I strolled around the campus for the first time, familiarizing myself with the buildings I would teach in and taking care of little details: getting a parking sticker, keys, and i.d. card. As I passed the tennis courts that a maintenance crew was resurfacing, the group of men stopped working and started hollering at me. "Hey, baby!" "Whoooooeee, baby!" "Hey, come here." "Hey I'm talking to you!" "Baby, come back." I was raised in a city with plenty of construction sites, and like most women, I had developed a screening mechanism for such "attention." And like most women, that didn't prevent my stomach from knotting up from the combination of fear and indignation that welled up in me each time. I wanted to scream, "Fuck you, you assholes!" and almost turned to do so. Then I thought of the dignity I had hoped for in my new job. No, I wouldn't scream. I thought of going over and demanding their names, but I could see how that might lead to more problems. What I did was what our mothers told us to do under such circumstances: pretend you don't hear and keep walking.

The next semester I taught our campus's first-ever Introduction to Women's Studies course to a small, brave coterie of women students. One day I was at the blackboard recording the students' responses to my question, "What are the myths surrounding rape?" As I turned to call on the next student, I noticed that the square of plywood propping open the window said "EAT PUSSY" in large letters. Underneath, like the signature under a work of art, was the name of one of the fraternities on campus.

I stopped in the middle of my response to a student, strode to the back of the room, and wrenched the sign from the window. The students jumped as the window banged closed. "How does this make you feel?" I asked, holding up the sign. The students stared into their notebooks, as if they might find some answer there.

"Gross," answered Michelle, normally an eloquent woman.

"Like a thing," Becky added. She was an effervescent redhead who could always come up with some kind of solution to each of the many dilemmas we faced in the course. Now she looked at me as though I might be able to explain away the sign. But there are signs all over. Signs that scream "Cow!" Signs that direct: "This way to your natural function." I could not wave a magic wand and make them disappear.

Tammy, who had told us at the beginning of the term that she thought women had "too many rights," raised her hand. She still insisted on raising her hand, even though for weeks now all the other students simply took turns speaking. "That word," she said, shuddering. "It makes me feel ashamed. Like I'm disgusting." There were tears in her voice. The students nodded. Michelle patted her arm.

"It makes me afraid," admitted Joanne, a determined thirty-year-old woman who often mentioned her young daughter. "And I resent it like Hell."

Mary, a soft-spoken black woman, raised her eyes from the doodling she was doing in a corner of a page and looked me in the eye. "It makes me feel like I don't belong here."

Of course, that was the sign's message. And it had been Dr. McBride's. And it was the message of all the syllabi every semester without a single woman's name on them. And it was the message of the work crew as I passed them. "This is ours." "You are ours." "You don't belong here." But we were talking now. And in the background of our talk, I kept hearing the echo of the window slamming shut as I yanked out the sign. I heard over and over the great boom of my own anger. And I vowed never again to be silent.

Judith Sornberger teaches English and Women's Studies at Mansfield University in Pennsylvania; her book Open Heart *will be published by Calyx Books.*

Jan Graveline Eliot

YOU WANT TO DO WHAT TO MY WHAT?

Laurel Speer

Have I ever been sexually harassed? (And I always put the accent on "harASSed," which is where it's frequently focused!) Hell, yes, I've been sexually harassed. What woman who's been alive more than five minutes on this earth hasn't? Here's the latest: During a period of six months (in the last year), I encountered a young man on a bicycle on my afternoon walk route. I would be walking on the sidewalk east and he'd be proceeding down the street west, so at some point we passed each other. He looked to be in his late teens or early 20s. I am not a young woman, but my body looks young because I do daily workouts at my health club. I am wearing a visor and dark glasses, shorts and a shirt, so he can't see my face, which would tell him I'm well past any consideration he might give to me as a sex object. In fact, I'm 51 years old. What in the world would a kid be doing ogling a 51-year-old woman!

He not only ogled me, he made a very obscene gesture *every single time* he passed me on that damn bike. He stuck out his tongue and vibrated it up and down as soon as he saw me in exactly the same way the truck driver did to Thelma and Louise in the film. That gesture says only one thing to the sex object he's addressing with it: I WANT TO SUCK YOUR PUSSY!

What did I do? I did nothing on the six or so occasions that it happened. I looked straight ahead and walked straight ahead, opaque as to my thoughts and reactions behind my sunglasses and visor. But I was more than mad. I was totally outraged. I would've liked to have tossed him off that seat to the street, then stood with my foot on his chest and yelled: "DON'T YOU EVER DO THAT AGAIN TO ANY WOMAN IN THIS WORLD!" Anything less would've deprived me of more dignity than he'd already taken by making the gesture in the first place. So like many women, weighing my options, I kept silent and walked on. Eventually, he didn't show any more. I can only hope, if he worked in one of the offices or hospital complexes along that street, that he was fired for having an attitude problem and that he was ganged up on by the women in his work place.

You can imagine my joy and sense of triumph when Thelma and Louise blew up that obscene truck driver's rig. It was as if they'd spoken for me, too, against my bicyclist. And what about when we saw Thomas confirmed by male senators over Anita Hill's reports of his severe sexual harassment? If there was *any* truth at all in her allegations, he should never have been seated on a court where he'll be passing judgments against the women of this country for generations to come. I felt as if my bicyclist had jumped behind Thomas (and all other males who've ever pinched, rubbed up against, slurred) and said, "Go get em, fella," where the "em" is every woman in these allegedly great United States.

Laurel Speer is a 51-year-old poet, essayist and book reviewer; she edits the journal Remark *and regularly contributes to* Small Press Review.

Throughout my Life

Kathy Stern

When I was twenty-one, I was hired as a waitress, by a young male who was managing a new Pizza Hut restaurant that had opened in my home town. I soon noticed how he gave me and the other attractive waitresses he had hired the most and the best hours for securing tips, while the less attractive waitresses got the least and poorest hours. I also noticed how he scheduled me to open the store alone with him in the mornings, at which time he'd be unusually friendly and helpful. I grew uneasy when one of my co-workers told me that she had slept with our boss, Al, and that another one of the waitresses had done the same. I then figured out what his plans were for me. A co-worker who was going out with the assistant manager told me that Al wanted to go to bed with me. After this, I approached Al and told him that I didn't think it was fair how he distributed the hours. His eyes twitched and his jaw tightened as he stared at me, yet he didn't say a thing. The following week, when I checked my work schedule, I discovered he gave me only four hours of work, as compared to my previous thirty-two. I did not complain. The next week was the same story. I still did not complain. The following week when I arrived to check my schedule, Al was lingering in the kitchen, close to my schedule, watching me read it. My name was still on the schedule, but dashes were drawn through every day, leaving me with zero work hours. When I asked him what was up, he looked me square in the eye, facing me, and snidely said, "You have just been x-ed off the schedule." As I stood there, looking shocked and puzzled, he smugly smiled, adding, "In other words, YOU'RE FIRED!" Today I realize this was sexual harassment on the job. Back then, you just kept your mouth shut because you knew it was a taboo subject and that there was little you could do about it, as men were in power as the bosses and superiors. If you went to a higher-up, who was a male, to talk about it, you knew they'd probably just have an amusing chuckle about it all, or perhaps worse, also begin to focus upon you sexually. I never told my friends, my boyfriend or my parents the real reason why I got fired. Because I was so angry, I did talk to the regional superior. I didn't tell him of how my boss sexually harassed me and others, but I did tell him that Al, who had the key to the restaurant, showed up really late one morning after a night of partying, while I waited outside for him to open the business. I also told this regional manager how unfairly Al scheduled workers. I later found out that the manager canned my boss, so at least, even though I lost my job, I felt some justice was served.

When I waitressed at this restaurant, it also alarmed me that some male customers would come on to me in a sexual way while I worked. Many would leave me extra large tips, and a few would even leave their phone numbers next to their large tips. This irritated me, as I felt as if I were an object, rather than a person, and that they were trying to buy me, much like the way a prostitute gets paid for sexual favors.

When I was twenty-four, I gave birth to my first baby at the Madison general hospital. I was sore from the episiotomy stitches. I had told my doctor before the birth that I didn't want an episiotomy if it could be avoided. My breasts were painful and swollen, engorged from the new milk that had come in. In a private room at the hospital, I sat nude in a sitz bath to heal the wounds on my bottom. I felt very embarrassed, flustered and upset when the obstetrician entered the room, closed the door, and sat on a chair directly facing me. My hospital gown and towel were too far away for me to reach to cover myself from him, and I did not want to get up, exposing my entire body to him. So I just sat there, feeling my privacy totally invaded. He sat there, relaxing, asking me all kinds of questions. I just sort of gave up, realizing from many of my past experiences with men, that this was just the sneaky way they operated and tried to dominate women. I knew full well that these were questions he could have waited to ask me when I was robed, sitting on my hospital bed. Instead, he deliberately chose to ask them while he could view my body, disregarding any respect for me or my personal privacy.

At age thirty, I worked at a Marc's Big Boy restaurant. The company policy specifically requested that female waitresses wear lipstick and eye make-up, to make ourselves more sexually attractive and alluring. Luckily, my superiors were both women, so I didn't have to deal with sexual harassment from a boss at this place. I had to deal with it only from a funny, strange little man who swept the floors and did dishes—and from the majority of male customers, of various colors, who frequented the place daily. I often felt scared opening this place alone at 6:00 a.m., as it was located in a rough neighborhood where two drug-related murders had recently occurred. Men would sometimes be hovering around the restaurant before it opened. Daily, I was sexually harassed by the male customers.

When I was thirty-three, I applied for a part-time lab job while I went to college. A man interviewed me, and I felt uneasy as he looked at me. He hired me immediately. On my first day of work, he offered to buy me lunch. His male friend and co-worker tagged along. I thought it was a company good-will gesture,

256

as we casually, during lunch, discussed politics, current events, the job. My boss later made it clear to me that there was no dress code in his lab, where I worked with him, his male friend and another woman. He also told me that he had hired me, even though I wasn't a chemistry or physics major, because I "had a more lively personality" than the "deadbeat male physics and chemistry students" he had interviewed. I found out my boss was married when his wife appeared at the lab one day. She hovered nervously around him, wearing high heels and a very short dress, as she glanced over at me. She seemed on edge. I felt his wife didn't trust him—and for good reason. When I took my work breaks outside, my boss would follow me out to smoke his cigarette. On one of these breaks, I was with him and his male friend. I started to feel awkward and uncomfortable when the two of them started throwing little innuendoes my way, indicating they were both interested in me sexually. Shortly after this, my boss started to crack some sexual jokes regarding women. Then, a few days later, the three of us again went outside for our break, together with another woman who worked in our lab. I felt nervous again, when my boss started to talk about some of the strip shows he had gone to in northern Wisconsin. He went into explicit, pornographic detail about the breasts of the women in these strip shows—about how some of the breasts were so huge that they sagged, how the women's nipples were shaped differently, how sweat dripped off one woman's nipple. My face turned red and I had to look away. My boss then bragged about how he and some buddies had shoved money up some of these women's "cunts."

A few days after this my boss and I happened to be working alone in the lab together. Once again he cracked a sexual joke, and began to describe women's anatomy to me. I then realized that the jerk was trying to come on to me, hoping he'd be able to set a date with me, to check out my anatomy, to see what I was like without my clothes on, in comparison to other women he had seen. At that moment, I quickly laid down a firm boundary to him as I said, "I never, ever want you to talk that way about women again, when you are around me." The very next day, he bragged how he had just ripped off two school systems for $75.00 apiece, for a five-minute asbestos sample reading. I was irritated, as I knew he was intentionally saying this to bother me because I had rebuffed him sexually. I said to him, "You're bragging about that?"

The next day when I came to work, he told me that he had to "let me go." When I asked him why, he told me I wasn't following the dress code, because I had worn combat boots to work one day. When I reminded him that he told me that there wasn't a dress code in his lab, he changed his line and told me that I wasn't reading the asbestos samples correctly. When I rejected that excuse, reminding him how he hadn't even sent me to the training classes yet, he didn't answer me. I then burst into tears, knowing that the only reason why I was being fired was because I didn't want to sleep with him. I never told a soul the real reason why I had been fired, and what my boss had said to me. I never sought recourse either, because I knew I couldn't prove a thing about being sexually harassed, as the other woman was not present when the two other incidents happened.

Strange men, who I don't even know, seem to feel that they have the right to kiss me on my face, or put their arm around my shoulder and hug me, or put their hands around my waist. Why they feel that I am public property, and that they can do this—touch me as they please—is something I do not understand. I've only had a couple men in my whole life who have asked me if it was okay to touch me; at least I respected these men who showed that much respect towards me. I immediately get turned off to, and annoyed by, men who touch me without asking—no matter who they are!

When I've gone for walks or ridden my bicycle I've received numerous car horn blasts, wolf whistles or sometimes derogatory obscenities thrown my way. I've also had men who were married, or involved with steady women lovers, come on to me sexually behind their woman's backs. These men I find to be the most deplorable of all—the most repulsive—for it shows me how low in character and dishonest they are, to break a woman's faith, trust and love for them. They are the lowest of the low.

My life has been affected by sexual harassment in many ways. It has warped my perceptions of the opposite sex. I view them now to be sneaky, overpowering, shallow, insensitive, incapable of loving, impure, deceptive, disrespectful, spiritually weak and undisciplined, as well as greedy and unrefined. I do not enjoy being compared to other women's photos in a porn mag, movie or advertisement. I feel many men do not know how to establish true intimacy—building up feelings of closeness and trust, getting to know a woman well and sharing their innermost selves, dreams, goals, likes, dislikes, values. Instead, my experiences seem to tell me that most men want the superficial excitement that lasts in bed a short time. To me, sexual harassment is a moral problem.

Kathy Stern is a divorced mother of two daughters with a degree in Psychology; she has worked many blue-collar jobs and is presently caretaking the elderly.

LONG DONG JUSTICE

© 1991 BY ALISON BECHDEL 122

Our gals at MADWIMMIN BOOKS are REELING with POST-THOMAS CONFIRMATION STUPEFACTION!

THE HEARINGS GOT THE MEDIA TO EXPLORE SOME COMPLEX ISSUES AROUND RACE, GENDER, AND THE WHITE MALE POWER STRUCTURE. IN THE LONG RUN, IT WAS A STEP FORWARD FOR WOMEN.

CAUTION: BOOKS

IT COULD BE A WATERSHED IN AMERICAN POLITICS, FORCING THE LEFT TO FINALLY UNITE AGAINST OUR COMMON ENEMIES.

AFTER ALL, THINGS ALWAYS GET WORSE BEFORE THEY GET BETTER.

BULLSHIT! THERE'S NOTHING GOOD ABOUT IT! THE BOYS WON! THEY PIT THEIR BIGGEST ENEMIES, THE BLACK COMMUNITY AND THE FEMINISTS, AGAINST EACH OTHER, THEY GET A BLACK JUSTICE WHO'LL VOTE TO **ABOLISH** CIVIL RIGHTS, THEY GIVE A TACIT NOD OF APPROVAL TO SEXUAL HARASSMENT, **AND** THEY'LL REPEAL ROE V. WADE IN THE BARGAIN! YOU GOTTA ADMIRE THEIR **TECHNIQUE!**

YEAH. IT WAS THE PERFECT SET-UP. THE SENATE DECIDED IT'S BETTER TO LOOK **SEXIST** BY DISCOUNTING HILL THAN **RACIST** BY REJECTING THOMAS, SO WOMEN TOOK THE FALL, AND BLACK WOMEN ARE ON THE BOTTOM OF THE PILE, AS USUAL.

THE REVOLUTION OF LITTLE GIRLS

THE DANCE OF RAGE

TIPS ON TERRORISM

SO WHAT ARE WE GONNA DO ABOUT IT?!

KEEP DOING WHAT WE'VE BEEN DOING. CONFRONT HARASSERS. PICKET. BOYCOTT. DO ANTI-RACISM WORK. FUND WOMEN CANDIDATES...

...GET A SEX CHANGE OPERATION. JOIN THE G.O.P.

LO-IS!

HEY, YOU THOUGHT ABOUT IT FOR A SPLIT SECOND THERE, DIDN'T YOU?

Hitting

Doreen Stock

For a housewife the home *is* the workplace, but the first time it happened was in the car. We were driving on a crowded freeway toward New York City. We must have been married about four years, because our two-year-old daughter was in the car. I remember I was saying, "But your aunt is expecting us for lunch," as he turned toward his cousins' house on Long Island. Filled with fury at the traffic and frustration with the long drive down from Boston, he lifted his right hand off the steering wheel and swatted me as hard as he could on the side of my head with the back of his hand.

Reaction? Stunned. Totally stunned. Then tears. Then silence. How many times does it take for you to feel that it's not your fault?

The second time we were packing to move out of Boston. I think I was overtired ("hysterical" is the term most often used for this state), and running around in a disorganized fashion, sort of like a gerbil. It was night. I don't remember what I said. He grabbed me and threw me away from him into a wall. I stumbled, fell, and hurt my foot so badly I wore sandals all the way cross-country to California. Reaction? It was my fault for being so disorganized. His fury and his action I accepted on some deep level as justified. The third time was several years later. It was in the dining room. I had just gleefully opened the mail: a check for a poetry reading I'd done in San Francisco. I don't remember the dialogue, if there was one. He hit me in the face with our middle child watching from the couch. I think she must have been six or seven. My right eye turned black. I think it was that visual evidence that finally galvanized me—up out of the stunned, crying state and into anger. *Seeing it*, in the mirror. The next day I confronted him. I took off the sunglasses.

"Go ahead," I said. "If you're ever going to hit me again, do it right now." He put down the newspaper (it took a lot to get him to do that). For a moment it looked like he might do it again. Then he explained, "It was the look of triumph in your eyes when you got that check. I just couldn't stand it."

Therapy was out of the question. He didn't believe in it. But I told him that day that if he ever hit me again I'd leave him. This was not a huge threat to him. He was full of power and money. I was just the opposite. An unpublished poet with three children under the age of ten. A full-time housewife.

"Why did she wait so long?" people say of Anita Hill. I have to laugh at their naivete. The ink is just dry on my divorce and the baby is in college.

Twenty-five years is how long it took me to stop feeling inferior. To get my children to a stage where the rage that seethed inside of him couldn't destroy all of us. To stop blaming myself for all of the ways I continually tried to flee from him. To break up a family that from the outside looked ideal.

The year before I left him I visited the Anne Frank House in Amsterdam. It was there that I saw the medals Hitler gave to perfect mothers; there where I experienced the ways I'd been in hiding; and there, staring at that little bookcase that closed the Frank family in, that I first felt a fierce yearning to be free.

Doreen Stock is a 49-year-old Jewish writer; her occupation was housewife.

FIRST EXAM

Emma Strong

My first visit to a gynecologist was when I was in my first year at college, away from home. I needed to get birth control and knew only about the pill. Without knowing about how to find a gynecologist, or that I could go to the student health services on campus, I turned to the yellow pages.

Not only had I never been examined by a gynecologist, I had no idea what to expect in the exam. The doctor, a man, seemed to me to be ancient; with the distance of nearly twenty years, I'd guess that he was in his mid-to-late fifties. He had a nurse who left us alone for the exam. During the exam I said I wanted a prescription for birth control pills. Were his actions that followed related to my request? As a young unmarried woman did I become something of a tramp in his eyes? After completing the medical portion of the exam, the doctor told me, as he fondled my clitoris, that exams shouldn't hurt; rather, they should be enjoyable.

Emma Strong is a 36-year-old teacher and writer living in the Boston area.

If even one woman is spared such a horrific experience or is helped through one, something useful will have been gained from our torturous experiences.

—Maxina Ventura

Women suffer from a case of apartheid far more severe than the blacks in South Africa, because they are almost totally unconscious about the subservient subliminal role they play in society. Not even equal pay, let alone 53% representation of women in congress, business, academia or the bureaucracy. We continually play into the game of sexual harassment, with a kind of unconscious sleepwalking mentality. At least the blacks in South Africa know they are harassed.

—Helen Caldicott

The deadliest lies are the ones in which all of us, black and white, male and female, collude in deceiving ourselves. So for me, the wonder is not the detail of Anita Hill's allegations, nor the fact that she spoke so late, but the fact that she dared to speak at all.

—Rita Williams

Without a doubt, Professor Anita Hill's act of courage in publicly exposing the odious treatment she endured has triggered the most massive outcry and mobilization of women's rage I have witnessed.

—Eleanor Smeal

REACH OUT AND TOUCH SOMEONE

Amber Coverdale Sumrall

My parents have just left for a dinner party. My younger brother is spending the night with a friend. I am alone in the house, a rare occurrence in my twelve years, and am looking forward to a long evening of reading the latest Nancy Drew mystery and talking to my friends on the phone. When the telephone rings I answer it in my parents' bedroom, where I can stretch out on the thick green carpet. It might be Karen or Jeanie.

"Hello."

"Why hello there sweetheart, how does it feel to be all alone in the house?"

"What? Who is this?"

"This is a friend of yours. Someone who would like to be a much better friend if you'll let him." I don't recognize the man's voice, but I know he is a man, not a teenage boy playing a trick on me. He sounds the same age as my father. A chill passes through me as I realize he's waiting for me to say something. I say nothing.

"I know your parents are gone, your brother too. I know you are in the bedroom. I want you to stay right where you are and take off your clothes for me. Show those new breasts off."

I can't believe this is happening to me but I am frightened. I don't think this is a joke. Is he a neighbor? Is he close to the backyard, or just beyond, where the botanical gardens border our property? How does he know I am alone? Did I lock the doors, all five of them? If I run out of the house will he grab me?

"Are you listening? If you don't listen I'm going to hang up and come over there right now. I know where you hide the spare key. You'll never get away."

"OK," I say, stalling for time. "I'll listen."

"Good girl. Now, I want you to take off all your clothes. Then I want you to lie down on your parents' bed and wait for me. I'm going to fuck you, little girl. I've been watching you for a long time. I'm going to fuck you in the mouth too."

"No, you're not," I scream into the receiver and slam it down. I run to each door, check to make sure it's locked, then grab the key from the back mat. I'm shaking and crying. The phone rings again. I let it ring seven, eight, times then pick it up and push the disconnect button before he has a chance to speak. I leave it off the hook until I can think what to do. What I do is dial my neighbor's house and tell my friend Gail to get her father and hurry here. Which they do. I can't remember ever feeling so afraid, so helpless in my own home.

Several nights later I get up in the night to go to the bathroom and find a man's face pressed against the window. I scream and my father runs outside but the man is gone. My father calls the police. I tell them about the phone call, but I don't repeat the word, fuck. They tell me if it happens again to call them right away. It does. The man calls one afternoon when my parents are away shopping but this time I tell him I'm calling the police and that they are monitoring our phone. I hang up before he can say anything and call Gail again.

I think he must have been a neighbor. In fact, now, I'm almost certain he was the neighbor directly across the street. Even though I'd been taught not to resist male authority, something in my twelve-year-old self realized that his words violated me as a human being. All my survival instincts came to the surface. This incident changed the way I carried myself. I began to hold my schoolbooks close to my chest, to hold my hips and body differently when I walked. To hold myself back and in.

It is 1978. I am living in a cabin in the Santa Cruz mountains and dating a musician who plays saxophone in local clubs. When he's not doing gigs in the Bay Area we spend entire days in bed, making love and talking, drinking tequila and getting high on homegrown. I ignore the telephone when it rings. One Saturday afternoon it doesn't stop ringing. I think it might be an emergency and get out of bed, leaving Ken curled up beneath quilts reading the newspaper.

An unfamiliar male voice says, "Hello, Amber. I know your nigger boy is there. I hope he's sticking his black cock up your ass like you deserve, you nigger-loving bitch. I hope his big cock makes you bleed. Cause if he doesn't I will. You fucking whore."

I slam the phone down, shaking, and go to the bathroom until I can breathe normally. I don't tell Ken. I say it was a wrong number. I cannot bear to repeat the words.

One night we come home late from a club where Ken has been playing and the phone starts ringing as soon as I open the door.

"You bitch, I'm watching and waiting for the right time. Your black stud is going to regret ever touching you and you, well, you are never going to go near a black man again after you've had a taste of what I'm going to give you." He laughs and hangs up.

This time I tell Ken, watch his face change from shock to anger. We decide to call the police. I'll do it. As a white woman I have more credibility. Which doesn't amount to much, I discover, as the police refuse to take any action, telling me instead, to buy a police whistle and blow hard into the receiver. "But he threatened both of us," I tell the officer on the phone. "Lady, you don't even know who he is," he says. "I thought it was *your* job to find out," I say, but am realizing that nothing will happen until something already has. Classic Catch 22.

I buy a floodlight for the yard, alert my next-door neighbors. I think about getting a doberman. Wouldn't my seven cats be thrilled with that? I buy a knife and carry it with me. I buy the police whistle. I blow into the phone. I'm furious, stomp around my cabin in a rage of frustration and worry. Ken assures me he can handle this guy. But what if it's more than one? What if he has a gun? Ken tells me his whole life has been about preparation for violence. But how can you live like that? I ask. I am not ready to acknowledge that mine has been like that too.

I am working with the Sanctuary Movement to aid Central American refugees who are fleeing the oppressive U.S.-backed regimes in El Salvador and Guatemala. It is 1983. My phone rings at all hours of the night. The calls could be important. Over and over that summer a man asks how I like fucking and being fucked by scumbags. He says, "I'm gonna get me some Salvador girls, young ones, and fuck them till they bleed." He says, "I'm having a party and I hear you really like to screw niggers, well I've got myself a few here for you." He says, "You lowlife cunt, when I finally get you alone you'll never fuck another wetback again." He says, "Bitch, I know where you live and I'm warning you, I'm gonna make you wish you'd never laid eyes on a Salvadoran."

When my husband started answering the phone at night the calls stopped. We finally bought an answering machine. There is no sexual charge, evidently, in leaving a message, which might be listened to by the police. A permanent record. An identifiable voice. These experiences and several others have left a bitter residue in my psyche. Sexual harassment is an act of cowardice. Men who harass women are insecure bullies, they have no concept of what *personal* power is all about. For them it's all about power *over* someone. They are, I suspect, the same men who clamor loudest for War.

Amber Coverdale Sumrall, of Irish, Dutch and Mohawk ancestry is a writer and editor.

STREET MUSIC

Lynda Tanaka

I was living in San Francisco with a boyfriend. One weekend day, I wanted to go shopping and asked my boyfriend to go with me; he was not interested, so I went alone. I went straight to Union Street, recalling some great shops in this area. I remember walking along the street, peacefully, enjoying the day while window-shopping. There were many people about.

It was the sixties. My attitude about life was extremely optimistic and hopeful—all people were my brothers and sisters, and every human being was essentially good. All living things were an aspect of some great being or energy, God.

While walking along, I was struck by music in the air and turned to see where it was coming from. A long-haired street musician was singing and playing his guitar as he strolled along. I thought to myself, how nice, and smiled. As I continued walking, the musician caught up to me. He politely invited me to have some coffee with him. I declined and said I was shopping for shoes. He continued to follow me, and asked again if I would have coffee with him. I apologetically said no. Perhaps my polite Asian heritage interfered in my ability to say what I really wanted to say: "Get lost!" He persisted, using a slightly different technique, and asked again if I would buy him coffee. I continued saying no without being rude. He then asked to borrow some money to buy drugs in North Beach! I decided it was time to get away from this guy, although I must admit, in those days and times, discussing drugs and openly using them was not so shocking.

The guy became more and more insistent. This peaceful street musician became an obsessive pursuer. My heart began to race; my mouth turned very dry. A fear-flight panic came over me. We were at a street corner when he pulled me towards a parked vehicle. He wanted to show me something. He was pulling my arm, and I was feeling afraid.

The more I pulled away, the more forceful he became. The guy was acting more and more hyper. He forced me across the street and pulled me into this long,

267

dark alley. He started coming at me and pushed me onto the ground. He forcefully raped me (he tried—I was so afraid, I was very tense). While this was going on, again I tried using psychology to talk my way out. I thought "Stay calm, you're a college coed, use your brain—talk to the guy—reason with him." He didn't hear a word I was saying. He threatened to use a knife on me if I didn't cooperate. I was scared and thought I could die there.

I kept trying to focus on God, but wondered why me? Why anyone? Could I have been a target as the result of inaccurate myths about Asian women being petite, sensual and subordinate? I tried rationalizing and confirming that all beings were an aspect of God, and that this was happening for a good reason. I kept thinking about yelling or screaming for help, but I didn't know how—I just remember my mouth being so dry! I remember seeing people strolling by, and hoped they would see me. I could see them, but they didn't see me. When he was finished, he apologized and began playing his guitar while singing to me! I was astonished. For an instant, I thought he was an angel in disguise here to teach me a lesson. It was so confusing to me. I had never felt shame, pain, humiliation, and anger—all at one time.

I felt dirty and wasted. The tears dried on my face. I found my way back home and immediately took a bath. My boyfriend realized something was wrong. I told him. He was very shocked and angry. He wanted to go back out and find the guy. I called the police with intent to file a report. Their attitude was cool. They kept inquiring whether I had behaved in any manner that could have invited such attention. I could not believe their attitude. I was frustrated and angry. How could a human being experience such suffering and violation and not get support, understanding and help? I want to express that despite such an experience I have not allowed it to prevent me from living a fairly happy, healthy and responsible life. It is not easy to share such an ugly experience with the world—but, it happened, and if anyone can gain insight or strength in any way, then it is good to tell it.

Lynda Tanaka is a fourth-generation Japanese-American.

Mother/Daughter Stories

Anna Strulo Taylor and Dena Taylor

_1988_

My mom and I are in the shoe store and I'm buying a pair of silver high heels for my eighth-grade graduation dance. I am walking around the store wearing my shorts, tank top and my first pair of heels.

I never wanted to own a pair of heels before, but I had a fancy dress and it seemed like they were the required shoes. They are so awkwardly uncomfortable when I put them on that they seem like a joke, a dress-up game. I fall every other step when I first wear them. I hardly ever wear shoes, let alone ones that barely touch the ground. I look over at my mom. She seems worried.

I'll buy you those shoes if you want, Anna, but you should know that they make you very vulnerable. You've got to watch where you put your feet and you can't really run in them.

The night of the eighth-grade dance, there are ten girls, all about 14 years old, each wearing a tight dress and all except one, high heels. We are walking home, feeling safe because there are so many of us and the distance is only two blocks. We are spread out in ones and twos, when one of the girls in front yells that she has been shot at. I take off my heels immediately and begin to run as fast as I can. I am the last one, behind everyone else. But soon, I am far ahead of almost all the others. I and one other girl, the one not wearing heels, run and hide in the bushes. The rest end up getting hurt and their dresses ruined by five guys in a jeep who are shooting paint pellets at us.

_1991_

Mom, I've been thinking about those boys that shot at us in the eighth grade, and how awful it was that they knew one of my friends and that they were waiting to get us. They got a thrill out of humiliating and hurting me and my friends.

Yes, Anna, a thrill out of using you as objects in their sadistic game—a game where the rules are learned as children. I remember a time when I was ten years old and the neighborhood boys I played baseball and kickball with every day asked me to come into one of their houses. It was nothing unusual; we hung around together all the time. But this day there was definitely a feeling of "them" and "me." A magazine was produced, and they wanted me to look at a certain page. On it were pictures of women's breasts, about 50 different shapes and sizes. The boys wanted me to point out which picture was like me. I looked, but said nothing. I suddenly felt awkward and somehow on the outside of what had been a group of pals, so I left.

Would you call that sexual harassment?

No, I think not. It was young boys being curious about a girl's body. But the fact that there was such a magazine, and that these boys were learning to objectify women and women's body parts, was laying the ground rules for the game.

Mom, do you remember when I was 13, and that guy was looking up my skirt? I was shopping at the little market on the corner, and wearing a short skirt. As I looked in the candy aisle I heard something drop on the ground behind me; I didn't turn around because I didn't think it was anything. When I *did* turn around I saw that the owner of the store had come out from behind the counter and was on his hands and knees looking up my legs.

And we like to think things are getting better, Anna! When I was five or six, and alone in the house with a man, a "friend of a friend" of my parents, he picked me up in his arms and began to toss me in the air, higher and higher. I was wearing only a bathrobe, nothing underneath. At some point I realized he was looking up my legs as he lifted me above his head. I told him I didn't want to play anymore, and after a while he put me down. When I told my mother, she was furious at the man, forbade him ever to come to the house again.

I have been sexually harassed so many times in my life already, and I'm only seventeen. By the time I was eleven I knew what it was like to stand on the sidewalk and be asked by a man with a luring voice if my name was Peaches and Honey. At the age of twelve I knew what it was like to be followed in and out of shops and to be asked by a forty-year-old man if I wanted to go to bed with him. At fifteen I knew what it was like to walk down the street and be asked if I was wearing a bra by a man in passing.

And last year, when I was visiting in Eugene, I was walking alone on a dark street on a moonless night, wearing black clothes. I was alert and kept watching all around me, when a car approached from behind. I didn't turn around, but I knew, because I could hear their voices, that it was a car full of men. They were asking me questions and wanted me to go with them. I walked with overflowing power and confidence. I looked straight ahead and sped up, yet showed no fear. They followed a couple of feet behind and began to insult me. Their voices turned to yells. When I had a chance, I turned a corner and they could no longer follow me so closely and be in the correct lane. The car sped past me and was gone. I turned around and ran to my cousin's house. It wasn't until I got there that I let myself feel the terror filled with anger.

And just recently, I was approached by a mentor of mine. He is a thirty-year-old man, an experienced actor, and we were in a dance class together. We talked, we danced, and we were friends. Once I remember him jokingly telling me he didn't like to see other men hugging me and I quickly responded that it was out of his control who I hugged. Then one day, in dance class, I was standing up against the wall and the rest of the class was gathered near me sitting on the ground. We were all listening and watching the teacher. The next thing I knew this mentor of mine had come up behind me and was pressed against my body, kissing the top of my head and neck. I immediately moved away. He told me to stop being such an "American" (he is Latino), that if I knew myself, I would see how much I wanted his body. I told him to stop being such a sleaze, and walked off. The next class meeting he told me that all the women's studies classes I was taking were giving me an attitude. That all I really wanted was his body. Again I walked away. Though I don't remember the exact words he told me, I will never forget the sudden pressure of his body and how he fell from mentor to someone I never wanted to see again. I was humiliated he would do this to me, especially while I was standing up in front of all these people. I knew this gesture of his was not a hug, was not a joke, and was not even a shoulder rub. This was an invasion of my space; this was him sexually coming on to me in front of an entire class. And then telling me that I did not understand myself, and that if I did I would desire his body.

I can't believe the arrogance and stupidity of some men who think we're just dying to go to bed with them. When I was in my late twenties I met a man in the insurance business who worked near where I did, and we had lunch together a few times. One day he asked if I wanted to come to his place for dinner; he'd invite a few of his friends too. Sure, I said. I drove to his secluded house in the mountains. He was the only one there, and the lighting was very dim. I felt uneasy, and wondered if I should leave right then.

"Where are your friends?"

"They're coming."

And they did. All men. Seven of them. I decided to just be cool, but to stay very aware of what was going on. We had some cheese and crackers and a drink and made small talk. I asked where the bathroom was so I could have a look at the layout of the house. When I came back to the group, my host's erect penis was sticking out of his pants. When the guys saw that I noticed it, they laughed.

"Come and touch it," he said.

I looked around at the faces of the group. Only one looked uncomfortable. I picked up my jacket and said I wanted to go, and headed for the front door.

"Oh, stay, stay, we just want to have fun!" they called after me. I walked quickly to my car, and saw it was blocked in. I was on a deserted mountain road, far from anything. I decided to go back in, where the men stood grinning. I looked right in the eyes of the one who seemed uncomfortable earlier.

"My car is blocked in."

He looked down. I kept my eyes on him. He looked at me again, and muttered to someone to move the car. I walked out again, followed by a guy who gave me a very nasty look as he got in his car and backed it away from mine. I didn't start shaking until I was well down the road and close to town. I was very frightened. And I blamed myself. I felt that I was really dumb to have gone to his house. And what had I done to make him think I would want to participate in some kind of sex night with him and his friends?

It wasn't until years later that I was angry: Angry at the men who treat women this way, who once were teenagers who shot girls with pellet guns, who once were boys who had access to pornographic magazines.

Anna Strulo Taylor is 17 years old, attending college as a theater major. **Dena Taylor** is 50, an Irish/Jewish mix, and makes her living with books.

Deja Vu

Ellen Treen

For a few days the media fretted about the national trauma suffered during the Anita Hill hearings. They projected long-lasting effects on the workplace, saw it so changed, that many men would be unnerved, rendered unable to function. What I saw was a rehash, a duplication of a small-town trial that happened ten years earlier, one where I was the mother sitting behind her daughter as she testified to her abusive treatment by her employer. In silent outrage I also listened as her character, actions, testimony, witnesses and judgment were questioned, examined, ridiculed and discredited. The tactics were the same ones used to undermine Anita Hill. In both instances, when grown men asked a woman to repeat over and over the details of her sexual abuse, I was reminded of children begging for yet another telling of a favorite story.

While the camera focused on Anita Hill I was conscious of the mother behind her, knowing what she was feeling, breathing for her. And wondering: how long did she know? Was she aware of the harassment as it was happening or did she learn of it only when it was about to become public knowledge? Of course, I knew my daughter brought charges of sexual harassment but, until the trial was imminent, she did not tell me the extent or the seriousness of it. More shocking than the revelations, was her tearful question: "You despise me, don't you?"

Despise her? No. I was outraged at what I heard, pained for her pain, and sorry that she had not confided in me. Long after the verdict was in, that question disturbed me. I couldn't understand how she might think I despised her—not until I went back forty years to my first job in Hartford, Connecticut, and looked at it honestly. The term "sexual harassment" had not yet been born, but certainly it was conceived out of the unending pawing, leering, touching, and pinching I and women like me endured. "Brush it off," we were told, a remedy about as effective as a mouse brushing off a cat.

It began the first day. Putting a cozy arm around my shoulders, my boss, a stooped man with a gravy-stained tie, led me down long aisles through lines of desks, pausing frequently to introduce me to one of "the girls" sitting behind them. With each introduction he gave me a fresh squeeze, and, if possible, the other "girl" too. By the time he deposited me at a desk of my own, I felt more like I was joining a harem than the accounting department of an insurance company. With the help of the surrounding women I soon learned to file and post, total and balance, all by rote. None of us knew what we were doing or why; for that information we had to turn to the men who patrolled the aisles, lounged on our desks, assigning tasks and collecting work. Their answer to any question was a pat or a pinch and a "Don't worry your pretty little head," or, "Why don't you just let me take care of it?" We left it at that.

What my co-workers did know was which men needed to be avoided and how. By the end of the first week I learned to avoid elevators, stay out of hallways, carry a file folder like a shield, let a dropped pencil lie, and the proper use of my wheeled chair to slide out from under advancing hands. One fatherly type was particularly adept at reaching across the desk and snagging the button on my blouse, even pulling it off. Once, in my rush to avoid him I fell off my chair, causing an embarrassing commotion I never lived down. Despite all our tricks we were sometimes caught: I still cringe, feel that hot flash of shame, remembering hands on my neck, sliding down to snap my bra strap, lower to feel for a girdle, and lower yet to fondle my garters, snap them. Any attempt to extricate attracted attention and made the situation worse. The most business-like encounter ended in the same degrading groping.

Possibly some people in that office thought it was fun and games; I did not, and I didn't know anyone who did. Most of us were young, newly married or engaged, many putting a husband through school as was I. We were not interested in middle-aged men, who seemed far removed from our world and we found their behavior disgusting and intrusive. At best we giggled and shuddered, at worst we cried and comforted one another, flocking together to plan a new strategy and describe the latest passes. Every day I was more tense and uneasy. I dreaded having to walk across that huge room for any reason, knowing that snickers and stares followed every step. I felt on parade, and never knew what the laughter was about. Were my seams crooked? A crucial button unbuttoned? Did my slip show? A bloody spot on the back of my skirt?

Crude, sexual jokes about the female employees were constantly circulated by the men, with the expectation women would appreciate them also. I resented that expectation, but not to laugh was to be seen as a humorless person, someone who couldn't take it. When we took our complaints to the one older woman in charge of the office staff, she shrugged, and told us it was a hazard of working, like a run in your nylons or ink on your favorite blouse. Reminding us we probably wouldn't be there long, she added, "disgusting male behavior" was part of the working conditions women had to accept. I accepted it, believing it was as much the way things were as snow in December. I also believed my real place was home in the suburbs raising children, a place I would inhabit as soon as my husband was financially fit enough to provide it.

Still, hoping for something better, I left the insurance company to become a department secretary at the university where my husband was a student. There, the hierarchy was strict, the protocol formal and the harassment worse. The department head, a full professor, with spiky white hair and a soft drawl, expressed his love for the ladies and showed it with long-armed hugs that extended to my breasts, knees, buttocks, wherever his fingers could probe. More than once I played the cartoon secretary, keeping a piece of furniture between us while I took dictation. Running from his touch, and the smell of his whiskey breath, I was denounced as a cold northerner, unlike the warm southern women he missed, the real women. It was the first, but not the last time I heard a man expound on the virtues of "real women" at the expense of the human female in front of him. At the time I felt confused and inadequate, anything but real.

Frequently, the professor traveled, leaving the associate in charge, a short militaristic man who threw red-faced tantrums. On better days he treated me to playful slaps on the fanny, and made sexual jokes about his wife, intimating she was frigid. I was embarrassed by his revelations and appalled when he wanted to broaden the discussion to include my sex life.

Finally I made it to the suburbs and in the twenty years I lived there, never once considered a job. The disappointments of a bad marriage seemed better to me than the degradations of the workplace. What I saw as a failure in the working world made me sure I could never take care of myself, let alone four children.

After the divorce I looked for jobs where I worked in isolation or with other women; presently I work for a woman in a job where I am valued, for my self as well as my work. When I consider those earlier jobs, I wonder which was worse, being groped or having my work trivialized. Without the drudgery of thousands of women, the insurance business would have floundered, but I saw my work as inconsequential. In fact, I had no idea whether I performed well at my job or badly; my goal was to get through the day unbruised.

Until lately I have been able to relegate those experiences to the past, a different time, different mores. If I did think about it, I blamed myself for being naive, stupid, trusting; I should have been stronger, smarter, handled it better. But listening to younger women, to my daughter, to Anita Hill, I hear the same thoughts.

The combination of harassment and trivialization is lethal, one important reason why women are underpaid, undervalued and underpromoted. And I know it damages self-esteem. I hated what happened to me, and hated myself because of it. I could not admit the past, thinking my daughter would despise me, exactly as she thought I would despise her. Forty years does not make what happened to me any different than what happened to my daughter, except it was not so bad. The media believe that the Anita Hill controversy will make a difference, that it roused the country to make drastic changes in the working world. Maybe. To me it feels more like deja vu.

Ellen Treen is a writer and a knitter, works in a yarn shop and lives in Santa Cruz, California, in a house full of women.

Christine Roche

THE FIRST DAY OF THE REST OF MY LIFE

Sherrie Tucker

My first real job—that is, a job where my employer was not a friend of my parents, but at a shop where there was an ad to answer and an interview to survive—was at a small Hallmark card and gift store in southern California. I was a cashier. I rang up greeting cards and sometimes made a big sale: a music box, or figurine, or a jigsaw puzzle, or one of those wooden plaques with a picture of a sunset or rainbow or small, fuzzy animal, and "Have a Nice Day" or some equally benign epigram plastered across the bottom.

Even at nineteen I knew the merchandise was a gross-out. But I was still proud to have that job.

My employer was a crude, angry, rotund man named Marshall Frank, who probably never said "Have a Nice Day" to anyone. He huffed and bellowed at his young female employees all day long. Because he was my first boss, and because he so resembled the stereotypical boss figure from TV and the comic strips—hot-headed, egotistical, babyish—I didn't think to question his behavior, not to mention his myriad rules and policies. One of Mr. Frank's edicts was that we must wear skirts. Slacks of any kind were "inappropriate in retail." I did not imagine fighting this rule, although there was a young woman named Pam, who had more work experience than the rest of us, who often broke the code. We were amazed that she was not fired. Pam never had to work evenings, but the rest of us often did.

The sunset and rainbow plaques literally covered the walls at Marshall's Hallmark, from eye-level to the ceiling. They were unbelievably ugly—photographed and touched-up pastoral scenes with trite sayings, shellacked to small slabs of wood—but Mr. Frank insisted that the reason they didn't sell was because they needed to be rotated and dusted on a regular basis. The best time to tend to the plaques was in the evening, when the store was quiet. Evenings at Marshall's Hallmark were so quiet, in fact, I often wondered why he stayed open. Only two people would be working: Mr. Frank and one of his skirted young retailers.

With Mr. Frank holding the ladder below, I climbed to the ceiling in my wrap-around skirt. I dusted "Have a Nice Day." I moved all the puppies to one area and all the hand-holding couples to another. I put plaques with blue writing in a row and purple writing in another. I alternated daisies with redwood trees. I staggered the poems. Several evenings later, I might be instructed to move all the poems together and stagger the puppies. Mr. Frank would bark his latest decorating scheme and I would work on the ladder, wondering if the idea that he was looking up my skirt was just my imagination. And if it was true, what should I do? Having no other employees or customers or witnesses of any kind in the store with whom I could exchange a glance and learn without a doubt that my discomfort was founded—that the rage I tried to suppress was the appropriate reaction—I teetered between confusion and clarity even as I teetered on the ladder, maneuvering plaques. Sometimes I would dust "Today is the First Day of The Rest of Your Life" and feel intensely depressed. Often, I thought of dropping it on my employer's head. In a feeble effort to maintain my dignity, I would tell myself to just concentrate on my work, hanging the plaques as straight as a regiment of flattened soldiers. Or sometimes I would silently smirk at how ugly Mr. Frank's merchandise was and marvel at his stupidity in ordering it. But neither of these methods could remove his gaze from my underwear.

It strikes me as sad, now, that we, the young women who climbed the ladder on different nights, never discussed this particular aspect of the job. We huddled occasionally in the gift-wrapping closet to complain about Mr. Frank's temper, about his unreasonable rules, about specific incidents that offended our senses of justice, but we never discussed how it felt to have an employer routinely look up our skirts. I knew Claire and Agnes had parallel experiences, because the plaques were in different places after the nights they worked, but I never asked them about it. I was afraid of being childish or wrong *or even vain*, would you believe it! My nineteen-year-old self-consciousness told me that if I said a man stared up my skirt, it would be interpreted as self-flattery and cause people to laugh and think, "Who does she think she is, Cher Bono?" I only mentioned it to my mother, long-distance, and in question form: "Do you think he might be looking up my dress?" My mother was no more prepared for this situation than I was. She thought he could be sneaking a peek, but it wasn't her style to suspect people of bad behavior. She suggested that I look for other work if it happened again. But mostly, I remember she wasn't outraged. We had an innocent respect for employers.

Then one day, Pam, the young woman who wore slacks and never had to climb the ladder, radiantly entered the store on her day off. It was five-ish and busy, with three of us working and Mr. Frank supervising. Over the hubbub of this rare rush on Marshall's Hallmark greeting cards, Pam announced that she had gotten a job at Emporium. She didn't hide her excitement or any of the details. Right in front of the customers and Mr. Frank and everybody, she shared her salary and benefits, vacation, sick leave (information which left us all amazed) while Mr. Frank fumed and paced. When she dropped her written notice next to the cash register and said goodbye, Mr. Frank acted the weirdest I had ever seen him.

"Pam is a man," he said all day long, as if that was the answer to some mystery and would prevent us from following in her shoes. "She cannot act like a girl. Pam is a man."

That night as I rotated the plaques, I tuned out Mr. Frank and his crazed "Pam is a man" litany and thought only about Pam and her new job. It was a triumph for us all. The ubiquitous "Today is the First Day of the Rest of Your Life" plaque should not have been illustrated with a sunrise over a golden wheat field, but with our faces, mine and Claire's and Agnes', as we listened to Pam explain the wonders of overtime pay and sick leave, and a "chain of command" which went beyond the immediate supervisor.

I would like to say that Pam's example gave us the courage to speak out against Mr. Frank's "peeping" ladder technique, but we simply did not have the language nor the public support to confront sexual harassment in Marshall's Hallmark, circa 1976. However, it did expand our horizons beyond his employ. Soon Claire had a union job at a meat-packing plant and I was stocking the shelves in a university book store. It was by no means the last sexual harassment I was to experience, but it was the last time I was ever caught completely clueless and off-guard.

Just recently, while Anita Hill spoke out against sexual harassment in the Clarence Thomas confirmation hearings, my mother telephoned to say, "I guess that was sexual harassment that happened to you at the Hallmark Store." I am in my thirties now, but it was still good to hear my mother speak in clear opposition to Mr. Frank staring up my skirt when I was nineteen. I hope it is easier for women today, daughters and mothers, friends and co-workers, to see such offenses as serious and unacceptable. And I hope we are headed for a future where men, in general, and male lawmakers, in particular, will agree.

Sherrie Tucker is a 34-year-old Creative Writing graduate student, half-time secretary, and part-time, fill-in jazz radio announcer.

As American as Apple Pie

Barbara Unger

I saw the sleazy side of life clearly enough to know that it wasn't for me. I had big dreams. I wanted to be a poet, a writer. I wanted to live in a world where little girls, teenagers and young women could be free from sexual harassment. But, since that world wasn't likely to come in my lifetime, I learned how to ward it off. I armed myself with defenses learned from Hollywood movies. I could always be Katherine Hepburn, Joan Blondell, Barbara Stanwyck or Gloria Graham. There was always a sneer, a shrug, a smart retort. But it hurt! I was never tough enough not to be bothered by it. I knew it was discrimination.

I figured that sexual harassment only happened to poor girls working in dead-end jobs and that when I became a teacher, I'd never have to endure it again. By and large, my assumption was correct. There were good years in the late fifties, working as a public school teacher, friendly male colleagues, supportive mentors. A sort of good-natured equality reigned in the New York City school system. In fact, I felt so comfortable that, in 1958, I decided to test one of the Board of Education's ancient bureaucratic rules...the pregnancy code. The rules were that a female teacher had to give notice of her pregnancy as soon as she was aware of it. Then, she had to resign. She received no pay of any kind after her resignation but could return to the Board of Education, if not to her old job, upon termination of pregnancy leave.

I didn't want to resign. I figured that if I could work until the end of the semester, I'd be able to earn quite a lot of money. I felt fine and fit. I needed the money. I thought the ruling was discriminatory. Only women got pregnant. Men didn't have to resign when they were about to become fathers. My husband was a schoolteacher. Nobody was suggesting that he should resign. As a result, I saw no reason to inform anybody of my condition.

By my fifth month, it was Spring vacation and I was wearing maternity clothing. My department chairperson, a male, was furious with me. When asked, I denied knowing that I was pregnant. Blithely, I gave him the old *sangfroid* look.

I considered this a challenge of a bad law.

If I was pregnant and I wasn't aware of it, then I could still be within the guidelines and continue to work. And so I refused to answer questions about my pregnancy. The department chairperson turned from a Dr. Jekyll to a Mr. Hyde. I could do nothing right. He was constantly in my classroom to be sure that my condition didn't interfere with my ability to teach. I realized that what I was doing made me into some kind of renegade, but I didn't appreciate being harassed for challenging an outdated irrational ruling. My supervisor, however, felt personally threatened. Maybe he thought I could get him into trouble.

Finally, in June, I "discovered" my pregnancy and filed for a leave. My first daughter was born three months later. When I left, there was no departmental party in my honor. My students, however, admired my chutzpah in confronting the outdated bureaucratic rules and chipped in to buy me a farewell gift. I guess they realized I was testing a law. Actually, I was a few years ahead of my time and eventually the ruling was formally tested and changed. In time pregnancy would no longer be considered a condition rendering a woman unfit for teaching service. I'm proud of having fought for this.

As revenge, my department chair refused to reinstate me to my former position when I wanted to return to active teaching. I could have brought a court case but didn't feel up to making a formal challenge.

I enrolled in a doctoral program in a different large municipal university and focused my energy on counseling psychology. My advisor was a tall, handsome transplanted Midwesterner just out of a California encounter group. From our first meeting, he started coming on to me.

This was a high-powered game of mind-fuck. The power this self-styled guru wielded over my success or failure in a doctoral program was total. Soon he began acting not only as my departmental mentor but also my clothing advisor and personal shrink. First, he warned me not to wear miniskirts because I'd be "sending out signals." He turned around my words to make me feel like I was coming on to him. He insisted on learning about my personal life, my marriage and my sexual history. When I displayed reticence, he assured me that everybody had sexual feelings. He even had sexual feelings for his fifteen-year-old daughter. He routinely experienced sexual feelings for his students. Didn't I? At the time, I was teaching pizza-faced junior high schoolers. I found the question more comical than offensive.

The more I pulled away, the more he insisted that I could never succeed in counseling until I stopped being so "up-tight." I needed, in particular, to have an affair in order to get in touch with my sexual feelings. It didn't matter if the affair was with him or not, so long as I had one. Our conferences turned into cat-and-mouse encounter sessions. My intellectual progress or papers were of little interest to him; only "feelings" mattered. If I planned to counsel students, I'd better "get in touch with my feelings." This led to a series of courses that were structured as little more than encounter groups that carried academic credit. Assaults on one's self-esteem and defenses were routine. During this time, I began to seriously doubt my abilities and goals. I was confused to see everyone around me expressing themselves through hugging, kissing and sexual contact, late-sixties style, when all I felt was anger and confusion. I wasn't comfortable in this role.

I knew sexual harassment, even without the word, even when it came in the guise of a "love guru" with beads and a peace symbol, a beard and a doctorate. When a teacher asks a student out on a date the first time she appears in his office for advice, it has to be something sleazy even if I didn't quite have the name for it yet. I knew I couldn't run to anybody in the department about my problem. Just because he represented the radical fringe of the profession, my mentor was inviolate and the rest of his department put up with his antics. Nobody wanted to be the whistle-blower. I never finished that Ph.D. I left graduate school.

In the early seventies I began teaching in college. My marriage ended. During this time, both a lawyer and a therapist who I consulted in connection with my divorce came on to me. By that time I came to see that sexual harassment was as American as apple pie.

I began to see sexual harassment legislation as a logical goal for the women's movement. My work with the women's movement developed into a course which I still teach.

During this time, a married male colleague began to put his hands on me in a hostile and sexual manner. He'd come up behind me and grab me, pretending to give me a friendly bear hug. I made it clear to him that I didn't appreciate being mauled in this manner but he continued.

At last our college had an affirmative action officer and I brought the case to her. The harassment ended and eventually the colleague left the college. After that, it became clear that sexual harassment would no longer be tolerated on our campus.

To me, sexual harassment is just another way for men to belittle women and remind them of their "inferior" status. It is clearly a power issue. I like the new euphemism for sexual harassment: "hitting on." The term captures the violent aspect of sexual harassment, for, after all, it is just another form of male violence against women.

How has it affected my life? It made me angry. At times it puzzled, confused and shattered me. It led me to doubt myself. It lowered my self-esteem. I felt powerless. I felt I had to quit, escape, leave, run, get away. As a result, I never did finish a doctorate. I continue to be highly suspicious of male colleagues' friendships. I have learned to endure, survive. Somehow, I managed to get stronger and today I consider myself a survivor.

I sometimes envy younger women whose careers developed during an era when sexual harassment, though hardly dead, was no longer tolerated in doctoral programs and on college campuses. I envy women who can chat freely about their pregnancies at work without fearing reprisal. I envy women who can relate to their male mentors without fear or prejudice. I envy women who went back to graduate school and who weren't victimized, tormented and belittled.

But I also know that, for every woman whose career advancement has been steady, without setbacks or false starts, there are others like Anita Hill who have been victimized by men and others who are still silent. And there are men out there (they know who they are) who have not had to pay for their behavior. In fact, I was not amused to learn that my two graduate advisors in education have both made fine careers for themselves. One rose to be chairperson at a highly prestigious university and the other is now considered a popular male feminist on campus, a man who younger women feel they can talk to and trust.

I suppose those of us who have survived can feel good about our role in talking out and, in some cases, naming names. I know I do. I used to think only young and vulnerable women got hit on, but even now, well into menopause and pushing sixty, I'm wary. You never know a sexual harasser until he strikes. Kitchen, corporation, home, college, university, therapist's office, legal counsel, street, office...he's out there waiting.

Barbara Unger is a writer, teacher and feminist; she has published six books of poetry and fiction.

DENIAL IS THE NAME OF MY STORY

Aileen Vance

My best friend and I walk side by side out of a local nightclub at about 11 p.m. on a weeknight. We have been sitting in the bar for several hours, listening to some friends play a few sets of Irish music. My friend, who intends to go back into the club to hear the band's final set, has offered to walk me to my car. We exit under the big marquee that announces the upcoming weekend's rock shows, and round the corner. There, on a well-lit side street, alongside a small shoe repair shop and a Chinese restaurant that closed an hour before, sits my car, a beat up, maroon-colored 1971 Chrysler Newport that often does not start on command. It is a hand-me-down from my in-laws, and its chief selling point is its roominess. We open the doors and settle into the spacious front seat, laughing and talking.

Suddenly, we hear a strange, loud, groaning sound, almost like a roar. We stop our talk and look up. A man is emerging from the space between the two buildings next to the car. He is walking with his pants unzipped and pulled down, his two hands holding his penis. He is pointing his penis at us, and swaggering towards the car, his wordless, guttural roaring getting louder as he approaches.

Without saying a word to each other, we both immediately lock the car doors, and I turn the key in the ignition. The car rumbles, sputters, then dies.

"Oh, God!" my friend moans.

I try the key again, my hands shaking. This time it starts, and I put it in gear while keeping my foot on the accelerator, so it won't die again, an act that seems to take long, slow motion-like minutes, instead of really just a few seconds. By now, the man stands almost directly in front of the car. I honk the horn, gun the engine, and pull out into the street, my hands trembling on the steering wheel. He shakes his fists at us, screaming out in anger. There doesn't seem to be another soul in sight.

"Thank God there was no car parked in front of me!" I let out a big breath.

I drive two blocks, pull around a corner, and stop. I say to my friend, "What should we do? What if he tries to hurt someone? I think we should try to call the

284

police." I feel confused about what action to take, and need her reassurance.

"But what if he sees us?" she asks.

"I'll go home and call," I say, trying to convince myself that I'm thinking clearly. I feel dazed, as if I'm not sure that this really just happened.

My friend agrees. She tells me she does not want to call the police, and wants to go back to the club, because her boyfriend will begin to wonder where she is. Her boyfriend is drunk inside the club, and is often wildly suspicious of her when he has been drinking. She is careful not to aggravate him.

I drop her off in front of the club, and watch her go in. Then, I drive the few blocks more home, still shaking. Perhaps ten minutes have passed.

I arrive to an unlit house, my husband having gone to sleep some time before. I walk into the bedroom, and wake him up.

"I need your help," I tell him. "I've got to call the police and I think I need some support. I'm scared."

I relate to him what has just happened. He blinks his eyes, and looks at me, bewildered.

"Why did you wake me up?" he asks, his voice tinged with both sleep and anger.

His response confuses me. I have a little talk with myself inside my head about what to do: I feel alone in my desire to call the police, yet at the core, I know that if I remain silent, and the next morning find out that this guy is some lunatic who has attacked a woman, I will feel responsible. I have heard the all-too-familiar statistics many times: a woman is raped every sixty seconds in this country.

So, I pick up the phone and dial the police station. I notice that the shaking has spread to my stomach. I stumble over the words: "Um, hi. I was just downtown and a man...a man came out of the alleyway by the shoe store on Cathcart street with his..." I hesitate, "...with his pants down, yelling at me and my friend. I drove home because I didn't feel safe trying to call from downtown, but I'm afraid he may try to hurt someone."

The woman on the other end of the line says they'll send someone right over to talk to me. I ask if they're going to send someone to look for the man. She says they will.

I turn on the porch light and the kitchen light. Twenty minutes pass. Twenty-five. Thirty. My husband and I sit at the kitchen table. He is still irritated because he was awakened for this.

Two policemen finally arrive at the door, and the questions begin. One of them has a small notebook and a pen in his hand. He asks me what happened, and I repeat my story. I am not prepared for what he asks next:

"Was he masturbating?"

I am silent. This question has caught me off guard.

He continues. "Did you notice if he had an erect penis?"

I tell them I can't remember if I noticed either one, that I was trying to get away from him as fast as possible.

"Well, what was he wearing?"

"It's hard to remember," I answer. "It all happened so fast. I think he had on a pair of Levis and a bluish-grey T-shirt."

"Can you give us a clear description of what he looked like?"

I try to close my eyes and remember. "It's hard to give specifics...I think he had sort of sandy blondish hair, he was white, he was medium height..."

The first police officer cuts me off mid-sentence, "Let's see, white, sandy blond hair, medium height...so, he looked just like *me*?" he asks, in a decidedly teasing manner, a wide smile on his face.

The two officers, facing me in the porch light, and my husband, who is standing behind me in the doorway, all burst out laughing in unison.

"I only saw him for a few seconds," I say, defensively. "I called because I was afraid he might try to hurt someone!"

The first officer is putting his pen back into his breast pocket and rolling the cover back over the pocket-size notebook. "Well, we did send someone over to the area, but they didn't find anything. We'll keep our eyes open."

"Thanks for comin' out, you guys," my husband calls congenially from behind me.

"Sure, no problem," the other officer says, as they walk back to their patrol car.

I close the door behind me. My hands are shaking again. I try to explain to my husband my anger and disbelief at the laughter. He returns to bed, still not understanding why I woke him up, why I was scared, or why the police officer's little "joke" wasn't funny.

"I don't think he meant anything by it. What's the big deal?" His words echo around me.

So, I sit alone in the dark living room, silently questioning myself. Have I made "a big deal out of nothing?" Was it justifiable for me to call the police? Then, I say aloud that tomorrow I will write a letter to the police department, describing the incident, and complaining about the insensitive treatment of the officers.

But the next morning, in fact, I do not write the letter, because by then I am convinced that no one will believe me. I am no longer sure if I believe myself. Even my friend, who was with me, talks about it on the phone the following afternoon as if it were my experience alone. She *does* express outrage and sympathy, but her words are those of one who believes it is futile to try to do anything else about it. And after our long, emotional conversation, in which I tell her about what happened after I left her the night before, I realize that *my* words sound the same.

And so, I begin to forget. I bury this night-time incident deep in my memory and do not give it another thought until some nine years later, when, while watching the TV screen one hot October afternoon, I watch one lone black woman facing a panel of fourteen white men. The men, all U.S. Senators, are grilling her about the validity of her charges of sexual harassment against her former boss and current Supreme Court Justice nominee, harassment she says occurred several years earlier.

After grueling hours of incredibly graphic testimony, her motives are repeatedly questioned. The Senators want to know *why* she would say these things happened, if the nominee says they did not.

The Senator from Alabama tries the psychological approach. He asks, "Are you a spurned woman? Are you a zealot civil rights believer? Do you have a martyr complex? Are you interested in writing a book?"

Laughter breaks out in the hearing room.

The woman answers, "No, Senator, no...I'm not given to fantasy. I can only tell you what happened." She reminds the panel that she had more to gain by remaining silent.

And hearing the laughter, it's as if a lid has just popped off an old, tightly covered, overfilled tin box. I see it all clear again in my mind, the long-held memory. I remember the laughter of that night long ago, and how it held me in its grasp.

I sit and watch the lone woman being questioned over and over again about the specific incidents of the harassment. Over and over again, she is asked why she did not come forward sooner. After many long hours of testimony, she does not buckle under the pressure; she does not recant her story. She repeats calmly, again and again, the dignified explanations of her fear, her disgust, and her confusion.

Yet the panel's joking continues into the next day and the next, occluding the power of the lone woman's forthright words. Later, the Senators are chuckling about the reading of *Playboy* magazines and the alleged sexual exploits of one of the male witnesses who has been called to testify in defense of the nominee. The Senator from Pennsylvania suggests that, if this woman's testimony is taken seriously, sons may no longer be able to kiss their fathers goodnight, for fear of their actions being misunderstood.

Then, the following Monday evening at about 11:00 p.m., after days of being glued to this drama, I finally get up and turn off the TV. I am aware by now that the Senators have made sure that the lone woman will *not* be taken seriously and that her former boss will be confirmed to the Supreme Court as planned.

I have turned off the TV, but the sound of the laughter still reverberates in my living room. It is a sound I have heard many other times, made by so many different kinds of men. U.S. Senators, Supreme Court justices, alleyway attackers, ignorant police officers, confused spouses, construction workers, bar hoppers, truck drivers, elderly bureaucrats, convicted criminals, utility company repairmen, teachers, bosses, friends, and nice neighbors down the block, all make this sound. The rich men and the poor, the famous men and the unknown, all are unwittingly united by this kind of laughter; all are bound together by the commonality of this fraternal complicity, which has been woven so tightly together by the strong, thick thread of denial.

But something else reverberates in this room, too. I sit here in the night and listen to it, taking in slowly the sound of myself and all women everywhere who have heard that mocking laughter and buried our thoughts beneath its constricting weight. This, too, is denial, this too a kind of complicity, one that feeds hungrily on the lies which both men and women are taught to believe, and one which only grows stronger when nourished by the deafening sounds of our own silence.

I get up from my chair and walk to the kitchen. I fish a pen and a piece of scratch paper from the basket next to the phone, and I begin to write. The first words that come into my mind are these: "Denial is the name of my story."

I'm not sure yet why I have written them, or where they will take me, but I write them down anyway and underline them. Underneath this, I put my name.

Tomorrow, I will begin writing the story that goes with these words. I will not stop until I have finished it.

Aileen Vance is a singer/songwriter living in Santa Cruz, California; she works all over the country, and in Canada and Britain.

I hope that white feminists have a better sense of the challenges women of color face when we make the commitment to confront sexual oppression.

—Barbara Smith

If Thomas had not been confirmed, every man in the United States would be at risk.

—Rebecca Walker

As long as the men of this country are comfortable purchasing women's sexuality cheaply and easily at newsstands and video stores, they will not appreciate the damage done by reducing women at work and elsewhere to the sum of their physical attributes.

—Patricia M. Keady

Do not vote for them unless they work for us. Do not have sex with them, do not break bread with them, do not nurture them if they don't prioritize our freedom to control our bodies and our lives.

—Rebecca Walker

I find sexual harassment to be degrading, repulsive and extremely boring.

—Kathy Stern

Anita Hill did ten years of education in one weekend.

—Rita Walker

Boys Will be Boys

Irene van der Zande

"Hey, Chick! You wanna play with my balls?" The smooth-looking young man stood in front of his fraternity house, juggling a couple of tennis balls. He bounced the balls on the sidewalk in front of me, blocking my way. "Not these, of course," he smiled. "I've got a special pair in my pants, just for you." He nearly fell over, laughing at his joke.

Yet another idiot, I thought, looking through him and walking away. It was my junior year of college. I'd left my small school and moved to a big campus in L.A. My apartment building was at the end of Fraternity Row. I'd gotten used to ignoring dumb comments from the men hanging around in front of their houses. But this fraternity had a particularly bad reputation. During parties, people whispered, women were sometimes snatched off the sidewalk and forced inside.

Very early the next Sunday morning, I passed this place again on my way back from buying groceries in the 24-hour market. Usually, Fraternity Row was dead on Sunday morning, but this time the Saturday night party wasn't over yet.

Several men—five, six, seven?—I can't remember exactly, surrounded me. Hands clutched me everywhere, pulling me towards the house. Looking around, I could see nothing but a circular wall of men's bodies. "Don't worry, honey," leered one man. "We're going to show you a good time."

Impossible! These nice young men were going to....Nonsense!

I dropped my bag of groceries and pulled against the men's hands to step as close as I could to the man right in front of me. "What would your mother think about what you're doing?" I asked, indignantly, staring into his eyes.

His mouth dropped open and he let go!

I turned to the man next to him. "If you have a sister, do you want someone to do this to *her*?"

He let go, too!

As I started to speak to another man about his girl friend, they all let go.

Somewhat ashamed and sheepish, looking at me with puzzled eyes and at each other not at all, they picked up my groceries and handed me the bag. The next day, I complained to the campus police department.

"Boys will be boys," laughed the officer at the desk. "It was just a joke!"

"I want to speak to the Police Chief!" I snapped.

"He's too busy!" snorted the officer.

"I'll just wait here until he's free," I said firmly, taking a seat.

The officer glared at me, made a few rude remarks, but finally ushered me into the Police Chief's office.

After I told my story, the Police Chief looked at me doubtfully. "It's funny," he said, "that no one has ever complained before."

He stood up and walked me to the door. "Don't worry," he said reassuringly, "I'll look into it."

I'll bet, I thought. I stomped down the street, trying to think of what else to do. Finally, I shrugged it off, telling myself, Oh, well, nothing really happened.

Later that month, I sat in the big lecture hall for my organizational psychology class. Dr. Benton, an impish man in his early 50s, was giving his usual humorous talk. I took copious notes, enjoying his jokes, not minding at all feeling alone in the middle of 99 other students.

Just before class was over, Dr. Benton announced, "The following four students need to stay to make an appointment with me." To my amazement, one of the names he called was mine.

Somewhat concerned, I walked up to the podium. "I'm Irene," I said, hesitantly.

"Good!" Dr. Benton smiled warmly at me. "Your paper about that community center in Watts was brilliant, Irene. The best I've seen in years. Why don't you come to my office around three this afternoon to talk about it?"

"I...I'm still in class," I said shyly.

"Well, what about four then?"

"Okay."

I left quickly, overwhelmed at the praise, puzzled about what exactly he wanted to talk about.

Precisely at four, I knocked softly at Dr. Benton's office door. The door opened abruptly.

"Come in!" Dr. Benton laughed. "Don't look so shy!" he took my hands and let me into his office. "Such cold little hands!" he exclaimed, then pointed to a chair. "Sit down!"

Wide-eyed, I looked around. In between the papers stacked everywhere, there were books, all sorts of art objects. A sculpture of a naked man and woman twined together. A framed painting of a woman doing something that had never occurred to me before.

Amused, Dr. Benton watched me. "What do you think about that?" he asked, pointing to the painting.

"I don't know," I said, flustered. "What did you want to say about my paper?"

"Your paper?...Oh, yes! It was brilliant!" Dr. Benton said, enthusiastically. "Did you really go alone into Watts?" Before I could answer, he leaned over and touched my hair. "Such pretty curls," he murmured. Then he said, "You're a smart girl. There's a lot I could teach you as my private student."

"What do you mean?" I asked, wonderingly.

"Oh, I could help you out...get you working on special projects," Dr. Benton explained.

Pleased that he thought so much of me, I scolded myself for feeling uncomfortable. He's just being friendly, I thought, and smiled at him.

"Would you like that?" he asked.

Still too shy to look at him for more than a quick glance, I nodded.

To my astonishment, he lunged forward and kissed me passionately. When I didn't respond, he asked gently, "Don't you know how to kiss?"

"Yes, but..." I stood up, forced myself to look directly into his eyes, and sighed, "This isn't what I had in mind. I think I should go."

"Too bad. You'll be missing a lot," Dr. Benton said, meaningfully. "Both scholastically *and* personally."

Still facing my professor, too full of bewilderment to feel anything else, I backed out of his office. On the way down in the elevator, I remembered that the other three people whose names he'd called had also been women. What were *their* appointments like, I wondered.

As I stepped out onto the sidewalk, a young woman shoved a leaflet into my hand. "Come to our meeting tonight," she said.

"What's it about?" I asked.

"About women's rights!" she explained. "So we can stop being oppressed."

I laughed at her. "You don't know what you're talking about!" I said. "I can do anything I want. Women aren't oppressed unless they're poor or minorities."

"You're just deluding yourself," she sighed.

"Nonsense!" I handed her back the leaflet and walked away.

For the next few weeks, I felt restless. I had trouble sleeping or concentrating on my studies. Finally, I decided to go to the Student Counseling Center.

The counselor assigned to me was a very respectable-looking, very plump black man. "What's the trouble?" he asked sympathetically.

For a moment, I hesitated. It would have been easier to talk with a woman. But, after all, he *was* a counselor. Talking was what I'd come to do.

"I think it's about relationships," I said. "Last year I was into all this free love, hippie stuff. But it just didn't feel right for me. What I'd really like, is to know a couple of men as real friends. But when I turn down sex, men just don't seem to want to bother with friendship. And then these strange things keep happening to me."

Without going into details, I told the counselor about the men on Fraternity Row and my professor. "What am I doing wrong?" I asked, wistfully.

The counselor listened attentively. Then he moved his chair close to me, and patted my knee. "I think," he said, warmly, "that you're just hung up about sex. You need a relationship with someone a little more experienced, that's all."

Oh, no, I thought. Not again!

"I'll take you out tonight, and we can get started," he offered.

I stood up, shaking my head. Polite as usual, I sighed, "No, thank you," and walked out.

For hours I wandered through that old ivy-covered campus, not knowing whether to laugh or to cry. This world is a pretty crazy place, I thought. You can't count on anybody. I'll just have to figure things out for myself.

Suddenly, I remembered the words of the philosophy professor from my small school the year before. "You keep asking me for The Answer, Irene," he'd say, sadly. "And I haven't got it." He'd killed himself a few days after school was out.

I can't let that happen to me, I told myself, walking faster. Suddenly, I came to an open place where the sunlight reflected a brilliant golden-green on the grass, blinding me for a moment. Standing there, soaking up the warm sun, I thought, there's no reason to look at anything it hurts too much to see.

I marched home to my apartment, right along Fraternity Row, smiling cheerfully into the face of each man hanging around outside. And for some reason, instead of harassing me as usual, each man smiled cheerfully back.

Postscript: This all happened over twenty years ago. I no longer feel the need to be polite when confronting harassment. Now, I have better tools than denial, though I must admit that pretending there was no problem served me well for a long, long time.

Irene van der Zande is Executive Director of the IMPACT Foundation and KIDPOWER, two organizations which teach personal protection skills.

"WHOSE WOODS THESE ARE I THINK I KNOW"

Patrice Vecchione

Last week I was walking my quick step in the woods when I heard a jogger coming up from behind. Alert, I continued on. The runner slowed down to run alongside me, an older, white-haired, heavy-set man. He said, "Good morning." "Hello," I replied. Then he said, "You sure walk fast. I've been trying to run you down for the longest time, but even jogging it took me quite a while to catch up." In response I laughed, but it was tainted laughter, curdled, the way one laughs at a joke that is supposed to be funny but isn't. It was a small girlish giggle that I let out, thinking he was trying to be funny, which he was. He was laughing also, a big vibrato laugh. I laughed the kind of laugh certain men might expect from a woman, a little woman's laugh, diminutive, not my usual whole body laugh. I think he was aware that what he'd said could scare me and he was laughing to cover up his awareness of this. But perhaps not. Perhaps I was only a woman jumping to conclusions again, having to think seriously of her safety. I didn't feel humorous, I felt afraid. Not terrified, but afraid. His words scared me. The litany of "what ifs" paraded through my brain. "Oh," I said. When what I wanted to say was, "You were trying to what, 'run me down,' that's what you said? Why would you want to do that? How can you possibly find that funny? Where in the hell do you get off laughing at such a statement?" But I felt I couldn't say any of that. I only laughed and said "Oh," remembering my physical vulnerability there in the woods where there were perhaps no other people for miles. Or not remembering it, rather knowing it so thoroughly that I just responded without having to think of how to respond.

During the summer I was fourteen I visited my Nana Ora in the Bedford Stuyvesant section of Brooklyn. At the end of our visit I walked to the subway station, despite her warning, "You can't be too careful in this neighborhood." I walked quickly through the quiet streets and only noticed the six men walking behind me when one man called out, "Ooohh, red, where'd you get that hair?" followed by another man's call, "Baby, what I could do with you," and "Hey, where are you in such a hurry to?" There is no word short of terror for what I felt. I pretended to ignore the men, tightened my belly, held my breath. They came up alongside me, taunting. And still I kept my face stonelike. I stayed silent. I thought of riding horses and how they say a horse can smell your fear. I swallowed my fear. I tried to be invisible, thinking, if I am not here they will not hurt me. Thinking: be invisible, unfeeling, unaffected, melt into the ground. When I arrived at the stairs to the subway I walked down steadily, to where it was dark, a long tunnel before the change booth. They did not follow me there. I do not know why. Had I become invisible? Did they wish only to frighten me? In order to speak to me in that way those men had to see me as something different from themselves, the other. A woman I know was nearly raped when she was traveling. But the men stopped hurting her when she said, "Look at me, I am a woman, the same as your mothers."

The ways in which women respond to men's harassment often fit under the heading: woman-swallows-her-tongue-in-order-to-save-her-ass. There are variations to the general theme. There is the give-me-this-job tongue-swallowing. And there is the please-reduce-this-item-so-that-I-can-afford-it tongue-swallowing. They are all related to the please-don't-hurt-me tongue-swallowing. They are all forms of it. And what they say is: "Look mister, I'm just a girl, and really, I don't threaten your power. See, you have all of it." Women know this kind of response. Our mothers teach it to us along with other etiquette lessons.

Two days later I was walking in the woods with my friend Robyn. We had walked for twenty minutes along the path, slick and muddy from the morning's rain, when she said, "Look, a deer." I looked into the thick brush where she was pointing, but didn't see anything. "I guess not," she said, but did not begin walking. Then she said, "Wait, do you see him? It's not a deer; it's a man and he's crawling through the bushes. Let's go," she said. Quickly we turned around, walking very fast out of the woods. We didn't talk right away, but I accepted one of the two big sticks she reached down for and handed to me. We walked-ran, looking frequently behind us, but did not see him coming. "He crawled through the bushes, stood up, stared at us," she said. "He had long hair and a beard, wore a plaid shirt." As we were hurrying out I just kept saying to myself, "No! This is my place. I want to be here. Do not disturb my haven." But it had already been disturbed.

Patrice Vecchione is an Italian-American who teaches writing in the schools and in workshops.

PEOPLE'S PARK

Maxina Ventura

Saturday, the 10th of August, 1991, I set out for People's Park in Berkeley for a march protesting the University of California (with the support of the Mayor and City Council of Berkeley) for having built the now-famous $1,000,000+ volleyball courts. These courts were built not to provide some nice courts for everyone's use, as UC and city officials would say, but rather as a most blatant beginning of the takeover of this free-speech gathering space which is surrounded by native plants and trees and has been successfully user-developed over two decades. City and University officials have been putting their heads together for many years to figure out how to get homeless people out of Berkeley rather than figuring out how we in Berkeley can deal with the results of a national crisis.

This day we marched and sang all around Berkeley picking up hundreds of people along the way. When we returned to the park, people flooded the sand courts and the cops went wild. I lay down in the sand as a gesture of reclaiming this land upon which I'd gathered with friends for so many years and was subsequently attacked and beaten and chokeheld over an extended period of time by about eight or nine cops. It was scary, they went for my throat and wrists. Eventually I was dumped in a police van near the park, hands cuffed behind my back. I was in the process of trying to get myself into a more comfortable position when the driver's door opened. I wondered what was going on since I was the only one in the van at the time and figured others would be taken to the jail in the same one. An officer climbed in on his knees facing the back of the van. He was directly in front of me. He looked at me with a sort of maniacal grin. Life as I'd known it came to a grinding halt as he reached his hand over the back of the driver's seat and clamped onto my crotch. As I sat helpless, battered and bruised with my hands cuffed behind my back, he rammed his finger first partially into my anus and then far into my vagina. As he stared beyond me, his face waxen, memories of having been raped several years ago flooded over me. It didn't matter who I was; I was a woman and I was totally helpless.

When he finally let go and climbed out, I knew I had to let somebody know what had happened. I was so stunned that I feared I'd forget on the conscious level as had happened with me when I was raped. I yelled out the window but no one could hear. No one could even see me since the van windows were darkened. People were so close yet I was never going to be able to contact them. It was just like a terrible nightmare in which someone drowning sees a lifeline only feet away but cannot quite reach it. This was the start of months of swirling through a whirlpool, just barely being able to surface for air most of the time. I don't know when I will resurface.

My friend Carol was badly beaten and hog-tied by this same officer while objecting to his searching down another woman's pockets in the cell across the way. Carol had been there for me steadfastly as I broke apart and tried to pick up the pieces and go on.

My whole damned life has been taken over by this thing. We've come forward publicly, and I feel like I've jumped off a cliff. Nonetheless, I understand how important it is that we do this, more for others than for ourselves. If even one woman is spared such an horrific experience or is helped through one, something useful will have been gained from our torturous experiences. Just that hope, that desire, that inspiration is what keeps me moving forward each time I feel ready to retreat from the world.

Maxina Ventura is a singer/songwriter/activist who is studying American Sign Language in Berkeley, California.

A Serpent Within

Elizabeth Weir

On a windy November night in England, when I am fourteen, scary sex snakes into my life. My friend Cherry and her family are expecting me to sleep over, and I stand in the flare of an orange street light at the end of our road waiting for the 408 bus to take me to Epsom. The green double-decker runs every half hour, but tonight there is no sign of it after fifty minutes. I stand in the lea of a young elm, but the sleet-laden wind sweeps around the narrow trunk, hurling itself against me. Stiff with cold, I am considering walking home when a car draws in to the curb.

A man, whose drooping moustache makes me think of my father, throws open the passenger door and asks where I am going. The heat from his car spills, wrapping itself around my chilled legs, drawing me into the warm interior.

"Epsom," I answer.

"Get in," he says, smiling. "That's where I'm going." His voice is soft and deep like Daddy's and, stifling my mother's warnings about strangers, I step into the car and settle.

"My wife always says you can't rely on buses after nine o'clock," my savior says changing gears and fumbling for something in his lap.

"You're so kind to help me. I'm frozen, and I was meant to be at my friend's house twenty minutes ago."

He doesn't reply. He drives with his left hand on the wheel, his other hand occupied.

After several miles, he asks, "Do you know what I'm doing?" I glance at his lap and gasp.

"Touch me," he says, his voice tight with desire.

"My mother told me about men like you." My heart thrashes against the cage of my ribs. "She says people like you are ill and can get help if you go to a doctor." How I wish I'd heeded my mother. She would be furious if she knew what I'd done. Since I was little she had drummed into me two rules: cherish your virginity until your wedding night and never talk to strange men. But this man

298

looked nice and I was cold and late.

The activity in his lap continues. I snatch another look. A fleshy shaft mounted by a knob strains upwards in the dim light of the dashboard. Is he going to force that inside me? My stomach drops like a rock leaving a rush of fear in my chest. What would Mummy do if she were here? She'd make him behave.

"You know what you're doing is wrong." I say. "Please stop it."

He makes no reply. I think of my three brothers and my father sitting by the fire in the lounge playing a noisy game of Monopoly. My mother will have escaped to the kitchen. Someone must have cornered the best properties and be winning by now. I wish I was with them, edging the little heeled shoe around the board. I wish Daddy was here to save me, and I picture the soft look on his face when he tells me I am one of the nicest things to happen in his life.

Instead of following the lamp-lit main road to Epsom, the man turns on the Banstead Downs road.

"You're taking me the wrong way."

"I'm dropping something off at Tadworth Station."

The few houses along the dark road yield to rolling heath and gorse bushes. In the exposed country, the wind collides with the car, knocking it off course, and I realize he could be planning to kill me and to dump my body on the heath. I consider opening the door and throwing myself out, but if I do, he will stop, and there will be no one to help me.

His breathing becomes heavy, and he begins to writhe in his seat.

I sit rigid.

The car cruises up a rise and tops the crest.

He moans and shudders.

As we ease downhill, he sighs, and the single light of the station comes into view. Instead of turning into the station yard, he stops on the side of the road. He mops himself with a handkerchief, zips, and leaves, slamming the car door. I don't believe he has anything to deliver.

The station will be deserted at this hour. I don't know whether to bolt into the darkness or to stay. Before I make a decision he is back.

"I'm late, and I must get to Epsom," I tell him in my mother's authoritative voice. He drives the half mile to the junction with the lighted Epsom Road and hesitates.

"Turn right here," I order with a firmness I don't feel. He turns toward the town. I pray for red traffic lights. The first set is green. And the second. The third is red as we approach but flicks to green. He slows for the van ahead, and I fling open the door and leap, staggering in the road from the momentum. Caught in blinding lights, I hear a blaring horn and the screech of brakes.

"Silly damn bitch!" an angry voice shouts from the brightness. "Play your bloody courting games..." The voice tears away in a blast of wind. The vehicle swerves around me, gets caught by the red light, and revs its fierce engine.

Hot tears whip from my iced cheeks in the wind, and I stumble to the curb. Cherry's apartment is at least a mile away and, as I set off, blown by the wind, I wonder if the man is really ill or if there is something in me that made him, a man as old as my father, behave like that. If it is my fault, will the problem always hound me? Will Cherry's mother and father want me to be their daughter's friend if they know what happened? The tardy 408 sways past as I turn on their street, and I decide not to tell anyone.

The car ride to Epsom remains a secret. Its terror haunts me, and I fear that I'm abnormal and will never marry and be happy. But, with time, I learn to coil the fear deep within my head, hidden under layers of soft gray folds, where it rarely slithers free.

My school friends and I gang around with groups of boys, but I don't have close boyfriends as they do; I have seen the tool of sex and fear it. We talk of careers, and I envy the boys, who have so many choices. Unless you are unusually clever, the options for girls are limited to becoming a secretary, a teacher or a nurse. I like the idea of helping people and, at eighteen, I leave home and start training as a nurse in a large London teaching hospital, where sex is woven into the warp and woof of each day.

Hundreds of young nurses and medics work long hours together and, as a first-year nurse on night duty, I am left in charge of thirty-two sick people when my senior nurse is taken to look after an acutely ill patient on another ward. I creep around in the dead of the night checking vital signs, intravenous feedings, and post-operative wounds, hoping my charges will continue to sleep and watching for the on-call intern to make his final rounds. I pray David Evans is not on duty.

I am applying an extra pad to Mrs. Manning's weeping scar, when I feel hands massage my hips. Dr. Evans.

"Now here's a tidy little rump," he says, leaning over me, his breath yeasty with beer.

"Look at this wound," I whisper, squirming from his grasp. "Do you think the loss is too heavy?"

"What's her blood pressure and pulse?"

I indicate the chart at the foot of the bed and continue applying the dressing.

"She's O.K., but you'll have to watch her. Half-hourly vitals and increase I.V. fluids to twenty drops a minute," he says, writing orders on the chart. "Come and give me a report. I'm knackered."

He walks to the red-blanketed nurse's desk and sits in a warm pool of light from the low-angled lamp, watching me with an appraising eye as I collect the charts.

"Plain but a magnificent body," he says as I approach. "Magnificent. And a nice mover. Are you good in bed?"

I ignore him and hope he thinks my flaming cheeks are a reflection from the red blanket.

"Ah. Sexy and a virgin. A challenging combination."

"Mrs. James, the Cholecystectomy, is nauseated. Can I have another phenergan order for her?"

"Anything you wish, sweetie," he says, stroking my thigh through my uniform.

I move my chair.

"Come back here," he orders.

"Look, you're tired, and I've got a ward full of sick people. Let's get on with it, shall we?"

"Exactly. Where shall we go? The linen cupboard?"

I shake my head but have an idea. "While we go through the charts, let me hold your hands."

He settles and listens as I give him the report, and neither of us hear the approach of Miss Crick, the night matron.

"I see you're occupied, Nurse Westover."

Her voice makes me start.

"Miserable string of piss," Dr. Evans mutters close to my ear as he rises and leaves.

"Explain yourself, Nurse."

"It's safer to hold his hands, Miss Crick. At least I know where they are then."

I think I see a flick of mirth in her hard eyes but discount it when she says, "You'll hear about this. We're a hospital, not a zoo. Now take me round to your patients."

At twenty-four I am a registered nurse and restless in London. Many of my friends are married. I have a boyfriend I really like, an aspiring urologist, but, although he enjoys my company, he is casual and shows no signs of committing himself to a long-term relationship. To prod him from his inertia and to prove to him how much he will miss me, I say, "I think I'll visit my friend in South Africa and work there for a while."

"If I were a nurse, I'd travel, too," he says, his eyes still on the journal he reads.

I'm hurt and disappointed, and I leave within a month.

South Africa is a young country that offers opportunities I can never have at home, and I decide to look for a better paid job than nursing. In Johannesburg I talk my way into a position as a personnel assistant in a small retail clothing company called On The Peg, where most employees are middle-aged, middle-class and married.

I work hard learning my new job, developing skills in maintaining files, placing advertisements, screening applicants over the telephone, conducting preliminary interviews, doing employee evaluation on lower-paid staff, and sorting out their problems. The work comes readily to me, and Major Ballscombe, my boss, says he thinks nursing is a good preparation for personnel work. He is kind and takes interest in training me. His favorite lunch spot is the shaded verandah of the Sunnyside Hotel, where he books a quiet table many Fridays and teaches me the basics of my job. I am enchanted with my switch from the heavy-duty toil of hospital life to the world of business in a new land.

Mr. Erasmus, a tall, rangy Afrikaner, who manages the Joffe Street store, comes often to the office. He fills the frame of my door and, leaning on the jamb, he says, "How goes it, Young England?" This greeting leads to tales of his life in the Cape. "Yes man, " he boasts, "I get around. When I stand in the Cape and shout 'Erasmus,' half the population stands up." I laugh, imagining all the little Erasmuses he has sired responding to his call.

Hugh Bartram-Jones from marketing likes to perch on the corner of my desk and confide in me as a fellow countryman. He has a better job with better pay than he can ever hope for in England, but his wife disapproves of apartheid with a passion and refuses to live in South Africa. His predicament tortures him.

Major Ballscombe doesn't approve of these men chatting in my office.

"You're young, Lindy," he says, adopting the same pet name my father uses. "I don't like Bartram-Jones and Erasmus hanging around you." And I appreciate his concern for me.

One day he gives me a new task to master. He asks me to learn to type and offers a bottle of champagne if I can teach myself. I find typing difficult. Many evenings I stay after work, eyes riveted to the typing manual, forcing reluctant pathways to transmit what my eyes see to my slow fingers. Sometimes Mr. Erasmus has late work to do, and several times he offers to drive me home; but I enjoy the walk to Hillbrow after being indoors all day.

One evening the daily summer thunderstorm arrives early; rain erupts from the turbulent sky, and I am not dressed to cope.

"Better take a ride with my ox team and wagon," says Mr. Erasmus, appearing at my side as I watch the storm from the window in the lobby.

"That would be lovely if it's not out of your way."

In Doornfontein he surprises me by stopping at a bar. I feel obliged to accept a drink. I have a beer, struggle through another but refuse more. He is disappointed, but I want to get home; my friends and I are going to a movie this evening.

I share an old house with six people, and he drives in to the overgrown yard with a flourish and turns off the engine.

"Thanks for the ride and for the drink," I say, searching for the door handle.

He lunges towards me wrapping me in his long arms.

"You're the most attractive woman I've ever met."

"You're married, Mr. Erasmus," I remind him, pushing him away. His grip tightens and he pulls me across the seat, holding me against him. I resist, and my mock-tortoiseshell link belt ruptures with a snap and chinks to the car floor.

"Let me go. You're a friend, that's all."

"Come on, girl," he says, twisting my face to his. "You want this."

My control explodes, and I fight like a cheetah cornered. My clawing hand finds the door handle, and I burst from the car. Mr. Erasmus flings a shoe and half my belt after me, slams the door, rams into reverse and drives off with screeching tires.

I have lost half a belt and my dignity; my elbow aches where I thumped it against the dash board, and my new stockings are torn. I feel cheap, guilty and bad for Mr. Erasmus. Have I given him the wrong signals? I think of him only as an amusing older man at work.

The following Monday he does not come to head office. Nor does he appear in the following weeks. I am grateful not to meet him and avoid having anything to do with the personnel in the Joffe Street store. I contrive for Major Ballscombe to deal with issues as they arise there.

Three weeks later Major Ballscombe summons me to his office.

"Erasmus isn't hanging around anymore, is he?" he asks.

I shake my head and shrug.

"Why are you passing along work at his store to me?"

I don't answer.

"He did something to you, didn't he?"

"No," I say, too vigorously. "I imagine he finished whatever it was that brought him here, that's all."

"He never needed to come here. He fancied you," Major Ballscombe says, winding himself into a rage, his military moustache bristling. "That's what brought him here, sniffing around like a bloody Kaffir dog. I'll take over Joffe Street, and if he ever bothers you again, I'll fire the uncouth lout."

"Thank you," I say rising, anxious to escape his unexpected tirade and sit in the peace of my office where I can think.

Mr. Erasmus has five children at home; by appearing to encourage him, I have put his job in jeopardy. Perhaps it is I who should leave the company.

The following week Hugh Bartram-Jones asks me to dinner at his apartment, his eyes soft and hopeful. "You're lonely and so am I," he says. "Please do come." I refuse and make him less welcome when he drops by to talk.

My job has become tarnished, but I persevere with the typing, hoping that by increasing my competence I can bring back the luster. Major Ballscombe asks the director's secretary to assess my typing speed and accuracy. I am nervous and slow, but, to my relief, she says I am reasonably proficient. The Major calls me to his office, asks me to close the door, congratulates me for my hard work and pronounces me ready for the bottle of champagne. I assume we will share the champagne with the clerks in the office, but he says, "You must come to my home tomorrow. I can pick you up, and I'll have the bubbly on ice. We'll celebrate in style."

"How nice of you. I'd love to see your house and meet your wife and sons."

"Well actually, Lindy my dear," he admits, curling his arm around my waist, "they're away visiting Mother-in-law in England," and he gives me a conspiratorial squeeze.

I am stunned like a cow when the bolt strikes it at slaughter—he, too, considers me available, a tasty morsel for consumption.

In a still second I make a decision.

"I've been meaning to talk to you, Major," I say sliding from his encircling arm towards the door, taking care to protect his dignity as well as my own. "I miss nursing. I've been thinking about resigning. It's time I picked up my career again."

"No," he says, taken aback. "You've worked hard, and I've worked hard to teach you. It's a waste, and you've got great potential."

I wonder to what potential he is referring.

"Sometimes it's better to stick to the work you know," I say, anchoring myself to the door handle. "I don't really belong here, and I can do more good with my nursing."

"Don't make a decision yet, Lindy," he urges, moving towards me. "Think about it over the weekend. Call me. I'm at home all by myself."

I open the door, reach for his right hand, pump it vigorously and say, "You've been very good to me, Major," and scuttle from his office pulling the door behind me.

In the quiet of my cramped office, I wonder if I imagined the squeeze, the implications of the invitation to go to his home. He has always been so helpful, so paternal. But I know I don't want to be in his office again with the door closed, don't want to see myself as the men at On The Peg see me.

I hand Major Ballscombe my resignation the following Monday.

"We'll miss you," he says.

I return to my desk and feel sad. I have enjoyed working in an office, enjoyed the freedom from weekend and night duty. But I am bad news; I disrupt the lives of married men. The racy but familiar setting of a teaching hospital beckons like a sanctuary.

I don't know whether I should apply to a hospital in South Africa or return to St. Luke's in England. I think of my boyfriend's infrequent letters—"Dear Linda, Glad you are having a nice time in sunny South Africa. It's raining here as usual..." There is no word of regret for my absence, no longing for my return, no spark of emotion; yet middle-aged men smolder and lick into flame around me. I remember the car ride to Epsom and, deep in my head, an old fear uncoils and slithers free.

Elizabeth Weir *grew up in England, has lived in South Africa, and is now a newspaper reporter in Minnesota where she lives with her husband and two sons.*

Marian Henley

TO PROTECT AND SERVE

Wenonah Williams

"You're lucky, in a way," he says peering at me over the expanse of his authoritative desk. "You could have developed ulcers which could be life-threatening. Once a pathway has been established, it is likely to continue. This is the way your body responds to stress."

I don't feel lucky. The pain alternates between a deeply throbbing ache and a searing burning sensation throughout my pelvis. The left side of my inner thigh and my vagina are numb. Sex is painful now. The diagnosis varies from doctor to doctor, all of whom are men. The neurologist says that I have weak ligaments; the osteopath says that my sacroiliac is torqued; the orthopedist can find no physical problems on x-rays and cat scans, but notices that my blood pressure is elevated; the chiropractor calls it subluxation and the psychiatrist says it's stress—psychological pain.

In the end they agree that I have to leave my job as a police dispatcher. Some doctors think that prolonged sitting is the problem; others that it is the stress of handling emergencies and some think that it is a combination of both. They don't know about the sexual harassment.

My psychologist, Dana, knows and is prepared to offer support if I choose to file a complaint, but she doesn't encourage me. She knows how difficult it is. She says that the agency's insurance company would send me to psychiatrists who would testify that I'm mentally unstable or that I hate men. She says I'm clinically depressed and she's concerned about what the additional humiliation would do to me.

My lawyer agrees with Dana. He described insurance doctors as whores, willing to sell their integrity to the highest bidder. They are paid thousands of dollars for a single evaluation of a plaintiff and they don't provide an objective opinion. Dana has had offers from insurance companies, but she's a feminist and won't sell out.

The dispatch center is a small operation. I work alone on graveyard and swing shifts. When I need to use the restroom, I have to call a police officer who

306

comes in and answers the telephones.

I hate going to work when Tony is on duty, but he likes swing shift. I don't have a choice. I don't have enough seniority for the day shift, when two dispatchers are on duty. I abstain from liquids all day, hoping to get through the shift without needing to use the restroom. I think if I don't invite him into the office, he might forget about me.

I sit at the console tensely watching the monitor. A video camera provides a view of the door outside, and I can see him standing there, punching in the door code. The door opens with a creak, its sound traveling across my nerves like chalk on a blackboard. It slams shut.

I'm trapped. My heart races. I am a small frightened animal huddled inside the trap as the hunter approaches.

Tony saunters in nonchalantly, chewing his gum and grinning. I never know what he will do or when he will make his move. He stops in the doorway of the inner room, my office. My escape is blocked.

I can't breathe. I try to calm myself. I tell him I have to use the restroom. That will buy some time. Maybe when I come back, a call will come in for him and he'll have to leave. Maybe I'll get lucky and he won't stay.

He doesn't move. He wants me to squeeze out past him, so he can catch me in the doorway.

I stand up, prepared to bolt for the door as soon as it's empty. He stands there leering at me. I hesitate, trying to think of what to do, thankful that the desk is between us. He looks so damned intimidating, with baton and gun hanging off his belt.

The telephone rings. Momentarily distracted, I sit down and answer it. Someone needs information and I try to concentrate as Tony approaches. My attention is split between the telephone call and Tony's shadow as he moves behind me.

He removes his baton, adjusts his belt so that he can sit, occupies the empty chair beside me and waits for me to finish the call. As soon as I hang up, I slide my chair back and slip out the door.

I return from the restroom to find Tony still sprawled out in the chair next to mine. I think maybe he won't bother me this time. Maybe we'll talk for a while and then he'll leave.

"What took you so long? I thought you musta fell in," he chuckles.

I ignore his attempt at humor and ask if there were any calls while I was gone. None.

He slides his chair towards mine. I inch away. He slides again, until his chair is lodged against mine and I'm wedged against the desk. Trapped again. I lean away from him, trying to put space between his body and mine.

He asks what I've been doing lately, as if he's there for a friendly chat.

I say, "Nothing." My body strains away from him.

He enjoys playing with his prey. I don't know when he'll pounce, but every fiber of my body is on alert.

The telephone rings. Someone is reporting a burglary. At last, he'll have to leave. I write down the details and hand the paper to him. He slowly stands, hitching his gun belt up. Leather creaks. I can smell freedom.

He stops behind my chair and leans over, sliding his hand down the front of my blouse, groping for a breast, asserting his dominance over me.

I slap his arm away and mumble, "Don't." I avoid eye contact.

He smirks and says, "See you later."

Now that the immediate pressure is off, I notice a throbbing pain in my pelvis and a burning sensation travels down my leg. I think I must have been sitting too long. I get up and pace around the small office.

Margaret is the youngest and prettiest of the dispatchers. She dates cops and her aspiration in life is to marry one. I don't like her much, but I'm sympathetic when she complains that Tony's partner, Jim, another police officer, is making sexual advances toward her.

Jim's wife doesn't speak English and never leaves the house without him. I suspect that she was a mail-order bride and that he couldn't handle a more independent woman. I feel sorry for her, alone in a strange country with no friends of her own. None of us has ever met her. I'm glad he isn't interested in me.

Three of us dispatchers are women of varying ages. Vanessa is the elder, in her fifties. I'm in my thirties and Margaret is the youngest, in her twenties.

Vanessa, the feminist, is outraged by sexual harassment. "They can't get away with it," she insists. Encouraged by Vanessa, Margaret files a claim against Jim.

Jim is incredulous. "That girl is trying to ruin my career," he tells the other officers. They discuss this situation in serious and hushed tones, each one feeling threatened. They characterize themselves as victims of the hysterical fantasies of unstable women.

A hearing is scheduled. After it's over, Margaret leaves the room in tears. She doesn't want to discuss it.

Jim brags that in the end, she apologized for bringing the charges against him. Now she is the brunt of jokes around the office; jokes that serve as a warning to the rest of us. We all know that the hearing itself was the real joke.

The officers are relieved. They can relax now and return to their old ways. Justice has prevailed.

Wenonah Williams has a deep appreciation for her Osage ancestors; she creates indexes for books and has recovered from the physical effects of sexual harassment.

Lynda Barry

MY CAREER AS A POLICE OFFICER

Pamela Cheatham Wood

My story of sexual harassment began when I was 29 years old. It happened in the work place. I wanted to be a police officer; after putting myself through the police academy, I was hired almost immediately by the Mill Valley Police Department.

I never had any experience of sexual harassment and probably didn't know much about it when it happened to me. I was a new officer in a training program under the direction of a Sergeant who was also the training coordinator. He could best be described as a very powerful person, intimidating, like a drill sergeant in the army. He also had a lot of power within the operations of the department, including influence in hiring and firing of officers.

I was the only female full-time regular officer. I wanted to be accepted, to fit in with "the guys." I'll never forget my first day walking into the shift briefing and how everyone stared at me. I had just completed the academy with twenty men and three women and I never had a problem. I finished in the top 10% of my class with a score of 91%.

The sexual harassment began almost right away. At first I was subjected to sexual jokes, innuendo, and comments that I was the "token female." I had a discussion with another officer who was also a training officer, and told him I was offended by the talk. He suggested that if I were to say anything to the officers that I would "just make waves" and not be accepted. He also said that I would be tested and if I could just joke back, then I would fit in better. I wanted to be accepted so I did what he recommended, ignored the comments, or even laughed at them. While in training, the sergeant I described earlier, whom I'll call Sgt. Mc, was very friendly and very attentive. I believed that he was doing his job as the training coordinator. However, things changed very rapidly. He would touch my knee while talking to me in the patrol car. He then said he was very attracted to me. I was embarrassed by this but ignored him and didn't say anything.

On Valentine's Day he purchased candy in a heart-shaped box; again, I just

310

didn't know how to respond and thanked him. I had thought it was for his wife. When I was promoted to regular officer status, I was talking to the captain when Mc came up to me, gave me a kiss on the lips and said, "Congratulations." The captain looked at him and Mc said, "I can kiss her, I'm her supervisor!"

He would approach me in the hallways at the station and ask for a kiss. I would laugh, say something like, "You're joking, right?" He would be insistent, trying to convince me that it meant nothing and he was just a very "affectionate" person. When I said no, he would get angry and remain that way for the remainder of our shift. He continued to ask me to kiss him and got very close to me, right in my face. I became afraid of him. He was so intense and powerful, he intimidated me. I was worried that his anger would affect my passing the training.

He continued to press me to kiss him and finally I gave in. He just wouldn't take no for an answer. I discovered that when I let him kiss me that his mood changed. He was nice to me again and didn't bother me for the rest of the shift. One kiss would satisfy him. Things went a lot smoother when he got his way. I found out early on that you don't cross Mc. There would be retaliation. While I was there at least four officers were fired. Mc was the training coordinator; he wrote the evaluations and recommendations to the Chief of Police.

Gradually Mc became very intense with me. One night while I was out having a beer after swing shift, we saw Mc patrolling outside as if to see who was in the bar. This bar was not in the city limits, where he normally should be.

When I left the bar to go home, Mc was waiting for me; he signaled for me to pull over. I was still in the training program, and had just purchased a new car. He said he wanted to see my new car, and talk to me. He wanted me to drive behind a school yard; it was about 1:00 a.m. I felt I had no choice. He was my sergeant, and I did what he asked me to do. He got in and closed the door. He said, "Don't these cars have a reclining seat?" He found the lever and pulled the seat all the way down, then pulled me over on top of him and kissed me. He put his tongue in my mouth and began to rub my breasts. He was holding me tight. I pulled away and said, "What are you doing? Stop!" He said, "I can't control myself with you." I said what would the administration do if they found out about this? He said, "They can't do anything to me. This is my personal life, and they can't touch me. My wife may divorce me, but they can't do a damn thing!" I asked him to leave and said I was not interested in this type of relationship with him. He did leave, but the next time I saw him, he asked to talk to me in the privacy of a room at the department. He closed the door, said that he had thought about it all weekend and had made the decision not to pursue me again. I was delighted.

After that meeting, things changed a little. But soon he began asking me to kiss him in the hallways. I tried to ignore him and walk away but he wouldn't take no for an answer. It became clear that in order for me to survive in the department and pass my 18-month probation period, I was going to have to keep him from being angry with me and go along with these kisses. I was too afraid to tell the department administrators for fear that I would be the one blamed for being a troublemaker. I was the only woman and had little respect and no support. I made requests for safety equipment that were denied. I was labeled as a complainer. I complained about locker room facilities that were inadequate. I requested a bullet-proof vest and a duty gun that fit my hand. These requests were denied. The men had vests. They changed the rules when I asked for one: "We don't buy them anymore."

I was suppressing the stress this was causing. I felt this was the only way to handle it. I just kept hoping that if I could make it through the 18-month probationary period, I would not be so afraid of being fired. I would then put my foot down and be more forceful with Mc. During this time I was also subjected to his crude comments. Mc would say things like, "I don't understand why you don't understand me, if you would just go to bed with me, you would see where I'm coming from...Let's fuck...Your tits are getting bigger."

He would inquire about anyone I was dating. He would say, "Does he kiss as good as I do? Did you get laid last night?"

When I walked into briefings he would say in front of everyone, "Look at Cheatham, she's smiling, she must have gotten laid last night!" If I got angry he would say, "You're just having PMS." I was called "flat chested" and "cheeks."

Mc didn't like me being with other men. He was jealous. He would call me into his office just to discuss who I was dating. He would want to know if we were having sex. He wouldn't let me leave his office until I told him. Sometimes I would cry with frustration. This seemed to please him. I felt totally controlled, under his influence. I was scared. He would talk about his penis and comment that "It's not the meat it's the motion."

He once took pictures of a stripper/prostitute who performed at a bachelor party for one of the officers. He brought the pictures into the briefing and passed them around. The pictures showed several officers' heads in the stripper's crotch. It showed the woman putting a dildo inside of her and it was described to me that she would push it out and aim it at the officers who would hold up their fingers and make a football-type goal. I was disgusted but he and all the officers were laughing. There was a contest with the pictures: they were posted on the men's bulletin board to name the back of the officers' heads.

I was told, "Don't be a woman here, be a cop. Be a woman at home. Leave your feelings at home, there is no room for feelings at work." Mc read a personal note that was addressed to me in a briefing to all the other officers. It was from a male friend, who was going to help me move to a new home. Mc knew this young man. He read the note and yelled at me, "Are you screwing him too? He's an asshole and cocksucker and you are a cocksucker for hanging around him!" Everyone laughed.

Mc yelled at me a lot. Like a drill sergeant trying to keep me stressed at all times, he could get away with anything. He had this power within the department that was hard to believe.

He tried to get me to meet him at a training class in Chico and wanted me to stay in his room. I refused but he kept asking me. He would say, "One of these days we really have to do it."

Finally I completed my probation. I had successfully passed a written test, and had received standard evaluations with positive comments from the other sergeants who had supervised me, as well as from Mc, who was my supervisor and sergeant during the last four months. I was assigned to a new shift and a different sergeant a few months later. I was relieved to be away from Mc; I still saw him frequently in the station, but he was not on my shift.

I began dating a fireman that I had known from high school. Once when I was leaving work, Mc stopped me and said, "Why are you smiling?" I said, "I'm in love," and he said, "Give me a little kiss." I said "No!" He tried to block me from walking, insisted I give him a kiss. I kept walking and left. The next time he saw me he demanded I come into his office and tell him about Mike.

He said, "I approve of Mike, maybe you will marry him, then we will both be married and then you will go to bed with me!"

When Mike moved in with me, Mc became very hostile. I wasn't afraid of getting fired for saying no because I was off probation and would have to do something really terrible for that to happen.

In the next rotation of shifts, I found I was assigned to graveyard with Mc. I would be working with him from midnight to 4:00 a.m. He was unbearable to work with and I complained to administration about how he was treating me, but I was too afraid to tell them about the kissing and sexual harassment. Mc would treat others in a hostile way and although he was not sexually harassing them, they would also complain about his demeanor. He was worse with me than anyone.

The administration wouldn't listen to me. They said, "You're just one of the boys...This goes with the territory."

During this time, Mc told the other officers that I was a danger to work with because I was afraid in dangerous situations. He told the other sergeants and officers to "write her up, even if she steps off the sidewalk." One officer said Mc said, "Watch this, I'm going to really fuck with her." I began to receive numerous memos citing "poor performance." I was written up for taking back a parking ticket from a handicapped person. I stopped a vehicle with a drinking driver and was not given credit for this but was written up because I already had a prisoner, the town drunk, asleep in the patrol car.

Anything I did that could be construed as poor performance was written up. I knew Mc was behind this but it wasn't until after I left that other officers confirmed it.

One night there was an incident that made another officer nervous that "he would have to protect me." This officer had not worked night shift as much as I had (they kept me on night shift more than the other officers), and this officer had not worked with me much. I also know now that he was told that I was "an officer safety problem," although I was never informed of this extremely serious accusation. If I was a danger to other officers, why wasn't I informed of this in a memo? Not even a mention by the Chief? This didn't make sense.

Anyway, I was called into the sergeant's office by Mc and given a two-hour lecture. I told him that it had been a peaceful arrest of a few guys who were too drunk to drive. No hostility, in fact I knew one of them personally! He yelled at me, and when I tried to leave the room, Mc demanded I stay. After two hours I started to cry. I said that I was being singled out for unfair treatment. I was being discriminated against! They wouldn't have treated a male officer this way. Mc then said, "Don't ever use the word discrimination here!"

The next night, he gave me a three-page memo that outlined what he thought had happened and about our counseling session. It was full of lies. I refused to sign it. He pressured me to sign for another two hours. Finally he said, "You're only digging yourself a deeper grave."

I wrote rebuttals and gave them to the administration. They refused to hear my side of the story. I was told if I did anything else I would be suspended.

I began walking on eggshells. I felt everyone hated me. I felt all alone. No one to talk to. I began talking to the department counselor. I would stop in his office and try to tell him about the problems. I was still afraid of talking about the sexual harassment. I didn't want it to get back to Mc.

I tried to work harder, write more tickets, do twice as much as the other officers. It didn't make a difference to them. I became nervous, full of anxiety. I began to have nightmares and couldn't sleep. I would have to drink wine to go to sleep. I would wake up in a cold sweat, afraid of going to work. I talked to the captain, told him I was being treated worse here than on the street. He said, "That's the way it is in police work, some things you just have to live with." Mc pulled me over again after he had seen I was at the bar with the shift. He insisted I was drunk and demanded I stop driving, but he didn't give me a sobriety test. He said, "I'll drive you home," then told me to get into the front seat of the patrol car. I lived in the next town. He had his K-9 dog with him in the back seat, a dog capable of biting anyone when agitated, even another police officer, which had happened. Mc opened the window separating the front and back seats and said, "Say hello to Bear." The dog was breathing down my neck. I was afraid to move.

314

Would Mc try to get me home and molest me? When he stopped in front of my house I jumped out of the car and ran inside. The next day he said, "This will be our little secret...I won't tell unless I have to."

I worked harder trying not to do anything wrong. At the end of the four months I was given my evaluation. The other sergeant gave it to me and said, "It's really bad, I'll leave you alone to read it." It was really bad, it was three pages of narrative, describing everything they could come up with to make me look like I was an unfit officer.

I cried and cried uncontrollably. I couldn't believe what I was reading. I knew Mc was behind this and that there was no way I was going to survive. I told the sergeant I wanted to resign. I didn't care any more. I was worn down and had lost all my desire to work. I left and went home. I cried hysterically at home and called the department counselor to make an emergency appointment. I saw him in his office away from the department. He tried to convince me to stay and work it out. I knew it was too late, they had destroyed me. I was not functioning at a safe level. I was weak and depressed. I finally told him about Mc and his sexual harassment. He then understood why I had to leave. I could not function at a level expected of a police officer. I was a danger now on the street in emergency situations. I didn't think I should be driving a car, much less have a gun. I wasn't thinking properly. I had to get out of there. Mc convinced them all to be against me.

I walked into the captain's office and resigned. He stated he didn't want me to do it but never gave me any support or help. I was crying. He said, "No crying in my office...Maybe you would be better off somewhere else." He told me how to write my letter of resignation.

At first I felt a brief sense of relief, that I was away from the stress and pressure. Then reality set in. I became more depressed. I couldn't sleep; when I did I had nightmares about the department and Mc. I would wake up in a cold sweat. I had numerous other physical ailments: headaches and stomach problems. I became withdrawn and afraid to see anyone. I became paranoid. I stayed in the house and saw no one. My career as a Police Officer had ended.

I didn't know if or when I could return to any type of work. I became afraid that Mc would try to physically harm me or kill me. A friend suggested I see an attorney and file for workers' compensation benefits. Three weeks later I began the process. The attorney recommended I see a psychologist. I was afraid to do this as I had never been to one before. I never dreamed I would need one, but this time I did.

I saw the psychologist for over two years and during this time initiated a lawsuit against Mc and the City of Mill Valley for sexual harassment and discrimination. For the next six years my life would be turned inside out. It was the hardest thing I have ever been through, but I knew I was right. I wanted to see justice. I had a great attorney and friend and if it weren't for her emotional support I would never have been able to complete the lawsuit.

The City fought back viciously and continued to harass me by heavy litigation and delays. They challenged the judge, and with four courtroom delays already, this postponed my day in court even longer. My civil case finally settled in 1991, for $240,000. My workers' compensation case is still pending, as is my disability retirement which I am also pursuing. I feel like my life has been irrevocably damaged because of the trauma and treatment I experienced at the police department and during the six-year litigation.

I have not told all the details. It would be a book in itself to do so, but this is a true story. What I have told is only some of the worst of what happened to me. I have learned a lot about myself. I look back, and it seems to me that I had been brainwashed to let them treat me like that. It's easy to look back, to know now what I would have done differently—not that it would have changed them, but I know who I am and that I will never let this happen again.

One of the hardest things about the settlement is that Sergeant Mc was never disciplined; in fact he was promoted to lieutenant during the litigation.

The city officials all believe Mc, that I came on to him, that a few kisses took place, that they were consensual. The newspapers quote the city manager in saying, "She was just a disgruntled employee looking for deep pockets," and "She couldn't make it as a cop."

This enraged me so much that I went to the city council meeting and demanded a public apology, reading to them a three-page letter I had typed in outrage.

No apology was given, only derogatory remarks by a woman on the council who refers to herself as a "feminist."

I have since become stronger. I am sure I did make a difference to the police department even if they don't want to admit it. A sexual harassment policy was written as a directive in the rules and regulations, written directly from my allegations. The women's locker room was remodeled in an attempt to make it more equal to the men's.

I have joined the National Organization for Women and other women's groups to get the word out and help other women who are suffering from sexual harassment. I am speaking at sexual harassment forums at the local level to educate others so that maybe it won't happen to other women in male-dominated occupations.

My husband and I are trying to put back our lives and we have recently adopted a baby. The legal fees have been excessive and the costs for the civil action were unbelievable! Of course the attorneys got a large percentage. The money wasn't worth it. It never can pay for all the suffering and loss of career. But I made them answer for what they did and I know they will never forget me.

316

It took several years to get my self-confidence and esteem back, but I don't know if I will ever be the person I was the day I walked into the police department and put on that badge.

Pamela Cheatham Wood, 38, is a new mother, and very involved with women's issues; she is working to form a sexual harassment task force in Sonoma County.

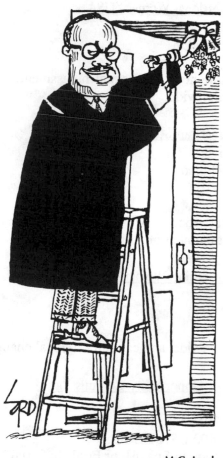

MISTLETOE TIME AT THE SUPREME COURT...

M.G. Lord

RESOURCES

Ad Hoc Sexual Harassment Coalition
c/o Lauren Wechsler
Ms. Foundation for Women
141 Fifth Avenue
New York, NY 10010
212/353-8580
A broad-based coalition of women's and civil rights groups organized in response to the "now what" question after the hearings.

Business and Professional Women/USA
2012 Massachusetts Ave., N.W.
Washington, D.C. 20036
202/293-1100
Information clearinghouse on sexual harassment. Also refers callers to local chapters nationwide.

Center for AfroAmerican Studies
Elsa Barkley Brown
University of Michigan
Ann Arbor, MI 48109
313/747-4887
Information on activities of African American women in response to the sexist and racist treatment of Anita Hill.

Coalition of Labor Union Women
15 Union Square
New York, NY 10003
212/242-0700
Has chapters nationwide, and can refer to local chapters.

Equal Employment Opportunity Commission
1801 L Street N.W.
Washington DC 20507
202/663-4264 or 800/USA-EEOC
For other information in Spanish or English: 800/872-3362.

Equal Rights Advocates
1663 Mission St., Suite 550
San Francisco, CA 94103
415/621-0505
Provides initial information and legal advice, and will refer to groups
nationwide. Provides counseling and advice in Spanish and English.

Feminist Majority Sexual Harassment Hotline
1600 Wilson Blvd., Suite 704
Arlington, VA 22209
FFM will help women learn what they can do to protect themselves against
sexual harassment and to expose the violators.
Hotline: 703/522-2501.

IMPACT International, Inc.
800/345-KICK
301/589-1349
Referrals to local programs for teaching women self-defense skills in an
atmosphere of strong personal support.

KIDPOWER
P.O. Box 1212
Santa Cruz, CA 95061
408/426-4407
Nationwide referrals to local programs to help children become safer and
more confident through effective self-defense skills. Workshops also for
parents, teachers and others on how to teach children these skills.

National Association of Commissions for Women
c/o Clair Bigelow
202/628-5030 or:
National Conference of State Legislatures Women's Network
c/o Sue Mullins
515/583-2156
Contact the above about media coverage, assessing laws and enforcement
mechanisms in your city, county and state.

The National Council for Research on Women
Sara Delano Roosevelt Memorial House
47-49 East 65 Street
New York, NY 10021
212/570-5001 or fax 212/570-5380.
Guidelines on organizing speakouts and forums on sexual harassment. Also available: *Sexual Harassment: Research and Resources, A Report-in-Progress*. Highlights current legal and scholarly definitions of sexual harassment, the extent of the problem, typical behavior of the harassed, myths about harassers, anti-harassment policy and procedures, and efforts needed to bring about significant change. $16 (discounts for bulk orders).

9 to 5, National Association of Working Women
614 Superior Avenue N.W.
Cleveland, OH 44115
216/566-9308
9 to 5 hotline: 800/522-0925. A toll-free service that advises women on sexual harassment and other job problems.

NOW Legal Defense & Education Fund
99 Hudson Street
New York, NY 10013
They will help find lawyers and will provide a legal resource kit telling where to go and what to do.

The Webb Report
A monthly newsletter on sexual harassment by Susan L. Webb
Premiere Publishing, Ltd.
145 Northwest 85th, Suite 201
Seattle, WA 98117
For questions or information: 800/767-3062
Also available from Premiere Publishing: "Twenty-Five Things to Do if Sexual Harassment Happens to You." $4 per booklet.
Susan Webb has videos on sexual harassment and how to stop it.

Wider Opportunities for Women, Inc.
1325 G Street, N.W. (LL)
Washington, D.C. 20005
202/638-3143
Will direct callers to local network of advocacy centers that deal with sexual

harassment and other employment issues.

W.R.A.T.H. (Women Refusing to Accept Tenant Harassment)
607 Elmira Road, Suite 299
Vacaville, CA 95687

Women can also contact their local ACLU chapter and their state human rights commission for advice and referrals.